Medical Ethics, Law and Communication
at a Glance

Edited by

Patrick Davey

Anna Rathmell

Michael Dunn

Charles Foster

Helen Salisbury

WILEY Blackwell

Library of Congress Cataloging-in-Publication Data

Names: Davey, Patrick, editor. | Rathmell, Anna, editor. | Dunn, Michael, 1980- editor. | Foster, Charles, 1962- editor. | Salisbury, Helen, 1963- editor.

Title: Medical ethics, law and communication at a glance / edited by Patrick Davey, Anna Rathmell, Michael Dunn, Charles Foster, Helen Salisbury.

Other titles: At a glance series (Oxford, England)

Description: Chichester, West Sussex, UK : John Wiley & Sons, Ltd., 2017. | Series: At a glance series | Includes bibliographical references and index.

Identifiers: LCCN 2016022212 (print) | LCCN 2016023250 (ebook) | ISBN 9780470670644 (pbk.) | ISBN 9781119266174 (pdf) | ISBN 9781119266167 (epub)

Subjects: | MESH: Ethics, Medical | Legislation, Medical | Health Communication | Professional-Patient Relations | Bioethical Issues | Great Britain | Handbooks

Classification: LCC R724 .M29424 2017 (print) | LCC R724 (ebook) | NLM W 49 | DDC 344.4104/1—dc23

LC record available at https://lccn.loc.gov/2016022212

Ethics, Law and Communication
at a Glance

Contents

Editors   vii
Contributors   vii
Preface   ix

Part 1 · Medical ethics and law   1

1   What is medical ethics?   2
2   Ethical theories and principles   4
3   Ethical reasoning   7
4   What is medical law?   10
5   The English legal system   13
6   Relationship between ethics, law and professionalism   16
7   Ethical decisions in practice   18
8   Negligence   20
9   Battery and assault   24
10   Confidentiality   26
11   Consent   28
12   Reproduction   34
13   Termination of pregnancy   37
14   Organ donation and transplantation   40
15   Mental health   43
16   Safeguarding children and adults   46
17   Public health   48
18   Allocation of resources   50
19   Clinical genetics   53
20   Human research   56
21   Care of older adults   58
22   End of life care   61
23   Health management   65
24   Primary care   68

Part 2 · Communication   71

25   The importance of good communication   72
26   The patient-centred consultation   74
27   Building the relationship   75
28   Listening and questioning   76
29   Explanations   78
30   Explaining procedures   80
31   The computer in the consultation   81
32   Shared decision making   82
33   Communication of risk   84
34   Talking about lifestyle changes   86
35   Breaking bad news   88

36 Bad news: patients' reactions 90

37 Dealing with anger and aggression 92

38 Talking about sex 94

39 Communicating across cultures 96

40 Communicating with people with disabilities 98

41 Communicating with colleagues 100

42 Professionalism 102

43 Feedback 104

44 Looking after yourself 106

45 Kindness 108

Index 109

Editors

Patrick Davey
Consultant Cardiologist
Training Program Director for General Medicine
    in Health Education
Northampton General Hospital
East Midlands, UK

Michael Dunn
Lecturer in Health and Social Care Ethics
The Ethox Centre
Nuffield Department of Population Health
University of Oxford, UK

Charles Foster
Fellow of Green Templeton College
University of Oxford, UK

Anna Rathmell
Medical Manager, Takeda Pharmaceuticals UK Ltd
Lay Member, Oxford C Research Ethics committee,
    Oxford, UK

[The contents of this book do not necessarily represent
the views of Takeda Pharmaceuticals or the Oxford C
Research Ethics committee]

Helen Salisbury
Honorary Senior Clinical Lecturer
Nuffield Department of Primary Care
Health Sciences
University of Oxford, UK

Contributors

Richard Ashcroft
School of Law, Queen Mary, University of London, UK
3. Ethical reasoning

Ben Bradley
Outer Temple Chambers, London, UK
9. Battery and assault

Jamie Carpenter
Hailsham Chambers, London, UK
22. End of life care

Grace Charles
Overlook Medical Center, Summit, NJ, USA
18. Allocation of resources

John Coggon
Law School. University of Bristol, UK
17. Public health

Liam Curren
Genomics Plc, Oxford, UK
5. The English legal system

John William Devine
Department of Philosophy, University of Birmingham, UK
5. The English legal system

Sharon Dixon
Donnington Health Centre Oxford, UK
32. Shared decision making

Michael Dunn
The Ethox Centre, University of Oxford, UK
1. What is medical ethics?
10. Confidentiality
11. Consent

Prem Fade
Poole Hospital, Poole, UK
21. Care of older adults

Elizabeth Fistein
Department of Public Health and Primary Care,
   University of Cambridge, UK
15. Mental health

Charles Foster
Green Templeton College, University of Oxford, UK
6. Relationship between ethics, law and professionalism

Imogen Goold
Faculty of Law, University of Oxford, UK
4. What is medical law?

Kate Greasley
Faculty of Law, University of Oxford, UK
13. Termination of pregnancy

Cara Guthrie
Outer Temple Chambers, London, UK
8. Negligence

Jonathan Herring
Faculty of Law, University of Oxford, UK
12. Reproduction
16. Safeguarding children and adults

Caroline Huang
Department of Bioethics, National Institutes of Health,
   USA
19. Clinical genetics

Liza Keating
Royal Berkshire Hospital, Reading, UK
2. Ethical theories and principles

Sam Mills
University Hospital Southampton, UK
33. Communication of risk

Christopher Newdick
School of Law, University of Reading, UK
18. Allocation of resources

Andrew Papanikitas
Nuffield Department of Primary Health Care Sciences,
   University of Oxford, UK
24. Primary care

Muireann Quigley
Newcastle Law School, Newcastle University, UK
14. Organ donation and transplantation

Anna Rathmell
Takeda Pharmaceuticals UK Ltd
Oxford C Research Ethics committee
10. Confidentiality

Suzanne Shale
Clearer Thinking, London, UK
23. Health management

Mark Sheehan
The Ethox Centre, University of Oxford, UK
18. Allocation of resources

Anne Slowther
Warwick Medical School, University of
   Warwick, UK
7. Ethical decisions in practice

Dita Wickins-Drazilova
School of Medicine, School of Dentistry and School of
   Nursing, University of Dundee, UK
7. Ethical decisions in practice

Ruth Wilson
Temple Cowley Health Centre, Oxford, UK
39. Communicating across cultures
40. Communication with people with disability
41. Communicating with colleagues
42. Professionalism
43. Feedback
44. Looking after yourself

Eliot Woolf
Outer Temple Chambers, London, UK
20. Human research

Preface

This book helps you to become a complete doctor. Technical prowess matters in medicine, but to be a good doctor it is not sufficient only to be technically competent: one must have additional skills. Technical ability comprises those crucial skills to make a diagnosis and deliver effective treatment, whether pharmaceutical, talking, surgical, radiation or whatever. These technical skills are not easy. Indeed, mastery of them is often difficult. One has to draw together the threads of a story, sift through contradictory examination and investigative findings, draw up a differential diagnosis, eliminate the impossible, degrade the unlikely and settle on the right diagnosis supported by the facts. Sometimes the diagnosis is easy; sometimes, indeed more often, it is not. Whether the diagnosis is known or not, treatment may be no easier. If there is uncertainty about the diagnosis, so there will be with the treatment. Even when there is certainty, the drugs may not work, and, if one operates, the surgery can be both mentally and physically demanding. The technical skills needed to be an effective clinician are considerable and they pose major stresses for clinicians. They are an absolute prerequisite to be a good doctor. These skills are often, indeed almost universally, undervalued by hospitals and healthcare systems. While essential, they are not sufficient by themselves to be an effective clinician. One must have additional skills: a good doctor must be part of a functioning team, must understand the political nature of the healthcare system, must perform within the law, within an ethical framework, and must communicate effectively, both with patients and managers. It helps if you understand and look after yourself, particularly emotionally. Many of these necessary additional skills are the subject of this book. The legal framework under which we all practise is outlined, medical ethics is introduced, and the principles of good communication demonstrated. These chapters provide the essential knowledge that turn excellent technical doctors into rounded clinicians, into those doctors that we all aspire to be. I hope you find them useful to gain that essential extra knowledge and skill needed to be an excellent doctor, and I wish you every success. It has been great fun writing this book with my colleagues. I hope you enjoy reading it as much as we all did writing it.

Medical ethics and law  Part 1

Chapters

1 What is medical ethics? 2
2 Ethical theories and principles 4
3 Ethical reasoning 7
4 What is medical law? 10
5 The English legal system 13
6 Relationship between ethics, law and professionalism 16
7 Ethical decisions in practice 18
8 Negligence 20
9 Battery and assault 24
10 Confidentiality 26
11 Consent 28

12 Reproduction 34
13 Termination of pregnancy 37
14 Organ donation and transplantation 40
15 Mental health 43
16 Safeguarding children and adults 46
17 Public health 48
18 Allocation of resources 50
19 Clinical genetics 53
20 Human research 56
21 Care of older adults 58
22 End of life care 61
23 Health management 65
24 Primary care 68

What is medical ethics?

Figure 1.1 What is medical ethics?

Medical Ethics, Law and Communication at a Glance, First Edition. Edited by Patrick Davey, Anna Rathmell, Michael Dunn, Charles Foster and Helen Salisbury.
© 2017 John Wiley & Sons, Ltd. Published 2017 by John Wiley & Sons, Ltd.

Introduction

Medical ethics is a discipline concerned with the systematic analysis of values in healthcare.

But this definition only gets us so far. We need to be clear about what healthcare values are, what it means to systematically analyse these values, and what it means to do so in the varied policy and practice contexts in which healthcare takes place. The first issue relates to the content of medical ethics, the second to its methods and the third to its scope. Each of these issues will be considered in turn.

The content of medical ethics

Medical ethics is founded on the idea that there are discrete ethical values specific to healthcare. Put another way, practitioners working in health owe something to those whom they care for precisely because they are involved in healthcare provision, and such provision is importantly different from other professions and the general obligations that human beings owe to each other. The justification for this special set of ethical values is usually articulated by observing that one's health is fundamental, in some sense, to one's life plan. Because being healthy is a prerequisite to pursuing other valuable goals, having access to healthcare, being able to make decisions about the care one receives, and being treated well within the healthcare relationship, is morally significant.

Much work in medical ethics is concerned with specifying the correct ethical values that underpin good healthcare. This project is one that is necessarily sensitive to moral theory, and that most commonly takes the form of identifying so-called 'mid-level principles' that seek to reflect and combine different theoretical considerations to provide a coherent, and ethically justifiable, roadmap for good practice (see Chapter 2).

Once ethical principles for healthcare have been determined, the medical ethics project broadens out. One other activity is to attend carefully to how these abstract principles ought to be applied to specific healthcare decision-making settings in diverse parts of the world. The challenge of translating ethical values into practice is no small feat. The varied social, cultural, and economic differences that are characteristic of different healthcare institutions means that careful analytic work needs to be undertaken to know precisely what it means to do good for a patient, **here**.

Another activity that medical ethicists attend carefully to is the common situation in which it is evident that value conflicts arise between competing principles, and therefore where there is genuine uncertainty about what a healthcare practitioner or policy-maker ought to do. Such conflicts can take different forms. On the one hand, they might be akin to a traditional moral dilemma, where there are good ethical reasons for pursuing two different and mutually exclusive courses of action. What ought to be done, for example, when a teenage patient refuses a straightforward and life-saving blood transfusion on the basis that such a procedure would go against the religious beliefs that they hold dear? On the other hand, the conflicts might be less fundamental in nature, perhaps where a doctor is clear about what ought to be done, but is unable to act as they ought due to practical constraints, such as institutional rules or cultural expectations in her workplace. Addressing conflicts of this kind raises questions about the role of medical ethics in advocating for policy or practice changes, and also shifts the locus of analysis onto issues such as 'moral distress' that can arise when practitioners are prevented from acting as they ought.

The methods of medical ethics

Medical ethics is a broad church. Those contributing to medical ethics use a variety of methodological approaches, including both ethical analytic and empirical methods.

Methods of ethical analysis are deployed in order to develop arguments that aim to settle these conflicts – to determine what ought to be done in a situation of ethical uncertainty. Justification and argument are the methodological characteristics of this normative enterprise. A defence to the claim that 'Doctors ought to do X' depends on providing a justification, based on the reasons in support of this argument, against the reasons supporting the claim that 'Doctors ought not to do X' or 'Doctors ought to do Y'. The extent to which a claim counts as a satisfactory answer to the question 'What ought a doctor to do here?' is judged in light of the standards of reasoning that apply to arguments generally. Thus, while rational argumentation of this form is generally seen to be philosophical in nature, it is in fact closely related to other analytic approaches, including the scientific method. Further information about ethical reasoning is provided in Chapter 3.

Empirical methods, on the other hand, are used primarily to describe how value conflicts arise within healthcare practice. Empirical methods can also be used to contribute to ethical argumentation by specifying evidence that can give substance to the reasons in favour, or against, a particular claim. If we think, for example, that a particular course of action is justified only if it would be widely accepted by the public, we need evidence that shows us whether the public would indeed accept that course of action. Finally, medical ethicists might draw on empirical methods to evaluate the impact of an ethical claim. If, for example, a research ethics committee is introduced in a healthcare setting to ensure that patients' well-being is safeguarded when these patients are recruited to a clinical trial, we need to be able to show that the intervention does indeed safeguard well-being. If not, there is no ethical justification for introducing the committee on the basis of this argument.

The scope of medical ethics

As well as being an academic pursuit, medical ethics is also practised 'on the ground' in healthcare settings. Ethicists provide ethical guidance by the bedside, in the hospital boardroom, or as part of committees working in health settings. These ethics support functions are described in Chapter 7. In addition to recommending a specific course of practice, arguments within medical ethics might also focus on the regulations or laws that govern healthcare practice.

Similarly, the boundaries of what counts as a medical ethics issue is also open to dispute. Medical ethics might be differentiated from healthcare ethics, where the former is more narrowly focused on the moral duties of doctors, while the latter broadens its analytic lens to other professionals and to non-medical settings such as social and community-based care services. Equally, the boundaries between medical ethics and bioethics are difficult to ascertain, with the latter orientated more towards biotechnological issues than the professional world of healthcare. In common parlance, these different terms are used interchangeably, and little hangs on where the boundaries are drawn.

2 Ethical theories and principles

Figure 2.1 The principles of beneficence and non-maleficence

Figure 2.2 Applying ethical theories and principles ... the clinician's dilemma

Medical Ethics, Law and Communication at a Glance, First Edition. Edited by Patrick Davey, Anna Rathmell, Michael Dunn, Charles Foster and Helen Salisbury.
© 2017 John Wiley & Sons, Ltd. Published 2017 by John Wiley & Sons, Ltd.

Introduction

Consider the relatively common scenario in a district general hospital late one evening: an elderly patient who collapsed at home with a large intra-cerebral bleed is now intubated and ventilated in the emergency department. Prior to intubation the patient is deeply unconscious, with a Glasgow Coma Score of three. His case has already been discussed with the neurosurgeons who feel that the transfer to the regional neurosurgical centre for further management is not appropriate because the predicted outcome are universally poor (Figure 2.1).

What is the next course of action? He could be admitted to the intensive care unit (ICU) for further assessment and review the following morning on withholding of sedation. Or should you consider a planned withdrawal of treatment that evening with his extubation and subsequent transfer to a medical ward for palliation? Does the knowledge that he is on the organ donation register make a difference? Will the situation change if this is the last empty bed in the ICU? Now consider your responses when it transpires that the patient is 96, not 69 as first thought. Are the wishes of the patient known to the clinical team? The family have been called and will not arrive this evening. How important is their input into the decisions that are required during the evening?

Ethical reasoning is critical to resolve ethical issues such as this one. However, if such reasoning is going to be able to guide clinicians' actions in ways that are justifiable, ethical theories and principles must be incorporated into this process. This chapter will provide the background to the main ethical theories, the ethical principles that are derived from those theories and that are relevant to contemporary medical ethics.

Three different ethical theories dominate the landscape of medical ethics. These function to determine how particular decisions or actions can be judged to be right or wrong in ethical terms. It is from these three theories that four ethical principles have been derived. The principles are well established in modern medicine. The method behind their application is intended to be simple and easy to apply across many clinical situations. These four principles are also described below.

Consequentialism

Consequentialist ethical theories claim that the rightness or wrongness of an action is judged solely by reference to the outcome of that action. For a consequentialist, the only morally relevant features of any action are its consequences.

Consequentialism is not a single ethical theory, rather it defines a category of theories. Utilitarianism is the most well-known consequentialist approach and the consequentialist theory that is most commonly applied and defended within healthcare. Utilitarianism gets its name from 'utility' – the value that ought to be maximised in determining the moral course of action. Utility is often interpreted in terms of 'welfare' or 'well-being'. There are at least three alternative forms of utilitarianism that can be differentiated by the way that welfare is accounted for:

- **Hedonistic** utilitarianism, where the right action is the one that involves the maximising of happiness.
- **Preference** utilitarianism, where the right action is the one that involves satisfying the maximum number of fully informed and rational preferences.
- **Ideal** utilitarianism, where the right action is the one that involves maximising particular goods in the world – those worthwhile things or activities that are taken to have objective value – beauty, or perhaps friendship.

Part of the strength of utilitarian theories is that they are simple to comprehend and appeal to common sense. They also chime closely with the central activity of providing optimal outcomes for patients and endorse 'well-being' as their central value – a concept that is well recognised and understood within medical practice. However the theory faces a number of practical problems when applied to healthcare decision making. There can be difficulties in predicting and in evaluating the consequences of any particular action. For example, several consequences can arise from one act and it can be difficult to predict the probability of certain consequences following an act. The question is whether there is one consequence that will outweigh all others. Furthermore, problems can be encountered when the act under consideration will benefit one person or group but may be to the detriment of others.

Duty-based ethics

Duty-based approaches define another category of ethical theories. These theories focus on the quality of the action itself rather than the consequences of that action. This ethical approach is also called '**deontology**' from the Greek for 'duty', *deon*. So duty-based ethics are concerned with what people are duty-bound to do, or how they are obliged to act. While such duties might extend to maximising the consequences of any action, it is not the maximisation of consequences per se that would make this action right, but that a relevant duty had been fulfilled. In other cases some actions will be wrong irrespective of the consequences. If one is duty-bound not to lie, for example, no reference to the benefits that might accrue from lying can provide an ethical justification for not telling the truth.

Much of the thinking behind duty-based ethics has arisen from the work of the eighteenth-century German philosopher Immanuel Kant, and Kantian deontology is the most common duty-based ethical theory. The basic premise of Kant's theory is that rational human beings have the capacity to make reasonable decisions and choose the right course of action. Kant formulated his theory and account of moral duties in a number of formulations of what he called the '**categorical imperative**', a rule that is true for all people in all circumstances. The right action must i) be one that is universal, ii) involve treating human beings as ends in themselves rather than merely as means to ends, iii) be autonomously willed by rational agents, and iv) establish the principles for a system of common laws.

More contemporary theorists have drawn upon and revised Kant's work on the morality of actions and rationality to reconfigure how moral duties apply and can be identified. Thomas M. Scanlon offers a different duty-based theory of ethics. He proposes that the judgement as to whether an action is right or wrong depends upon individuals identifying principles that can be mutually recognised and justified by reference to the value of ways of living with others that it would not be reasonable to reject. Scanlon offers a view into the complexities of determining universal duties, which he summarises as 'what we owe to each other' – a form of contractual moral agreement.

Virtue-based ethics

Arising from the ancient Greek philosophies of Plato and Aristotle, virtue ethics are based on an understanding that the rightness or wrongness of an action is based upon the character of the individual, rather than by reference to the action at all. In addition, virtue ethics provides guidance on the characteristics and behaviours a good person will demonstrate.

Virtue-based ethics focuses on the character of the person rather than their actions. The traditional virtues included prudence, justice, fortitude or bravery and finally, temperance. While one of the strengths of a virtue-based approach is that it centres on the person, the weakness is that it is unclear whether this theory can provide any guidance for action in the face of a moral dilemma.

Alasdair MacIntyre has been a key figure in contemporary virtue-based ethics. He has called the virtues or qualities of character 'internal goods'. MacIntyre has been a proponent of how virtues change over time while at the same time emphasising the historical context of ethics. The combination of the qualities of character viewed within both the historical and social context gives an understanding of how ethical issues arise and how the good life can be cultivated.

The four principles

Principlism is a method for ethical decision making in medicine that promotes the application of four principles. These four principles are second-order principles that have been derived from the three main ethical theories to form a useful and universal approach to working through ethical decision making. The aim is to be simple, easy to apply and culturally neutral. Henceforth, when confronting a problem, it can be helpful to apply each principle to allow some clarity and transparency to the situation, taking each different ethical theoretical insight into account.

The first principle, **respect for autonomy,** is the obligation to allow patients to self-govern their own lives, and to make decisions about their medical care in line with their own conception of their life plans. Respecting patient autonomy is usually understood as allowing healthcare providers to discuss and, if necessary, educate the patient about the different options available, but it does not allow the healthcare provider to make the decision for the patient. Implicit within this is the premise that medical practitioners must respect and follow those wishes, even if they believe that the decision is bad or incorrect.

The principles of **beneficence** and **non-maleficence** are closely related. Beneficence is the obligation to do good for patients: balancing the objective benefits of treatment against the risks and costs involved to provide the best medical care. This principle centres on the idea that welfare of patients is the main concern. This is often understood to mean that we must act in the 'best interests' of patients, a principle that has been invoked in English law although with rather different requirements. Conflict can arise when respecting a patient's autonomy means allowing the patient to make a decision that conflicts with what is thought to be in their best interests.

Non-maleficence is the obligation to avoid the causation of harm. As many treatments involve some degree of harm the principle of non-maleficence implies that the harm should not be out of proportion to the benefit of the treatment.

The final principle is **justice.** Justice requires medical practitioners to treat patients, and potentially the patients' caregivers, in a fair or just manner. What justice requires in any given situation will depend on which theory of justice is invoked in order to account for fair or equitable treatment. On some accounts, fair treatment will require equal treatment, but on other accounts a patient could be treated unequally but fairly. Justice considerations most commonly taken priority in dilemmas about the allocation of limited health resources between patients.

Applying ethical theories and principles

When applying theories and principles to real-world decisions such as the one detailed above a range of different considerations will need to be taken into account. From a utilitarian perspective, it is worth considering admitting the patient to intensive care and undertaking a sedation hold in the morning. At that point, a withdrawal of active treatment decision could be made and the process of liaison with the organ transplant coordinator could begin. From a deontological perspective, this approach should perhaps be reconsidered given that this is the last ICU bed available and the doctor is under an obligation to benefit the patient. Adopting a virtue-based approach, it is likely that the appropriate decision will have been reached having taken the time to assess the clinical situation and then seek the views of both the patient and his family, and also taken the time to explain the decision reached to the entire clinical team.

Following discussion with the elderly patient's family, it transpires that the patient would not have wanted admission to an ICU and would not have wanted to be resuscitated in the event of a cardiac arrest (Figure 2.2). Tissue donation is still a possibility and would have been in keeping with his wishes. The patient's autonomy has been respected. In view of the likely clinical consequences, this is likely to be in his best interests and no harm has been done: so beneficence has been practised. Given that there is now still an ICU bed available, it would appear that justice has been done. The application of the four ethical principles allows satisfactory resolution of a potentially complex situation.

Different outcomes may have followed. There is no single approach that is right or wrong but an understanding of the ethical theories and principles allows a decision to be made. The application of an ethical framework allows greater transparency and accountability in justifying the decisions that are reached while at the same time allowing different aspects of the problem to be taken into consideration together.

Further reading

Gillon, R. *Philosophical medical ethics*, 1986. Oxford: Wiley-Blackwell.

Danbury, C., Newdick, C., Waldmann, C. and Lawson, A. *Law and ethics in intensive care*, 1st edn, 2010. Oxford University Press.

Scanlon, T.M. *What we owe to each other*, 2000. Cambridge MA, London: Harvard University Press.

MacIntyre, A. *A short history of ethics*, 2nd edn, 1998. Oxford: Routledge.

3 Ethical reasoning

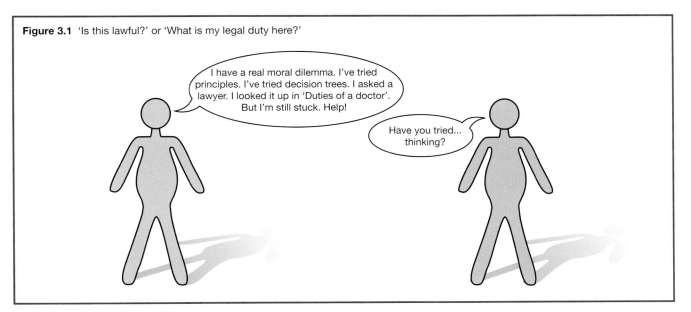

Figure 3.1 'Is this lawful?' or 'What is my legal duty here?'

Medical Ethics, Law and Communication at a Glance, First Edition. Edited by Patrick Davey, Anna Rathmell, Michael Dunn, Charles Foster and Helen Salisbury.
© 2017 John Wiley & Sons, Ltd. Published 2017 by John Wiley & Sons, Ltd.

Introduction

Most of the time in clinical practice, the essence of knowing what to do (and what not to do) in a given situation is fairly clear, given good medical training, experience and sound management. Ethical reasoning, as such, is rarely called for. Indeed, it would be hard to practise medicine in any useful way if one had to stop every 5 minutes and think hard about what to do, whether it was morally justified and so on. What is called for quite routinely is good practical judgement, well-developed communication skills, and medical and surgical proficiency. Compare legal knowledge: most of the time most of us are able to go about our daily lives rather successfully without knowing more than a few things about the law, and without needing to worry too much about what is lawful. While medicine does require doctors to have a good basic legal knowledge of matters relating to medical practice, and a thorough grasp of the guidance and rules of the General Medical Council (GMC), only occasionally will doctors need to stop and ask 'Is this lawful?' or 'What is my legal duty here?'

So much for preliminary reassurances: there are nevertheless occasions when ethical reasoning is necessary. One kind of occasion when it is important is when thinking reflectively about one's practice. It is impossible to practise medicine well without spending at least some time thinking quietly about one's work, one's motivations, one's hard cases, one's challenging colleagues, and patients and family members. It is no accident that so many great doctors have turned to the arts as a medium for this sort of reflection, nor that the arts have turned so often to medicine for subject matter when they wish to reflect on the human condition. But even on a more everyday level, reflecting on the choices that one makes, the tensions and difficulties that one faces, the values one tries to realise and live up to are part and parcel of the necessary 'backstage' work for successful and humane medical practice. It is also useful practice for the second kind of situation where ethical reasoning is called for: the hard case. And indeed it helps in the third kind of situation where ethical reasoning is essential: the making of policy.

Policy making might seem a bit remote from the everyday concerns of medical practice, but in fact 'policy' doesn't just mean law making in parliament or the development of guidance by regulatory bodies like the GMC or professional bodies such as the BMA and the Royal Colleges. Policy, as a consensual decision about how to handle a specific issue or situation, can be made at any level of the profession or within an organisation, even down to the individual general practice or hospital ward. However, the test of good policy is how it helps guide in particular cases, and for that reason this chapter concentrates on ethical reasoning in cases.

It is only a slight exaggeration to say that ethical reasoning begins from a feeling – often just a feeling of unease, sometimes a feeling of anger or sadness, or perhaps shame or embarrassment or guilt: 'There is something wrong here', 'I am not sure what to do here', How do we get out of this one? The feeling gives us a clue to a mismatch or tension of some kind: between theory and practice, principle and willpower, conscience and orders, competing demands of different interested parties. So the critical first point in any process of ethical reasoning is tuning into that feeling, identifying what prompts it and trying to figure out what the question is. Once we've identified that question, we can start to refine it, probe more deeply, test whether we've really got down to the fundamental problem. The fundamental problem is not likely to be anything very metaphysical or profound – in most cases – but rather it will be something difficult, which will make a difference to what we should actually do.

For instance: a baby is born after 25 weeks' gestation. It is in serious respiratory distress and has a low birth weight even for its gestational age. There is disagreement in the neonatal care team about what the best course of treatment for the baby should be – essentially, whether intensive efforts should be made to keep the baby alive, or not – and the baby's parents are under great stress.

A couple of preliminary observations: first, in reality, no neonatal intensive care team would approach this case as a novel challenge, and there would be policies and protocols in place. Second, in reality, decision making would focus on the fine clinical details of how to give the best medical support to **this** specific baby (and our case example is far too coarsely described to allow for us to follow that reasoning in detail here). Nonetheless, what the case does illustrate is a **type** of scenario that does challenge and concern paediatricians and intensivists and nurses, and which also makes a fairly common appearance in public debates (not only about caring for sick babies, but also about abortion and end of life decision making). From this case, or more precisely, from a much more richly detailed clinical situation, we start to think. We think: What sort of case is this? Have we seen one like it before? How did we decide then? Were we happy with the decision we reached? Did it work out as we expected? Is there a **principle** we can identify in that previous decision that explains it and justifies it? Does this principle apply to the current case?

This kind of approach is known as **casuistry**. It can be developed with great subtlety and sophistication, but at its simplest it requires only three things: a sensitivity to and awareness of the ethical features of situations; an attention to consistency in argument; and an extensive range of settled cases for use in testing and comparing claims about the present situation. In this respect it is very like legal argumentation. Critics of casuistry claim that it falls into the trap of 'mere' pragmatism (doing what seems least likely to cause trouble or will be most popular without proper attention to principle) or even relativism (since it finds its principles in the habits and values of a particular community and doesn't appear to rely on these being in any way objective or true). Many defenders of the use of principles in medical ethics make just these criticisms. But in practice, arguing from principles is never as deductive as it first appears, and the test of a principled argument is often how well it coheres with past experience, 'common sense', conscience and consensus among interested parties. Philosophers often call this process of testing one's conclusions against empirical facts 'well-understood comparison cases', and the consensus in a group of well-informed people 'reflective equilibrium'.

The other point to make is that it is a mistake to think that ethical reasoning is like mathematical reasoning: we don't start from axioms and make deductions and proofs. It is more like scientific reasoning, in that it is a mixture of induction and inference to the best explanation. Casuistical reasoning seeks to identify principles that emerge from the disciplined consideration of cases, and which can be applied – and tested and refined – in novel cases. Casuistry is not unprincipled, but it has a healthy scepticism about principles. In most situations, if your principle leads you to an unexpected or shocking conclusion, the casuist is more likely to think that something has gone wrong with your reasoning than that something has gone wrong with your moral common sense. On the other hand, unlike a moral conservatism (including many versions of 'communitarianism' – the test of what is right is basically what the moral community you are a member of says is right), casuistry is open to novelty and innovation. It's just that if you are going to draw radical conclusions, you need to give strong and compelling reasons, and show why your conclusion rests on a principle that works better at making coherent sense of a whole range of cases than the alternatives. Unlike in science, where we'd test the different claims by experiment, in ethical reasoning all we have is a test of coherence among the principles we've identified and the cases we can accept as relevant to the issue we are thinking about.

This then is a crucial feature of moral reasoning. It is not something you do on your own. Even if you are obliged to make a decision entirely on your own, for some reason, moral reasoning is a practice of arguing and giving reasons, and dealing with objections and criticisms, before drawing final conclusions. Moral reasoning does not depend on personal charisma or arrogance: it depends on drawing conclusions you can and should be able to explain and justify.

So, in conclusion: ethical reasoning is at the heart of good healthcare, as indeed it is at the heart of most worthwhile human activities. It is not always necessary: well-designed institutions, good management and good training make good ethical practice almost a matter of routine. But where it is necessary – in hard cases, in disputes or in making policy – good ethical reasoning is necessary. It will inevitably depend on the **intellectual virtues** of prudence, patience, tolerance and awareness of one's limitations and the merits of others' arguments and points of view. It requires patience, and can be slow and painstaking. Its outcomes may be somewhat provisional and open to challenge and revision. But there is no shortcut to good decision making and good patient care in ethics, any more than in any other branch of medical science and clinical judgement.

Further reading

Daniels, N. *Justice and justification: reflective equilibrium in theory and practice*, 1996. Cambridge UK: Cambridge University Press.

Jonsen, A. and Toulmin, S. *The abuse of casuistry: a history of moral reasoning*, 1988. Berkeley CA: University of California Press.

McGee, G. (ed.) *Pragmatic bioethics*, 2nd edn, 2003. Cambridge MA: MIT Press.

Williams, B. *Ethics and the limits of philosophy*, 3rd edn, 2011. London: Routledge.

Zagzebski, L. *Virtues of the mind: an inquiry into the nature of virtue and the ethical foundations of knowledge*, 1996. Cambridge UK: Cambridge University Press.

4 What is medical law?

Figure 4.1 Failed sterilisation

Figure 4.2 End of life

Figure 4.3 Non-consensual C-section

Figure 4.4 Breaching surrogacy arrangement

Medical Ethics, Law and Communication at a Glance, First Edition. Edited by Patrick Davey, Anna Rathmell, Michael Dunn, Charles Foster and Helen Salisbury.
© 2017 John Wiley & Sons, Ltd. Published 2017 by John Wiley & Sons, Ltd.

Introduction

'Medical law' refers to the laws that cover the wide range of issues that arise in the context of medicine. These include clinical negligence, ensuring adequate consent has been obtained for treatment, resource allocation decisions, measures to protect confidentiality, a raft of laws designed to regulate reproductive decision making, laws determining how those suffering mental disorders should be treated and, finally, provisions restricting what may be done as a person approaches the end of his or her life. It is an area of law bound together by its subject matter, rather than a discrete body of rules. It encompasses aspects of both criminal and civil law, as well as EU law, human rights law, administrative law and family law. This chapter will summarise some of the key areas of medical law, and provide a brief introduction to the legal dimensions of the chapters that follow.

Criminal and civil dimensions of medical law

There are criminal law aspects to a number of areas of medical law:

• It is a criminal offence to terminate a pregnancy (in the absence of one the statutory defences provided under the Abortion Act 1967).
• Mental disorders may have an impact on the charges brought against a defendant, as well as implications for sentencing.
• The Human Reproductive Cloning Act 2001 made reproductive human cloning a criminal offence punishable by up to 10 years' imprisonment.
• Police may access otherwise confidential medical records if investigating a 'serious arrestable offence' according to the Police and Criminal Evidence Act 1984.
• Euthanasia falls within the ambit of criminal laws against killing human beings.
• A doctor who kills a patient through gross negligence may be criminally liable for manslaughter.

In addition to these and other criminal laws covering medical issues, a range of civil claims may be brought for harms suffered in the medical context. The most common are clinical negligence claims against medical practitioners (and hospitals) for injuries suffered as a result of carelessness.

The roles of the criminal and civil areas of law are quite distinct. The function of the criminal law is largely punitive – to punish a wrongdoer. Such laws may also have a deterrent effect. By contrast, the civil law, particularly tort law, aims to compensate the victim for the harm suffered (or vindicate a breach of his rights). There are some areas of overlap, such as gross negligence, where the careless practitioner might be open to both criminal punishment and a civil claim for compensation.

These two means of dealing with misconduct are augmented by the regulatory role taken by the GMC. Medical practitioners cannot practise without registering with the GMC, and hence the council can use this power to deal with medical misconduct via restricting, suspending or even refusing registration of a practitioner whose conduct falls below the required standard.

Areas of medical law

Consent and capacity

A basic premise of medical law is that treatment should be consensual. This means that patients should decide for themselves whether they want to be treated, and which treatments they will accept. Medical practitioners are almost invariably bound to comply with a patient's wishes, even if they will result in disability or death.

• Consent operates 'negatively', in the sense that a competent patient is entirely free to refuse treatment, but does not have the right to demand it.
• The law recognises that a child's capacity to make decisions increases with age and maturity.
• Mental disabilities, both congenital and acquired, can affect a person's ability to understand information or make decisions, while some conditions mean a person is likely to lose some or all of their capacity to make competent decisions. The Mental Capacity Act 2005 outlines how medical practitioners are to determine what to do in these situations, including those where the person has made an advance directive.

Clinical negligence

At times, medical practitioners make careless errors. These errors include:

• delayed diagnosis or misdiagnosis, leading to a worsening of the condition;
• failure to perform a procedure correctly, such as a botched surgery, resulting in physical injury;
• failure to warn of the risks of a procedure, affecting the choices made by the patient;
• pursuing the wrong course of treatment;
• providing incorrect information, such as information about the health of a foetus that might affect a decision as to whether to continue a pregnancy.

The law in this area aims to provide people who have been harmed by a medical practitioner's negligence with compensation for what they have suffered. Only those harms that are actually **caused** by the practitioner's negligence will be compensated.

The law requires a medical practitioner to meet a minimum standard of behaviour, which is defined as 'a practice accepted as proper by a responsible body of medical men skilled in that particular art' (*Bolam* v *Friern Hospital Management Committee* [1957] WLR 582). If a practitioner's actions do not meet this standard and result in harm to a patient, they may be liable to pay compensation.

Reproduction

Having children is important to many people, and consequently when there are problems with reproduction the result can be emotionally distressing. Reproduction also involves the interests of more than one person, and potentially many people. In some cases, there may be clashes between the conceiving couple only, such as whether or not to continue a pregnancy. But assisted reproductive technologies like *in vitro* fertilisation bring other people with different interests into the mix, including egg and sperm donors, surrogates and commissioning parents. Our increasing ability to detect traits in foetuses *in utero*, and even in embryos before implantation, also brings the interests of future children into this complex equation. Medical law in this context attempts to regulate the difficult conflicts that can arise, and also sets some limits on the reproductive choices people may make.

- Sometimes a woman will want to end a pregnancy. Although widely regarded as lawful, aborting a pregnancy is actually a criminal act under the Offences Against the Person Act 1861, with the Abortion Act 1967 operating to provide limited statutory defences.
- Surrogates may be used to help infertile people have children. The Surrogacy Arrangements Act 1985 does not prohibit surrogacy, but makes surrogacy agreements unenforceable. The law also determines who will be the mother and father of the resulting child and how legal parenthood may be transferred (Figure 4.1).
- Assisted reproductive technologies (ARTs) like *in vitro* fertilisation can help some women conceive. Access to, and use of, these technologies is regulated by the Human Fertilisation and Embryology Acts. These Acts also outline when ARTs may be used to select embryos to avoid unwanted conditions, or to create a so-called 'saviour sibling'.
- The courts have developed principles about how much, if any, compensation will be paid if an unwanted pregnancy arises after a failed sterilisation (Figure 4.2).

End of life

As a person approaches the end of life, they may be faced with a range of difficult circumstances and decisions. Our choices about how we would like our lives to end are by their very nature tremendously personal. They may also have profound impacts on our quality of life during our final months and weeks, as well as on those around us (Figure 4.3). Some people suffer greatly as they approach the end of life. They may experience intolerable pain, frustration at their incapacitation or embarrassment at the indignities to which their condition exposes them. In such cases, they may wish to end their lives.

The laws relating to end of life attempt to balance a belief in the intrinsic value of human life with compassionate recognition that people should have the freedom to choose how they will end their days. The law continues to evolve as we try to determine how to strike the best balance between these considerations. In recent years, suicide has been decriminalised, while the Director of Public Prosecutions has released guidance on when those who assist another to commit suicide are unlikely to be prosecuted. Active euthanasia by a medical practitioner is still legally considered a criminal offence (most likely murder), although the courts have been sympathetic to doctrine of double effect arguments in favour of acquittal.

Mental health

There are both criminal and civil aspects to the law on mental health. Under the criminal law, a person suffering from a mental disorder who commits a crime may be able to invoke a range of defences. These include diminished capacity, insanity and automatism. If successfully raised, a mental disorder defence may affect the charges made against the defendant, and/or give the judge discretion to take account of the disorder during sentencing.

The civil aspects of mental health law address the treatment of people with mental disorders, including:

- capacity to consent to treatment;
- voluntary admission (and treatment) for mental health disorders;
- compulsory detention;
- compulsory treatment for mental health disorders;
- criteria for discharge;
- care of mentally disordered patients in the community.

Changes in our understanding of, and attitude towards, people with mental disorders, coupled with the European Convention on Human Rights and the Human Rights Act 1998 have prompted reform of mental health law in recent years. The law now takes greater account of the need to promote the welfare of the mentally disordered through greater care in the community (as opposed to incarceration) and provides measures to protect their socio-economic interests as well.

Confidentiality

Medical information is often highly personal and sensitive. Effective patient care is promoted by protecting confidentiality as it encourages patients to give full, honest information to their medical professional. Confidentiality of medical information is protected via both the common law and the Data Protection Act 1998, as well as provisions in legislation covering specific areas of medicine such as the Human Fertilisation and Embryology Act 1990 and the Abortion Regulations 1991. The GMC also uses its powers to ensure that patient confidentiality is respected.

Resource allocation

Medical resources are finite, and choices have to be made about which individuals and which conditions should receive priority. An obvious tension between the interests of individuals and the community arises in this context. Human rights law therefore has a role to play in this area of law.

Resource allocation decisions are made by government agencies under the provisions of the National Health Service Act 2006. The courts can be involved if an allocation decision is challenged. Judicial review of such decisions is available on the grounds of irrationality, illegality or error. It is not the court's role, however, to judge the merits of the decision itself beyond these grounds.

Compensation culture

'Compensation culture' is the belief that people are increasingly keen to bring legal claims if they believe their medical treatment has resulted in harm (Figure 4.4), and it is true that the number of negligence claims brought against doctors has increased hugely in the past four decades.

The term is often used pejoratively to suggest that many of these claims are unwarranted. This may be because the treatment was not negligent, despite resulting in injury. Or, it may be argued that errors are an inherent aspect of medical practice and should in some cases be accepted, leaving the loss to lie where it falls.

One problematic consequence of this supposed cultural shift is that NHS resources that could be spent on patient care are instead used to pay legal fees to defend medical practitioners. Another possible consequence is that practitioners' fear of being sued may affect their treatment decisions. This might mean pursuing less risky, but potentially less effective treatments. High litigation rates also drive up insurance premiums for some medical practitioners. For example, obstetricians face particularly high rates of litigation over things that go wrong during birth, and are as a result subject to very high premiums.

5 The English legal system

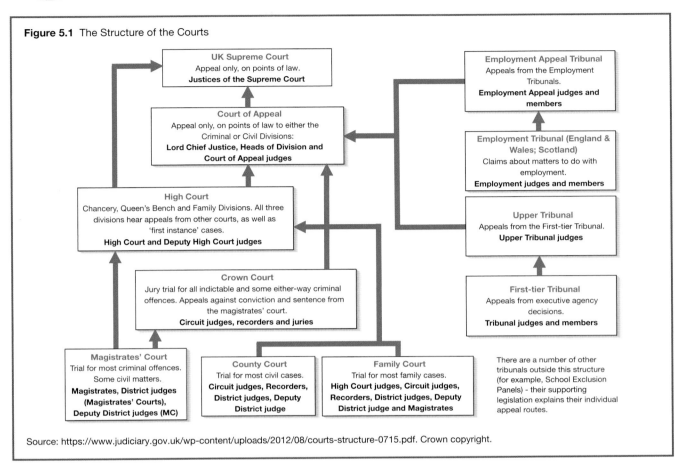

Figure 5.1 The Structure of the Courts

UK Supreme Court
Appeal only, on points of law.
Justices of the Supreme Court

Court of Appeal
Appeal only, on points of law to either the Criminal or Civil Divisions:
Lord Chief Justice, Heads of Division and Court of Appeal judges

High Court
Chancery, Queen's Bench and Family Divisions. All three divisions hear appeals from other courts, as well as 'first instance' cases.
High Court and Deputy High Court judges

Crown Court
Jury trial for all indictable and some either-way criminal offences. Appeals against conviction and sentence from the magistrates' court.
Circuit judges, recorders and juries

Magistrates' Court
Trial for most criminal offences. Some civil matters.
Magistrates, District judges (Magistrates' Courts), Deputy District judges (MC)

County Court
Trial for most civil cases.
Circuit judges, Recorders, District judges, Deputy District judge

Family Court
Trial for most family cases.
High Court judges, Circuit judges, Recorders, District judges, Deputy District judge and Magistrates

Employment Appeal Tribunal
Appeals from the Employment Tribunals.
Employment Appeal judges and members

Employment Tribunal (England & Wales; Scotland)
Claims about matters to do with employment.
Employment judges and members

Upper Tribunal
Appeals from the First-tier Tribunal.
Upper Tribunal judges

First-tier Tribunal
Appeals from executive agency decisions.
Tribunal judges and members

There are a number of other tribunals outside this structure (for example, School Exclusion Panels) - their supporting legislation explains their individual appeal routes.

Source: https://www.judiciary.gov.uk/wp-content/uploads/2012/08/courts-structure-0715.pdf. Crown copyright.

Medical Ethics, Law and Communication at a Glance, First Edition. Edited by Patrick Davey, Anna Rathmell, Michael Dunn, Charles Foster and Helen Salisbury.
© 2017 John Wiley & Sons, Ltd. Published 2017 by John Wiley & Sons, Ltd.

Overview

Sources of law

The principal sources of law in the English legal system are:

- legislation;
- case law; and
- European law.

Legislation

Parliament is the supreme law-making body. Parliament passes laws in the form of Acts of Parliament. Laws that arise in this way are known as statutes ('primary legislation') and statutory instruments ('secondary legislation').

Case law

Interpretation is the responsibility of judges in the courts. In their interpretation of statutes and in their application of the law to the facts of particular cases, judges play an important role in developing case law. The English legal system is a common law system.

In applying the law, courts are bound to follow the legal principles that have been set out by higher-ranking courts. The principles that judges use in deciding cases generally bind lower courts. This is known as the doctrine of binding precedent, or *stare decisis*. If a case has been heard by a court of a higher standing, the judge in the new case will be bound to follow the principles established in the earlier case. The body of precedent is referred to as the common law.

European law

European Union (EU)

The United Kingdom joined the European Economic Community (EEC) on 1 January 1973. The EEC eventually became the EU. Since joining, the UK has been obliged to incorporate rules of law prescribed by the institutions of the EU: the European Commission, the Council of Ministers and the European Parliament. European law encompasses a wide variety of areas, including the creation and maintenance of a free market of goods and services between EU member states, standards for the manufacturing of goods and employment law. Currently, where a dispute arises in the English courts relating to the interpretation of European law, such disputes can ultimately be referred for determination to the European Court of Justice.

European Convention on Human Rights and Fundamental Freedoms

The European Convention on Human Rights (ECHR) 1950 protects several basic human rights such as the right to life (Article 2), the right to a fair trial (Article 6) and freedom of expression (Article 10). Since the Human Rights Act 1998 came into force on 1 October 2000, the ECHR has been incorporated into UK law. This means that the human rights protected by the ECHR are directly enforceable in English courts without having to take a case to a European court. UK courts must decide cases in a way that is consistent with the ECHR. If they decide that a piece of legislation is incompatible with the ECHR, they issue a 'declaration of incompatibility' – a direction to parliament that there is an incompatibility and a non-enforceable invitation to make it compatible.

The constitution

While the United States, South Africa and Ireland, for example, all have a single document that serves as their constitution, the British constitution comprises a web of statute law, case law, custom and conventions. To say that the UK has no written constitution is not to say that it has no written constitutional material. Rather, it means that there is no **single** written document that serves as **the** constitution.

The UK constitution rests on three principles:

1 Sovereignty of parliament.
2 Rule of law.
3 Separation of powers.

Sovereignty of parliament

The doctrine of parliamentary sovereignty maintains that the parliament can make or unmake any law whatsoever, and no person or body can set aside the legislation of parliament [Dicey]. Parliament has the right to make any law whatsoever, however unjust or irrational. Once parliament has made a law, those within the jurisdiction are legally obliged to comply with it, whether or not they agree with it. This extends to the courts having the duty to apply whatever law parliament makes, irrespective of the content of the law. Provided that the law is made by parliament, the courts are obliged to apply and enforce it.

Rule of law

Power should not be exercised by the state in the absence of legal authority for such action. That is, the state should not be free to exercise its powers arbitrarily. The law regulates the legitimate use of state power. The rule of law also dictates that everyone should be subject to the same law – that is, no one is above the law and the same law should be applied to everyone. There should be equality before the law.

Separation of powers

Under the separation of powers, the three main functions of government – rule making, rule execution and rule adjudication – are kept apart by dividing them into three branches to prevent the concentration of power in a single body. The rule-making function is taken up by parliament (the legislature). This branch consists of the members of parliament in both the House of Commons and House of Lords. The rule-execution function (implementing and enforcing the law) is taken up by the Executive. This branch comprises the government (the Prime Minister and other ministers in cabinet) and the civil service, including local authorities, and the police. The rule-adjudication function is taken up by the judiciary. This branch consists of the judiciary, which is independent of parliament and the executive. Indeed, it is a central function of the judiciary to adjudicate impartially disputes between citizens and the executive.

UK courts and tribunals

Jurisdictions and judiciaries

The UK is made up of three separate jurisdictions – England and Wales, Scotland, and Northern Ireland. This separation is reflected in three distinct national court systems, or judiciaries. Operating above each of these judiciaries is one overarching senior UK judiciary: the Supreme Court, the final UK destination for the majority of disputes started in each of the national jurisdictions (Figure 5.1). Beyond the UK courts, certain matters can be escalated to the Court of Justice of the European Union (http://curia.europa.eu) or the European Court of Human Rights (www.echr.coe.int).

In addition to the courts, there are also several types of tribunal. This chapter will focus only on the hearings, tribunals and courts operating in England and Wales that are relevant to the provision of healthcare.

Professional standards hearings

A new adjudication framework was created in 2012 to convene non-judicial hearings applying the professional standards of the General Medical Council (GMC) (www.gmc-uk.org). The Medical Practitioners Tribunal Service (MPTS) (www.mpts-uk.org), which is operationally separate from the GMC, is responsible for the conduct of all adjudication hearings relating to doctors' fitness to practise in the UK. Under this new system, the GMC will continue to issue formal professional guidance, grant licences to practise in the UK and carry out investigations into alleged breaches of professional standards, but the MPTS will conduct disciplinary hearings independently of the GMC. There have been, and will be, some significant changes in procedure, such as legally qualified chairs in hearings; a greater reliance on written, rather than oral, evidence; and allowing the GMC to appeal against the decisions of MPTS hearings.

MPTS fitness to practise hearings follow a three-stage process:

1 **Findings of fact** (panel decides if allegations/admissions are proven by evidence);
2 **Decision on impairment** (a warning will be issued if fitness to practise is not deemed to be impaired); and
3 **Decision on the sanction** (if an impairment is proven, a doctor's registration can be restricted or removed).

Findings of the MPTS can be appealed by the doctor(s) in question (either against a warning, or a removal/restriction of their registration), or by the Commission for Healthcare Regulatory Excellence if the decision is deemed too lenient. Appeals must be made to the High Court of Justice in England and Wales, which must decide whether to dismiss the appeal, allow the appeal and quash the MPTS decision, impose a different decision or refer the case back to the MPTS for reconsideration.

Tribunals

Tribunals are specialist judicial bodies that decide disputes in particular areas of law. Two tiers exist: the First-tier Tribunal and the Upper Tribunal. The Health, Education and Social Care Chamber is one of six chambers in the First-tier, and will deal with matters in four areas:

1 **Care standards** – Appeals against decisions about an individual's right to work with children or vulnerable adults, and the registration of the provision of some types of health care, childcare and social care;
2 **Mental health** – Reviews of cases concerning the detention or discharge of patients under the Mental Health Act;

3 **Special educational needs or disability** – Appeals against decisions made by local education authorities about children's education; and
4 **Primary health lists** – Appeals by health professionals about the management of the lists of those permitted to provide healthcare services on the NHS.

Appeals from this chamber of the First-tier can be made to the Administrative Appeals Chamber in the Upper Tribunal. Appeals from the Upper Tribunal can be made to the Court of Appeal.

Most tribunals are administered by panels made up of a legally qualified chairperson and other members who possess particular professional expertise. Tribunal proceedings are more informal than court proceedings and the parties will often not use the services of an external lawyer. The scope of a tribunal to impose penalties is quite limited compared with the courts.

Courts

In England and Wales, Magistrates' Courts deal with the vast majority of criminal cases. County Courts deal with many civil cases. Only certain civil matters (for instance, some cases concerning the welfare of children) will be heard by a Magistrates' Court. Proceedings in Magistrates' Courts will be overseen by legally qualified District Judges, or unqualified (and unpaid) justices of the peace. Only Judges or District Judges sit in the County Courts.

More serious criminal cases, and appeals from Magistrates' Courts, are heard at the Crown Courts. Claims for damages for clinical negligence may be heard either by the County Court or the High Court.

Appeals from the High Court and Crown Courts will be made to the Court of Appeal, to the Civil and Criminal Divisions, respectively.

In 2009, the Supreme Court replaced the House of Lords as the highest court in the UK, a move to ensure a more tangible separation between judicial and political or legislative functions. The Supreme Court hears appeals either directly from the High Court (known as a 'leapfrog procedure') or, more ordinarily, from the Court of Appeal.

Further reading

Boylan-Kemp, J. The legal system. Part 1: It's not just for lawyers. *British Journal of Nursing* 2009; 18:2, 106–108.

Boylan-Kemp, J. The legal system. Part 2: It's not just for lawyers. *British Journal of Nursing* 2009; 18:3, 178–180.

Dicey, A.V. *Introduction to the Study of the Law of the Constitution*, 8th edn, 1915. London: Macmillan.

Partington, M. *Introduction to the English legal system 2013–2014*, 2013. Oxford University Press.

Rivlin, G. *Understanding the law*, 6th edn, 2012. Oxford University Press.

Slapper, G. and Kelly, D. *The English legal system*, 14th edn, 2012. London: Routledge.

6 Relationship between ethics, law and professionalism

Figure 6.1 The relationship between ethics, law and professionalism

(a)

(b)

(c)

A patient comes into a GP's surgery, complaining of a 10-week history of rectal bleeding. 'It's nothing to worry about,' says the GP briskly, without conducting any sort of examination. 'This sort of thing happens a lot. It's probably just piles. It'll sort itself out. Come back in a couple of months if it hasn't cleared up.' The patient, reassured, goes away.

By the time he returns, in a couple of months, even this incompetent GP can palpate a mass. The patient is referred. There's an adenocarcinoma of the colon. The prognosis is now poor.

The patient, outraged, makes a complaint to the GMC. The newspapers get to hear of it and several other patients, having read about what's gone on, make similar complaints. Apparently the GP is notoriously lazy. An examination is the exception rather than the rule – particularly on a Friday afternoon.

The GMC is concerned. After an investigation, the GP is referred to a 'fitness to practise' panel of the MPTS. The case is characterised as one of misconduct rather than merely inadequate performance. The GP, it is alleged, consistently put his own interests (e.g. in knocking off early) ahead of his patient, failed to perform the examination or institute the investigations required of a competent GP, and hadn't even heard of the guidelines governing referral in cases of rectal bleeding. By calling this 'misconduct', the GMC was saying that the case smelt of bad ethics.

The GP is also sued in the civil court. Sadly the patient dies. His death, says the evidence, would probably have been avoided by earlier referral. The allegations of breach of duty in the civil claim are essentially the same as the 'ethical' allegations made by the GMC. Yet the High Court judge, giving judgment against the GP, emphasises, rightly, that 'this is not a court of morals'. What's going on?

It's common for 'medical law' and 'medical ethics' to be mentioned in the same breath – for instance, in the title of this book and in the name of many university courses. Yet the relationship between medical ethics and law is complex and obscure. Medical law isn't just medical ethics with judicial teeth. There are plenty of purely ethical courts (the GMC fitness to practice panel, for instance) with very sharp teeth. The better position is that these are tribunals of professionalism rather than ethics, but the distinction between ethics and professionalism is, in practice, blurred to the point of non-existence.

In *Airedale NHS Trust* v *Bland* (1993), Lord Justice Hoffmann said: 'I would expect medical ethics to be formed by the law, rather than the reverse.' It's not immediately obvious that this is right. It looks rather like judicial wishful thinking. The *Bolam* test (see Chapter 8) says that a doctor will be liable in the civil law of negligence if what he has done would not be endorsed by any responsible body of opinion in the relevant specialty (Figure 6.1). And often (for instance, in the law of consent) an important source used in determining what responsible doctors do and don't do is the guidance issued by the authoritative professional organisations such as the GMC. Some of that guidance has a distinctly ethical flavour. So ethics often gets carried into the law on the back of *Bolam*. Sometimes the connection between ethics and law is said to be even more direct. Here, for instance, is Simon Brown LJ summarising his review of the cases on clinical confidentiality in *R* v *Department of Health ex p Source Informatics Ltd* (2000):

> To my mind the one clear and consistent theme emerging from all these authorities is this: the confidant is placed under a duty of good faith to the confider and the touchstone by which to judge the scope of his duty and whether or not it has been fulfilled or breached is his own conscience, no more and no less …

If that's right, an ethical doctor will be a legal doctor. Ethics leads the way.

But it's not so simple. Who drafts the ethical guidelines? Very often there's a significant input from lawyers. Ethicists are often too deferential to lawyers on matters of ethics. They often assume that lawyers are more philosophically literate than they really are, and that the lawyers have accordingly taken into account, in articulating legal principles, ideas of moral philosophy that have really never occurred to them. This is dangerous. The stuff of medical law – human life and death – continually begs philosophical questions. There should be a fecund, mutually respectful marriage between medical law and ethics. And indeed there is a marriage. But too often Lord Justice Hoffmann is right: ethics listens meekly to the law like an uncritically adoring wife in a bullying patriarchy.

Generalisations are difficult. Perhaps all that can usefully be said, without generating a flurry of footnotes, is that a doctor who acts professionally will be both ethical and lawful, a doctor who acts ethically is likely to act lawfully, but that a doctor who acts merely lawfully might nonetheless be found by a regulator to have acted unethically. The law is often more forgiving than the statutory regulator.

7 Ethical decisions in practice

Figure 7.1 Resolving dilemmas and conflicts

Medical Ethics, Law and Communication at a Glance, First Edition. Edited by Patrick Davey, Anna Rathmell, Michael Dunn, Charles Foster and Helen Salisbury.
© 2017 John Wiley & Sons, Ltd. Published 2017 by John Wiley & Sons, Ltd.

Making ethical decisions in practice

Doctors are required to make ethical decisions on a daily basis. Indeed, all decisions made regarding patient care should be ethically justifiable. Sometimes the right course of action is straightforward and practical judgement is all that is required: for example, the challenge of communicating effectively with an adult patient who has just awoken from a surgical procedure in order to obtain consent for additional interventions. Often, however, it is the ethical considerations themselves that create difficulties or conflicts in decision making. Deciding what is in a patient's best interests when they cannot decide for themselves, or whether it is justifiable to share patient information with a member of their family, can create dilemmas for the doctor or conflict with patients and families, or within the healthcare team. Resolving these dilemmas and conflicts requires ethical awareness, ethical knowledge and reasoning skills (Figure 7.1).

Identifying ethical issues

In order to make or implement ethical decisions, it is necessary, first, to identify that there is an ethical issue that requires attention. Knowledge of ethical principles and concepts will help to increase your awareness of the ethical dimension of your practice: for example, recognising potential breaches of confidentiality or the importance of appropriate consent. But often ethical concerns are complex and only become apparent if there are conflicting views about the right course of action in a particular case, or when a health professional has a sense of unease about a particular decision or situation. Conflict or unease do not necessarily mean that there is an ethical problem to resolve, but they should act as a flag to prompt further reflection about the decisions being made.

Understanding the context

Ethical decisions are not made in a vacuum. Good ethical decision making requires knowledge of the relevant facts of the case. Knowing the risks and benefits of a treatment may influence how to respond to someone who refuses it, or inform the assessment of whether it is in their best interests to have it. If a patient's lack of capacity is temporary, it may not be necessary to make a decision about whether the proposed treatment is what they would want, but appropriate to wait and ask them when they regain capacity. Information about a person's home circumstances or available social support may help to assess the consequences of the management options available.

Recognising different perspectives

Ethical decisions are primarily about values, specifically moral values, and ethical dilemmas arise when there are conflicting values at stake. Given the diversity of moral theories, it is clear that there will be differences in the relative weight given to particular moral values by different individuals in a particular clinical situation. It is not only moral values that are important in clinical practice. How we value certain aspects of our lives will inform how we make decisions about medical treatment. If being independent is a priority for me and I am paralysed, then I may be prepared to risk significant harm from surgery for a small chance of being able to walk again. Cultural and religious values are closely linked with moral values and will influence how a person, whether patient or healthcare professional, approaches particular decisions. Recognising the different perspectives being brought to bear on a case, and particularly being aware of one's values and how they influence thinking, is crucially important in making good ethical decisions.

Ethical decision making

Ethical decisions require ethical justification and, in the case of healthcare, these decisions may have to withstand public scrutiny and challenge. So a sound knowledge of relevant ethical theory and principles is necessary both to help work through dilemmas and reach ethical conclusions, and to articulate the reasoning process to others. It is important to recognise that any situation may involve several ethical perspectives or principles. For example, decisions about whether to commence tube feeding in a patient with advanced dementia might draw on considerations of best interests, minimising harm, the sanctity of life principle, the acts and omissions distinction, and patient autonomy (if there is evidence of an advance statement of wishes). Often there is a need to balance conflicting or competing principles, taking account of the particulars of the individual case and the overall context, in order to decide what the ethically appropriate course of action is. Part of the context of ethical decision making in clinical practice is the legal and professional regulatory framework within which health professionals must work, and knowledge of these is an essential requirement for ethical decision making in practice (see Chapter 6).

Good communication

Ethical conflicts often arise because of failure of communication between doctors, patients and families, or between members of the healthcare team. Given the range of values and perspectives that can be involved in these situations, resolution is only possible with open respectful communication between those involved. Deliberation is an important ethical tool, emphasising the importance of process and dialogue in resolving ethical concerns.

Seeking advice and support

Doctors make independent ethical decisions every day but, when faced with ethical difficulties or conflict, it is important that they seek support and advice from colleagues. The multidisciplinary team provides a forum for seeking the perspectives of others, testing ethical reasoning and reflecting on the values of all individuals involved. Difficult ethical decisions, like difficult clinical decisions, are often made by teams and not individuals, and benefit from the expertise and experience of a range of different people. When ethical difficulties cannot be resolved within the team, there may be other resources available in the organisation. Many NHS trusts have a clinical ethics committee or group that provides support to clinicians on ethical issues relating to patient care: www.ethics-network.org.uk. These provide another space for deliberation with a specific ethical focus. Clinical governance leads should be able to advise on organisational policies on ethical issues such as consent and confidentiality. There are also external sources of support:

- The GMC (offers advice to doctors): www.gmc-uk.org
- The British Medical Association (BMA; provides ethics guidance and has a telephone advice line): www.bma.org.uk/ethics
- A doctor's medical defence organisation (provides advice on ethico-legal issues).

8 Negligence

Figure 8.1 Negligence

Key Case Summary 1 : *Bolam* v *Friern Hospital Management Committee* (1957, High Court).

• John Bolam was treated for depression at Friern Hospital with electro-convulsive therapy (ECT).

• During his second session of treatment, Mr Bolam was given ECT 'unmodified', i.e. without any muscle relaxant drugs or manual restraints.

• As a result of his convulsions during ECT treatment, Mr Bolam sustained a fractured pelvis. He alleged that Friern Hospital was negligent in treating him in the way it had.

• At trial, much argument and expert evident focussed on the correct way to perform ECT treatment. The expert witnesses had a range of different views. In the end, the defendant hospital was found to have not been negligent.

• The judge, Mr Justice McNair, defined the test for negligent medical treatment as follows:

> ... in the case of a medical man, negligence means failure to act in accordance with the standards of reasonably competent medical men at the time... as long as it is remembered that there may be one or more perfectly proper standards; and if he conforms with one of those proper standards, then he is not negligent;
>
> the real question is whether the defendants, in acting the way they did, were acting in accordance with a practice of competent respected professional opinion; and
>
> he is not guilty of negligence if he has acted in accordance with a responsible body of medical men skilled in that particular art.

Key Case Summary 2: *Bolitho* v *City and Hackney Health Authority* (1997, House of Lords).

• Patrick Bolitho, a 2 year old child, was treated at the defendant's hospital for respiratory difficulties in 1984.

• When in hospital he suffered two episodes of acute respiratory difficulty, from which he recovered. He was not intubated after these two episodes.

• However, a third episode triggered a cardiac arrest, which left him with severe brain damage.

• At the trial, a key issue was whether any competent doctor attending after the second episode would have arranged for prophylactic intubation (which Patrick Bolitho had not received at the time). In the end, the trial judge decided that the claim should fail.

• On appeal, the House of Lords discussed the well-established 'Bolam test' and concluded that:

> ...the court has to be satisfied that the exponents of a body of opinion relied upon can demonstrate that such opinion has a logical basis; and
>
> if, in a rare case, it can be demonstrated that the professional opinion is not capable of withstanding logical analysis, the judge is entitled to hold that the body of opinion is not reasonable or responsible.

Medical Ethics, Law and Communication at a Glance, First Edition. Edited by Patrick Davey, Anna Rathmell, Michael Dunn, Charles Foster and Helen Salisbury.
© 2017 John Wiley & Sons, Ltd. Published 2017 by John Wiley & Sons, Ltd.

Introduction

If a clinician provides 'negligent' care to a patient, that patient can bring a claim against the clinician (or the relevant NHS trust) for clinical negligence in the civil courts. The purpose of these proceedings is to determine whether the defendant (the clinician or NHS trust or hospital) is liable to pay the claimant (patient) compensation (damages). This chapter addresses the civil liability of clinicians with regards to negligent care. It is not concerned with either criminal liability or professional disciplinary issues.

It is important to note that competent doctors occasionally provide substandard treatment or, through no fault of their own, form part of a team or system that results in a patient receiving sub-standard care. The fact that a clinician is criticised in clinical negligence proceedings does not, of itself or even usually, lead to any professional disciplinary proceedings. Nor is it likely that any clinician will have to pay a claimant compensation from their own pocket. Such compensation is paid by the relevant NHS trust or the clinician's professional indemnity body.

Clinical negligence claims – the four stages

For a claim in clinical negligence to succeed, a claimant must succeed at each of the following four stages:

1 The defendant owed him a **duty of care**.
2 The defendant **breached that duty** by providing negligent or sub-standard care.
3 The alleged breach of duty **caused** the patient's injury.
4 The claimant suffered **injury, loss or damage** (and to what extent).

These are exactly the same considerations that apply in a claim for personal injury sustained in a road traffic accident, where a claimant alleges that another party's driving was negligent. This chapter will consider each of these four stages in turn.

Stage 1 – duty of care

The existence of a duty of care is not usually in dispute because all clinicians readily recognise that they owe their patients a duty of care. However, there are circumstances where it is less easy to identify to whom a duty of care is owed. For example, does a doctor performing a vasectomy owe a duty of care to the man's wife, or indeed his future partner, if the vasectomy is performed negligently and she becomes pregnant?

Issues can also arise about the scope of the duty of care. A doctor will only be liable for injury caused to a patient that is within the scope of the duty of care. By way of illustration, a doctor who negligently fails to admit to hospital a patient suffering from appendicitis will be liable if that patient's appendix subsequently ruptures. However, if the same patient is mugged on the way home from work, the doctor will not be liable for injuries sustained during the assault even though the patient would not have been mugged had he been admitted to hospital.

Stage 2 – breach of duty

The question of whether there has been a breach of duty is usually far more controversial. A clinician will only be found to have been in breach of duty if the care that he provided would not be regarded as competent by a 'responsible body' of practitioners specialising in the same discipline. This is known as the 'Bolam test' (Figure 8.1).

If the standard of care would be supported by even a minority of equivalent specialists, the claimant would not establish breach

of duty unless they could show that there was not a 'logical basis' for such care. This requirement that there must be a logical basis for the care provided is sometimes referred to as the 'Bolitho gloss' (Figure 8.2).

In all clinical negligence cases, because the judge is unable to determine what is or is not an appropriate standard of care, the court will hear evidence from at least one expert witness who will give their opinion about the standard of care. However, if the care was provided by a junior doctor and other junior doctors would have provided the same standard of care, the junior doctor will still be liable if the court finds that the patient should have been treated by a more senior doctor who would have provided a higher standard of care.

Stage 3 – causation

Not all breaches of duty cause harm. Most clinicians will be aware of mistakes that they or their colleagues have made but which, fortunately, have not resulted in harm. In such circumstances, no liability in negligence arises, despite the common use of the term 'negligence' to refer to the provision of sub-standard care.

By way of example, a GP who fails to refer a patient with a suspicious lump when he should have done will not be liable if it turns out that the lump did not require treatment, or indeed if the patient requires exactly the same treatment as he would have required anyway with no health repercussions. Perhaps more surprisingly, the GP will not be liable if the lump was malignant and the patient subsequently dies if the GP is able to establish that even with an appropriate referral the patient would have died anyway. The question of whether the patient would have died anyway will also be a matter of expert evidence, and will be assessed on the balance of probabilities – did the patient have a greater than 50% chance of survival with earlier referral? Nor will the GP be liable if the patient always would have required surgical removal but their prospects of survival fall from, say, 90% with earlier referral to 60% with later referral because, in both cases, the court will find that on the balance of probabilities the patient would have survived and will still survive.

In most cases, the question of causation will depend on expert evidence. Normally, an expert witness will give evidence that, on the balance of probabilities, the negligent treatment has caused the damage complained of. The corollary of this is that with appropriate treatment the patient would not have suffered the damage complained of – i.e. 'but for' the negligence, the patient would have had a better outcome.

However, there are cases in which it is not possible to establish that the negligence caused the injury. In such cases, it is sufficient for the claimant to establish that the negligence 'materially contributed' to the bad outcome. Consider, for example, a patient who sustains a head injury and develops hydrocephalus that is negligently not diagnosed and relieved. The patient suffers permanent brain damage in consequence of both the original head injury and the hydrocephalus. They will be able to recover damages if they can show that the brain damage is undoubtedly worse than it would have been had the hydrocephalus been appropriately diagnosed and treated, even though it is not possible to identify how much worse.

Stage 4 – injury, loss or damage

The question of 'negligence' tends only to arise when a patient has had a less good outcome than either they or their treating team would have wished.

Figure 8.2 Negligence

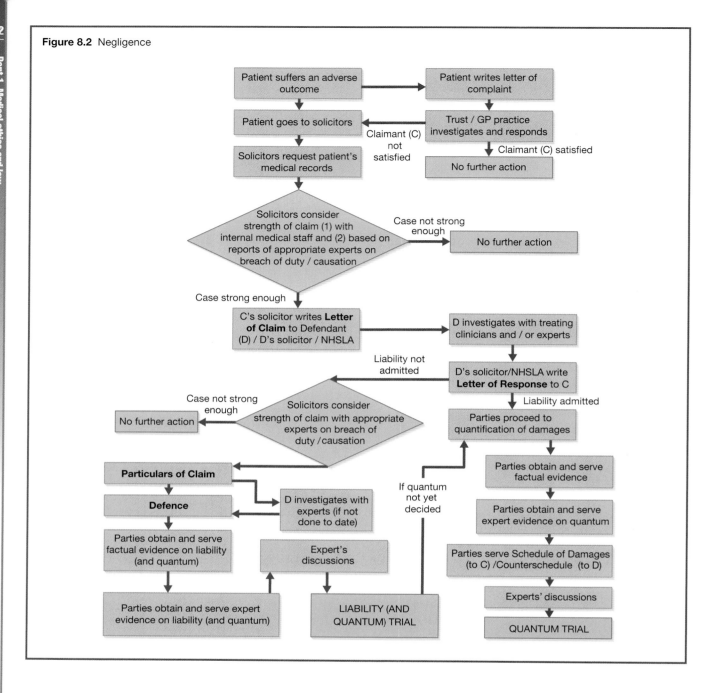

A claimant is only entitled to recover compensation for damage that was reasonably foreseeable. However, in clinical negligence cases, it is almost never a dispute that it is reasonably foreseeable that sub-standard treatment could result in personal injury to a patient, whether physical or mental or both. The patient will be entitled to receive compensation for the physical or mental injury and all the consequences thereof. However, where sub-standard treatment results only in economic loss, without any personal injury, the clinician or trust will not be responsible for this loss unless the patient was being treated on a private basis.

When a patient suffers a worse outcome than would be expected because of a feature peculiar to them, the defendant will nonetheless be liable for that worse outcome because a defendant must take their claimant as they find them. This is known as 'the eggshell skull principle'.

The damage that gives rise to a right to compensation falls into two general categories: (i) pain suffering and loss of amenity (non-financial loss), and (ii) financial loss.

The sums of money awarded for pain suffering and loss of amenity are conventional figures that depend on the severity and duration of any pain or injury and the extent of any resultant disability. For example, the maximum sum awarded for a young person rendered quadriplegic and utterly dependent on others for all care is about £260,000. Awards can be as little as £1,000, or even less, when the period for which pain is suffered is very short.

Damages for financial loss fall into two sub-categories: money necessary to meet the needs of the claimant that arise as a result of the sub-standard care – for example, the costs of medical treatment, therapy and care; and money necessary to put the claimant in the position that they would have been in had they not been injured – for example, loss of earnings.

The quantification of damages is a very large area that is not within the scope of this chapter. Suffice to say that the sums awarded by the courts can be very large indeed.

Other matters – timing, parties and procedure

Timing – when can a claim be brought?

The theory is that a defendant should not be liable for ever and there are some time limits for the bringing of a claim. The general rule is that a claimant should bring a claim for personal injury within 3 years of injury or within 3 years of their 'date of knowledge' if later. The date of knowledge is the date when the claimant knew, or should have known (i) that they had suffered a significant injury, (ii) that this injury was attributable to an act or omission that might be negligent, and (iii) the identity of the potential defendant. The time limit is longer for children who can bring a claim until 3 years after their eighteenth birthday. There are no time limits for claimants who do not have capacity to litigate. Furthermore, the court has the discretion, in all personal injury cases, to extend the relevant limitation period if it considers it appropriate to do so.

Parties – who will be the defendant?

When treatment has been provided within the NHS secondary healthcare system, a claimant will almost always sue the NHS trust that employed the treating clinicians rather than the clinicians themselves. This is because (i) the trust is legally responsible for the negligence of its employees, (ii) as part of the contract of employment, the trust will have agreed to indemnify the clinician for liability incurred in consequence of their employment, and (iii) the trust has deeper pockets from which to pay any damages.

When treatment has been provided by a GP, even if within the NHS, the practice is for the claimant to sue the GP personally as the primary care trust does not employ or indemnify GPs.

When treatment has been provided on a private basis, the claimant will sue the clinician personally unless the clinician is employed by, for example, a private hospital. If the clinician is employed, the claimant may sue the hospital instead.

Parties – liability for deaths

When a patient dies as a consequence of clinical negligence, members of their family can bring a claim on behalf of their estate and for financial loss that they have suffered as a result of their relative's death.

Procedure – pre-action and post-action

It is not within the scope of this chapter to explain in detail the procedure that is followed when a claimant brings a claim for clinical negligence. In summary, there are two distinct phases: (i) the 'pre-action' stage when the claimant notifies the defendant of their potential claim and the defendant responds in correspondence, and (ii) the 'post-action' stage when the claimant issues formal court proceedings and the parties then set out their respective positions in a 'particulars of claim' and a 'defence', and serve evidence in support.

These claims are not resolved quickly and it is by no means unusual for more than 2 years to pass between the start of a claim and its conclusion. Indeed, some cases can take more than 5 years. The other point to make is that the vast majority of clinical negligence claims are settled or compromised, and that it is only a small percentage of cases that conclude at trial. However, it is impossible to predict in advance which cases will end up in court, so all cases must be prepared as though for trial.

Procedure – evidence

The court will determine the issues in dispute based on the evidence before it. There are two main categories of evidence: factual evidence and expert evidence. The court will also consider documentary evidence and in clinical negligence claims the medical records, any report or investigation into the incident, and complaints correspondence can be particularly important. Factual evidence is simply an account of what happened. Expert evidence is the expert's opinion about what or why something happened, whether there was a breach of duty and what the consequences of that breach had been.

9 Battery and assault

Figure 9.1 Obtaining consent

Figure 9.2 Withdrawing consent

What are battery and assault?

Acts of battery and assault can amount to criminal offences. They can also give rise to civil causes of action (i.e. the possibility of being sued) and are commonly referred together as two kinds of trespass to the person. They are likely to be viewed as acts of serious professional misconduct by the GMC. Adherence to simple acts of good medical practice will safeguard the medical practitioner from these potential difficulties.

There is a technical legal distinction between assault and battery, but for practical purposes the distinction makes little difference to the way in which medical practitioners should deal with their patients:

- Battery will occur where a doctor touches a patient without valid **consent** or lawful justification.
- A 'common assault' may occur when a patient **anticipates** that they are about to be touched without valid consent or lawful justification. The touching need not actually take place: fear on the part of the patient is sufficient for the act of the doctor to amount to common assault (Figure 9.1).

The need for consent

Physical contact with a patient is obviously likely to be a necessary part of the vast majority of medical consultations. The risk of committing battery or assault can always be avoided by:

- effective communication: ensuring that at all times a patient is aware of what the doctor is doing **or about to do**; and
- obtaining **effective and valid consent** from a patient prior to making, or attempting to make, any form of physical contact.

Chapter 11 deals with the issue of consent in detail. If valid consent is obtained, in turn, any medical examination is likely to be lawful. Remember that:

- consent can be withdrawn at any stage by a patient, and continuing to treat or touch a patient in these circumstances will almost certainly amount to battery;
- providing treatment that goes beyond the scope of that discussed with a patient will also ordinarily amount to assault or battery.

The law adopts a fairly 'common sense' approach when applying the above principles. Thus, if a patient were to yelp and say "Ouch! Stop!" during an injection, this might be viewed as an expression of pain, rather than amounting to withdrawal of consent. The doctor must judge the situation and consider whether consent has been withdrawn (Figure 9.2).

Similarly, it is crucial to ensure that a patient gives proper consent for the **precise** operative procedure that they are about to undergo. If, for example, there is the possibility that a laparoscopic procedure might be converted to on open procedure during the operation, the patient must be informed of this risk materialising, and in effect must give consent for both possible procedures. That said, if in an **emergency situation**, a medical practitioner needs to provide what is immediately necessary to save their life or to prevent a serious deterioration of their condition, consent need not be obtained.

Good practice

The above issues arise in all areas of medical practice. However, particular areas of practice may be more problematic than others.

Surgery

The task of obtaining consent from patients for surgical procedures can be left to more junior doctors who must understand the full extent, scope, risks and implications of the procedure(s) to be undertaken.

Intimate examinations and chaperones

The use of chaperones provides protection for medical practitioners and patients by mitigating against the risk of misunderstandings arising between doctor and patient, thus reducing the risk of allegations of assault being made. Chaperones should always be offered during intimate medical examinations (regardless of the sex of the patient). Chaperones can be a member of practice staff, or a relative or friend of the patient. Always note the name of the chaperone, or alternatively note if a chaperone has been refused.

The purpose and nature of an intimate examination should be explained to the patient. Seek the patient's permission and be prepared to stop in the event that consent is withdrawn. For the reasons given above, any attempts to continue the examination for clinical reasons could amount to assault. At the time this publication went to press, the GMC was considering whether to revise its guidelines in respect of intimate examinations and chaperones. The draft guidelines in respect of chaperones are expected to be broadly identical to the current guidance already in place.

More detailed guidance is expected to be given in respect of obtaining consent prior to any intimate examination. The current draft guidance requires doctors to obtain specific, clear consent prior to the examination taking place, and to record in the notes that such consent has been obtained. No assistance should be given with removing a patient's clothing, unless the doctor has clarified with them that such assistance is required. Any misconstrued attempts to provide assistance without express consent can lead quickly to allegations of assault being made against a medical practitioner.

Life-sustaining treatment

Note that when a patient has full capacity they have the right to refuse life-sustaining treatment, regardless of how rational, irrational, unknown or non-existent the reasons are for that refusal. Thus, in *B v NHS Hospital Trust* [2002] 2 All E.R. 449, a High Court judge was highly critical of a patient's treating clinicians, in circumstances where they had kept a tetraplegic patient ventilated against her wishes. The court held that the continuation of such treatment amounted to unlawful trespass to the person.

Further reading

GMC consultation on explanatory guidance: see www.gmc-uk.org/guidance/12022.asp

GMC guidance: *Consent – patients and doctors making decisions together*, June 2008.

GMC guidance: *Maintaining boundaries – guidance for doctors*, November 2006.

Grubb, A. *Principles of medical law*, Chapter 8, 2nd edn, 2004. Oxford University Press.

10 Confidentiality

Figure 10.1 Confidentiality: which approach is correct?

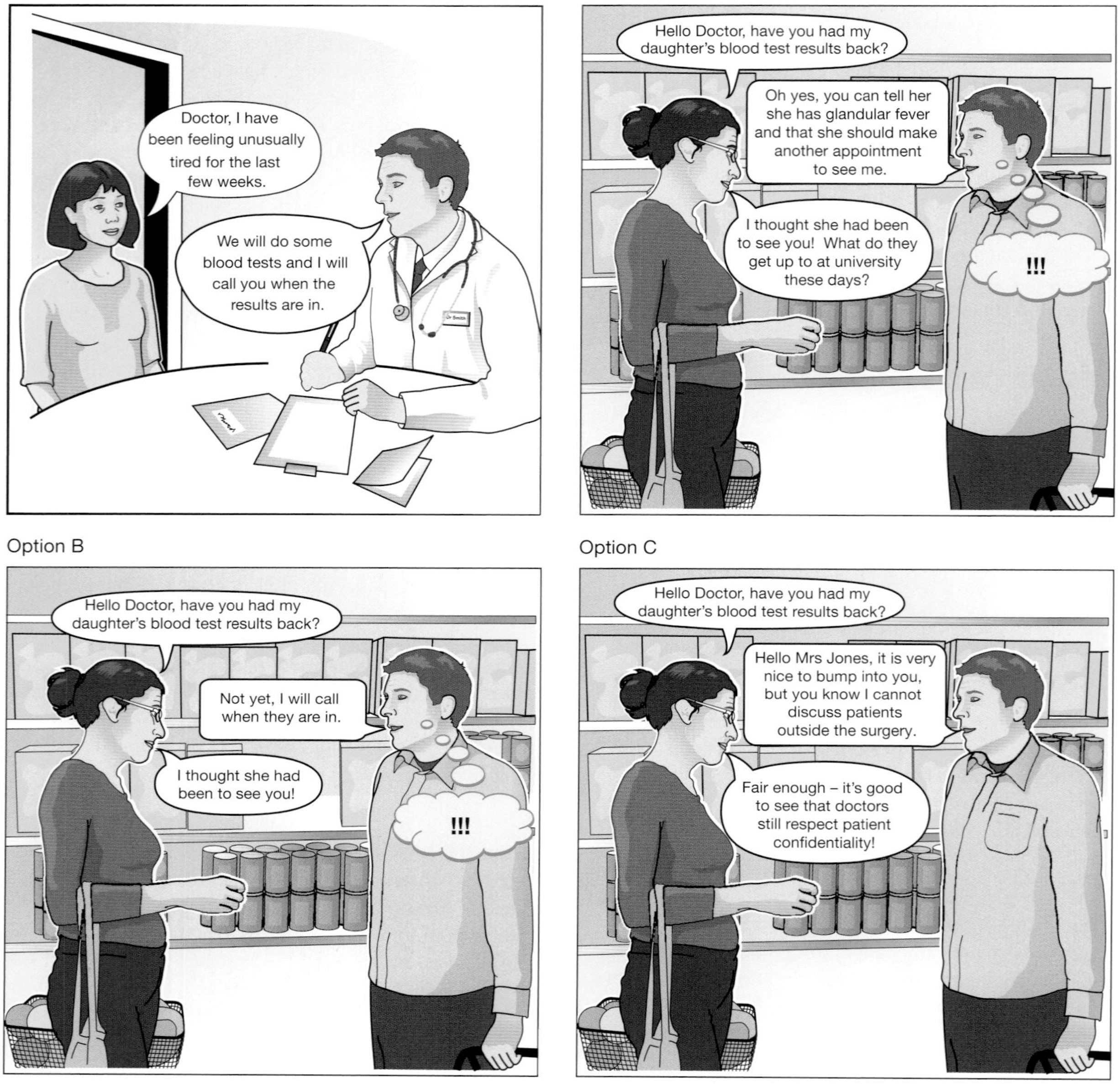

Source: Davey P (ed) (2014) Medicine at a Glance, 4th edn. Reproduced with permission of John Wiley & Sons, Ltd.

Introduction

The duty to respect patient confidentiality concerns what is owed to patients with regards to medical information about them (Figure 10.1). This duty stems mainly from two ethical principles. The first, 'respect for autonomy', is usually interpreted to mean that the patient ought to be in control over who has access to personal information about them. The second principle is based on the idea that there is a duty to act to bring about the best consequences for the individual patient and for other patients making use of the healthcare system.

The consequentialist argument proceeds by claiming that good health outcomes are contingent on the maintenance of public trust in the profession, and that public trust would be undermined if personal medical information were shared without the consent of patients. The premise here is that patients would feel less inclined to be open about their conditions and symptoms if doctors were in the habit of unilaterally sharing personal information, which would ultimately lead to the patients receiving a lower standard of healthcare.

The duty to maintain confidentiality

Both of these ethical arguments place clear value on the moral significance of maintaining patient confidentiality. This position is endorsed in English law. From a legal perspective, patient confidentiality is interpreted as a public interest rather than as a private interest, reflecting the consequentialist position outlined above. Although the Human Rights Act 1998 acknowledges that there is also a private right to confidentiality, in practice this makes little difference because of the weight given in the common law to the public interest in maintaining patient confidentiality.

Consent to disclose confidential information

Often, consent to share a patient's medical information can be presumed. It is generally accepted that information about the care of a patient will be discussed within the medical team, even if it is only shared with one member of that team. Express consent would not normally be required to seek specialist advice or a second opinion. The key question is whether the patient's interests are best served by sharing the patient's information among other professionals.

In most other circumstances, express consent should be obtained unless there is a legal obligation to disclose the information, or unless the practitioner believes that the public interest in disclosing the information requires it (see below). Importantly, the law also recognises duties to show appropriate respect to the patient, even if the decision has been made to breach confidentiality. Consent should always be sought, even if it is judged unlikely to be given, unless there are overriding reasons for thinking that the act of obtaining consent would itself act against the public interest justifying the disclosure of the information. Equally, the person should be informed that a breach has taken place, with the reasons for this decision being clearly outlined to them.

If an adult lacks capacity to give consent, doctors should consider the patient's 'best interests', and consent requirements in relation to the disclosure of medical information for children ought to adhere to the laws regarding consent for this group (see Chapter 11).

From a legal standpoint, it should also be recognised that confidentiality has not been breached if the patient has given valid consent for the release of the information. If a patient's medical information has been anonymised prior to being disclosed, issues concerning confidentiality do not arise. However, it is important to attend carefully to how this information is rendered anonymous, particularly when used for educational purposes. Simply removing a patient's name is unlikely to be sufficient.

Breaches of confidentiality

While the law endorses a duty to maintain confidentiality, this is not an absolute obligation. There are circumstances in which practitioners are legally obliged to breach confidentiality, and circumstances in which breaching confidentiality is permissible.

Situations where there is a legal obligation to breach patient confidentiality

Statutory legislation lays out the situations in which there is an overriding obligation to breach confidentiality when certain information comes to light. Alternatively, the obligation to breach confidentiality might be laid out in a court order. Some examples of situations where practitioners are obliged to breach confidentiality include:

- the presence of notifiable diseases;
- reporting of terminations of pregnancy;
- reporting of births and deaths;
- details of anyone alleged to be guilty of an offence under the Road Traffic Act 1988 (on request by police only); and
- evidence of terrorism activities, or knife and gunshot wounds.

Situations where it is permitted to breach patient confidentiality

These situations involve weighing up the public interest in disclosure versus non-disclosure. The GMC offers detailed guidance in this area and this guidance carries a lot of weight with the courts (see www.gmc-uk.org). The general idea is that disclosure of confidential information without consent would normally be justified in order to prevent risk of death or serious harm to others.

The position endorsed in law, and clarified by the GMC, here is entirely consistent with a more developed version of the consequentialist argument above. One can imagine circumstances in which, if doctors do not breach confidentiality, the outcomes will be such that trust in the medical profession is likely to be undermined to a greater extent than if confidentiality had been maintained.

The GMC also recognises that professional obligations relating to confidentiality continue after death, and gives specific advice concerning confidentiality and genetic information (see Chapter 19).

Confidentiality, privacy, and data protection

Duties in relation to confidentiality are closely related to duties regarding patients' privacy and laws relating to the protection of personal data more generally. In contrast to confidentiality, which concerns situations in which a practitioner is in possession of personal medical information, privacy concerns what is owed to a person when the practitioner is not in possession of that information – and is part of a more general set of duties relating to respecting those aspects of a person that concern their private realm. In England, medical legal obligations concerning confidentiality are now seen as being closely related to privacy rights. In contrast, data protection duties are separate, and less rigorous, than those relating to medical confidentiality. In practice, laws relating to data protection are more pertinent to the ways in which healthcare organisations use personal data to audit, report and manage their services.

11 Consent

> **Figure 11.1** Key case – *Montgomery* v *Lanarkshire Health Board* [2015] UKSC 11
>
> **The facts**
> In 1999, Nadine Montgomery gave birth to a baby boy with severe disabilities due to complications arising during birth. Nadine Montgomery had an increased chance of having a larger than average-sized baby, with an indicated 9–10% of shoulder dystocia during a vaginal delivery. The severe risks associated with shoulder dystocia are uncommon. Attempts to dislodge the infant's shoulders would occlude the umbilical cord resulting in death of the child, or causing cerebral palsy, in only 1 in 1,000 cases.
> According to the obstetrician, Dr McLellan, the risk of shoulder dystocia and the possible alternative of an elective Caesarean section was not something that he would disclose in a case like this because the risk of a severe side effect was very small. Dr McLellan claimed that this was standard practice. Mrs Montgomery sought damages on the grounds that Dr McLellan had been negligent for not properly informing her. Her case failed in the lower courts in Scotland. However, seven Supreme Court judges were of the unanimous view that Mrs Montgomery's appeal should be allowed: the surgeon had indeed been negligent in not informing her of the risk of shoulder dystocia and its associated complications.
>
> **The background**
> In allowing the appeal, the judges overturned the House of Lords' 30-year-old majority judgment in *Sidaway* v *Board of Governors* of the Bethlem Royal Hospital. In 1985, the *Sidaway* case established that informed consent required doctors to inform patients of side effects when these side effects involved a severity and degree of risk recognised as significant by the profession (the so-called 'Bolam test' – see Chapter 8). There had been growing dissatisfaction amongst judges about the position articulated in *Sidaway*. Other jurisdictions had moved firmly away from a professional standard test to determine what information should be disclosed to patients. The GMC's guidance on consent emphasised a partnership approach whereby doctors worked with patients to determine what patients are told within the consent process, and, in subsequent English cases and that a subtle shift away from the position articulated by the majority in *Sidaway* had already taken place.
>
> **A new legal standard for informed consent in health care**
> The new doctrine of informed consent established in *Montgomery* is one that is underpinned by a patient-centric, rather than profession-centric approach. A patient should be informed about material risks associated with a medical procedure, and 'the test of materiality is whether, in the circumstances of the particular case, a reasonable person in the patient's position would be likely to attached significance to the risk, or the doctor is or should reasonably be aware that the particular patient would be likely to attach significance to it.' (para. 87). At first glance, it seems reasonable to think that this new standard will track the kinds of information that professionals already disclose to patients. However, context is crucial. Patients are invested in different ways in different medical decisions, and so what reasonable people will be concerned about in these settings will also differ. This is particularly the case when value judgements are part of the decision, as Lady Hale suggests in relation to the requirement to offer patients the choice between different methods of delivery when there is any increased risk of harm to the mother or baby. Equally, if the patient expresses particular preferences or concerns, then the information should be tailored to these concerns.
>
> **Three additional points are worthy of note:**
> 1. It is legally justifiable to not tell a patient any information about risks or side effects, if they expresses such a preference.
> 2. The doctor is excused from conferring with the patient in circumstances of necessity, and can withhold information from a patient in rare cases when disclosing a risk is likely to be seriously detrimental to the patient's health (the so-called 'therapeutic exception').
> 3. The requirement to tailor information to the patient's concerns does not imply that any request made for an alternative treatment is overriding; resource constraints and the clinical appropriateness of that option remain relevant in deciding whether the patient's request should be respected.
>
> **Immediate implications for practice**
> The ramifications of *Montgomery* will take time to play out as subsequent cases clarify the expectations of reasonable patients in different decision-making contexts. However, in the short-term, this legal requirement is likely to require modifications to the consent process, with doctors needing to outline precisely what information has been shared, and to provide a rationale for sharing (or not) this information, particularly when this might depart from established norms of information provision in that clinical setting. More generally, the evolving law of consent in healthcare places even stronger importance on doctors to build collaborative relationships with their patients in ways that are focused on shared decision making. Doctors clearly need time and extensive communication skills in they are going to fulfil their new legal obligations in consent.

Medical Ethics, Law and Communication at a Glance, First Edition. Edited by Patrick Davey, Anna Rathmell, Michael Dunn, Charles Foster and Helen Salisbury.
© 2017 John Wiley & Sons, Ltd. Published 2017 by John Wiley & Sons, Ltd.

General principles

Consent is typically seen as the cornerstone of medical practice. At a time when patient-centred approaches dominate public discourse about healthcare, it is not difficult to see why this might be. Consent provides the means for patients to authorise treatment, in a way that reflects and respects their own values and commitments in life. The concept and practice of consent places clear limits on doctors acting on the basis that they know best.

Precisely why consent is seen as such a crucial ethical component of medical practice, and how regulatory regimes function to protect the patient's ability to exercise control over the medical treatment they receive, will be the focus of this chapter.

The ethical foundations of consent

The justification for the practice of consent in medical practice stems from the ethical foundation of respect for autonomy, and no treatment can proceed unless the patient themself has authorised it.

Immediate difficulties arise, however, with an autonomy-based justification for consent. Perhaps the most pressing concern is that there is significant uncertainty about how the value of personal autonomy ought to be explicated and, therefore, precisely what the practice of consent requires. Personal autonomy has been interpreted variously as self-rule, as self-determination and as the ability to live freely and independently. One might think that personal autonomy is respected only when a person is able to act on the basis of their considered desires, rather than on the basis of their ability to gratify their immediate inclinations. Alternatively, autonomy can be seen less as an individual capacity worthy of moral consideration, and more as one that can only be respected within interpersonal or caring relationships.

These different ways of understanding autonomy can lead to different ways of practising consent, particularly with regards to how doctors and patients share the process of decision making (see Chapter 32), and whether and how the patient's caregivers, family members or loved ones are brought into the process of authorising the decision to provide or withhold treatment.

Other ethicists, particularly those who view personal autonomy as more substantively linked to one's overall life plan rather than the day-to-day decisions that one makes in one's life, claim that consent is better justified by reference to other moral values. Most notably, trust is identified as an alternative ethical foundation for the practice of consent. Enabling patients to make choices about their care builds their trust in doctors, leading to better care and a more respectful and humane basis for medical practice.

Valid consent and informed consent

In law as well as ethics, the validity of consent is typically seen as tripartite, requiring a patient to be i) appropriately informed, ii) deciding voluntarily, and iii) competent (or having the capacity) to make the decision.

The failure to inform patients correctly is now recognised as falling within the tort of negligence. Judges have paid significant attention to regulating information provision requirements. Precisely how the practice standards underpinning the doctor's duty to ensure that a patient is sufficiently informed are to be articulated has been the focus of much deliberation.

Over time, these standards have shifted inexorably towards a patient-centred interpretation. The Montgomery judgment (Figure 11.1) represents the culmination of this shift, with doctors being expected to consider what the 'reasonable patient' would expect to know, given the nature of the procedure, the risks, benefits and alternatives associated with it, and any features about the patient and their expressed concerns that are judged to be relevant. This more qualitative approach to determining information requirements means that the doctor needs to tailor precisely what they disclose carefully to the context in which each decision is being made. No longer can the completion of a consent form be seen as a 'tick-box exercise' in which the doctor confirms that predetermined, clinically significant facts about the procedure have been disclosed.

This shift in information provision requirements brings the law more closely into alignment with the GMC's professional guidance on consent. The GMC's guidelines also clarify that a patient should generally be informed of anything she asks a question about, and that merely being told the relevant information is not significant: the patient must also understand it (and so a doctor must take appropriate steps to ensure understanding).

Because legal actions concerning consent in healthcare are brought in negligence, a patient must be able to show that they have suffered a loss in not being appropriately informed. Damages are not awarded if the patient shows that they were not informed about a side effect that should have been disclosed, but the side effect did not materialise when the procedure was undertaken. Moreover, a patient must also show causation between the failure to be properly informed about a side effect and that side effect occurring. In practical terms, this now means that a patient needs to prove that, had appropriate information been provided, they would not have gone ahead with the procedure at the time and place proposed. If this counterfactual is proven, the courts will allow for damages to be awarded to compensate for the patient being deprived of the ability to make a fully informed decision about their medical care (see Chapter 8).

Valid consent and voluntary consent

Reflecting an ethical account of personal autonomy that treats patients as self-determining agents, medical ethicists are generally wary of the imposition of coercion, pressure or undue influence on decision making. While these concepts need to be clearly specified, the common view is that a person's consent is voluntary only if the decision is reflective of the person's own will, rather than the will of another person. The difficulty here is in articulating thresholds to determine when a decision is truly the patient's own. When does persuasion or the good advice offered by a loved one or a doctor shift from mere influence to undue influence? Or, when does the obvious fact that a person's decisions are shaped by that patient's social context become ethically problematic in healthcare encounters?

These open ethical questions are reflected in a lack of clarity around the concept of voluntary consent in English medical law. The very limited cases in which voluntariness has been raised as a concern have focused on ascertaining whether the patient's will is overborne by the actions of a third party. In applying this standard, doctors ought to attend to i) the strength of the patient's will, ii) the nature of the relationship between the patient and the third party, and iii) whether religious beliefs are involved. No further guidance is available concerning how these considerations should be interpreted.

Figure 11.2 Substitute decision making under the Mental Capacity Act 2005

• Determine that no steps can be taken to enhance the patient's capacity in order to enable that patient to make their own decision.

• Establish that
  i) the decision to be made for the patient who lacks capacity concerns an act in connection with the patient's care or treatment, and
  ii) the decision does not concern an act that can only be made by the Court of Protection.

• Find out whether the patient has made an '**advance decision to refuse treatment**' (often referred to as an 'advance directive' or 'living will'), and ascertain whether this advance decision is 'valid' and 'applicable'. If so, follow the advance decision to refuse treatment without exception.

• Find out whether patient has a '**lasting power of attorney**' relating to matters of 'personal welfare'. Obtain consent from the appointed person, but only act accordingly if it is in the patient's best interests to do so (see next step).
Act in the **best interests** of the patient. This is a professional judgement.

• A patient's past and present wishes, feelings, beliefs and values are relevant in judging best interests (as is any advance statement that the person wrote to set out their wishes when they had capacity).

• Relatives and friends are to be treated as sources of information to judge best interests, and should be consulted. They cannot give or withhold consent unless designated as a 'lasting power of attorney'.

• Act in the best interests of the patient in the **least restrictive** way, and review whether it would be in the patient's best interests to wait to act until they regains the capacity to make the relevant decision for themselves.

Note: If the action to be taken in the patient's best interests involves a **deprivation of liberty** then the Mental Capacity Act 2005's 'Deprivation of Liberty Safeguards' must be used.

What care or treatment can an adult patient give, or refuse to give, consent to?

When it is established that an adult patient is making an informed, voluntary and competent decision, that patient is – by and large – able to give, or refuse, consent to all medical interventions, even if they are unable to give a clear or logical reason for this decision. This 'right to refuse' extends to life-sustaining treatment. Note, however, that the primacy given to patient autonomy does have limits. A patient is not able to demand that they be provided with whatever treatment they would like, on the basis of their values. The range of appropriate options that a patient is presented with must be reasonable, and such options will be constrained by resource considerations.

The exceptions to an adult patient's absolute right to refuse medical care are strictly limited. A patient suffering from a 'notifiable disease' can be detained on public health grounds. There is also scope for providing mental health treatment without consent (see Chapter 15). While the law is open to the idea that there may be more general public interest grounds to force treatment on patients, the legal right to autonomy as it relates to the control over one's health is seen as almost insurmountable, and so such situations are likely to be extremely rare.

Mental capacity and consent

It is common for doctors to encounter situations in which an adult patient is unable to give consent to medical treatment. This inability is usually referred to as the patient being incompetent – or, more commonly, lacking the mental capacity – to give consent, capturing the idea that patients in some scenarios will be unable to make autonomous decisions. In both ethics and law, two issues have been the focus of discussion: i) what does it mean to lack the capacity to make a decision, and ii) how should decisions be made when a patient lacks capacity. These issues will be considered in turn.

What is mental capacity?

The dominant philosophical account of decision-making capacity, endorsed in English law, is one that interprets mental capacity by reference to a set of cognitive and communicative abilities. This so-called 'functional' account of capacity situates the notion of decision-making ability firmly inside the person's head. Put another way, one reason why a person might not be autonomous is because that person lacks the cognitive processing abilities to reason as part of the activity of deciding about their life. The Mental Capacity Act 2005 supports this position, endorsing a two-stage test of capacity that requires the presence of an impairment of, or disturbance in the functioning of, mind or brain, which leads a person to be unable to i) understand the information relevant to the decision, (ii) retain that information, (iii) use or weigh up that information as part of the decision-making process, or (iv) communicate their decision.

In healthcare, it is important to be able to make continuous and very practical judgements about whether a person has the capacity to decide. This is because it is recognised that capacity, understood in this way, is a decision-specific phenomenon. Mental incapacity might be temporary, for example in cases of intoxication. Alternatively, capacity can fluctuate in progressive neurological conditions such as dementia, or because of the complexity of the information that needs to be processed in order to make a decision. The Mental Capacity Act 2005 endorses the general principle that, whenever it is appropriate to do so,

no substitute decision should be made until all steps have been taken to maximise the person's ability to make their own decision. Adopting easy-read forms of presenting information, or making use of communication aids, enable this legal requirement to be met in practice.

Concerns have been raised about the validity of the functional test of capacity. A number of patients, particularly those with mental disorders, look to have difficulty with decision making but to retain their cognitive abilities. By examining personality disorder, anorexia nervosa and intellectual disability, philosophers have taken issue with the 'cognitive bias' underpinning the functional account. The response here is to connect capacity and autonomy with, inter alia, a person's emotional state, their authentic or stable values, or by recourse to features of the relationships within which they are supported to make decisions.

A core concern in these discussions revolves around whether a value-neutral account of capacity is coherent. This account is one that does not explicitly or implicitly rely on a normative judgement about whether the decision being made is right, good or in some other sense appropriate. The functional test is explicitly value neutral because it commits to standards relating to the **basic set of abilities** that enable a person to reason, but not the **content** of that person's reasoning.

How should decisions be made when an adult patient lacks capacity?

When a person lacks capacity, a decision needs to be made on that person's behalf. Ethical and legal engagement with substitute decision making has exposed three distinctive principles.

First, **proxy decision making** refers to a set of procedures that aim to ensure that incompetent patients' **known wishes** guide the decision-making process. In the ideal scenario, patients would have made an advance statement and/or appointed a proxy decision maker, when competent, using a power of attorney. The proxy decision maker is then required to uphold the patient's known wishes if relevant. Despite academic debate about the nature of personal identity, advance directives are believed to best reflect autonomous choice.

Second, **substituted judgment** requires another person to attempt to make the same decision that the incompetent patient would make, if they were able to do so. The need for this surrogate decision maker to be able to 'speak' for the incompetent patient means that the next of kin has become established in a number of legal jurisdictions as the most appropriate surrogate. This subjective approach requires a detailed inquiry into the patient's life to make a **best guess** about their preferences.

Third, the **best interests** principle requires a decision to achieve the **best outcome**. Traditionally, patients' best interests were interpreted in terms of their objective welfare interests – typically, requiring treatment that is clinically indicated. However, ethicists are now sensitive to best interests having both an objective and a subjective component. This means that decision making should incorporate medical evidence relating to the decision at hand, filtered through an account of the person's own values, wishes and beliefs.

These principles have been adopted, combined and refined in different ways across legal jurisdictions. In England, a complex procedural hierarchy for substitute decision making has been endorsed under the Mental Capacity Act 2005 (Figure 11.2).

International conventions, most notably the UN Convention on the Rights of Persons with Disabilities (CRPD), endorses value commitments that pose a new challenge to the very notion of substitute decision making. Endorsing a 'supported decision-making'

Figure 11.3 Should the parents' refusal of consent be respected?

approach, the CRPD takes the view that passing the decision-making responsibility to another person disempowers people with disabilities. It remains unclear whether the Mental Capacity Act 2005 is compliant with the CRPD's focus on supported modes of decision making, and some commentators have argued that compliance depends on modifying the best interests checklist to adopt a person-centred approach. In practice, this might mean giving primacy in law to evidence about the person's current expressed wishes or behaviours, over and above evidence about previous values, beliefs or preferences.

Consent and children

When children (or 'minors') are being treated or cared for, it can be uncertain who can give or withhold consent to treatment, and on what grounds consents or refusals should be respected.

Two conflicting principles

In addressing these uncertainties, one important ethical principle that has been posited reflects the view that children ought to be treated differently from adults because of their developing capacities and autonomy. In the face of disease, preserving a child's 'open future' and stabilising their journey into adulthood requires healthcare practitioners to attend to the child's **welfare**, maximising health outcomes where possible. This is a view endorsed within English law, with the Children Act 1989 being founded on the core principle that children's welfare is paramount, regardless of the age of the child. In relation to consent, this opens up the possibility of denying children or parents the right to refuse medically beneficial interventions.

In contrast, it might be seen that treating children differently from adults fails to recognise the wide spectrum of capacities, abilities and maturities that define the early years of life, and the arbitrariness of age cut-offs in differentiating childhood from adulthood. Our duties to support children to develop into adults foreground the values of **empowerment** and **involvement** in order to advance educational goals or otherwise to promote the child's developing autonomy. Denying the right of children to make decisions about their lives when able to do so, or excluding their voices from the process of making such decisions, looks to be clearly at odds with these values.

In England, the law has struggled to reconcile these competing principles, leading to a patchwork landscape of complex regulations that is ripe for criticism.

Consent by a child

It has been long recognised in statute that 16- and 17-year-old children are permitted to give consent to medical treatment when they have the capacity to do so. If judged to lack capacity, these 16- and 17-year-olds fall under the requirements of the Mental Capacity Act 2005.

Children who are 15 years or younger are able to give consent to medical treatment only if they are judged as 'Gillick competent'. A Gillick-competent child is one who has 'sufficient understanding and intelligence to enable him or her to understand fully what is proposed'. In contrast to the legal concept of mental capacity for adults, this extends beyond the child's cognitive abilities to considerations of the child's maturity, interpreted as the child's ability to grasp the moral, familial and personal considerations that surround the decision.

Importantly, children aged 17 or below cannot refuse consent to treatment that is judged by practitioners to be in their welfare interests, all things considered. Welfare here includes an assessment of clinical outcomes, but it will also extend to considering the likely impact of forcing treatment on an unwilling child who fully understands what is happening. How this balance is struck is a matter of professional judgement, but it is clearly a judgement that needs to attend carefully to the risk and severity of harms that are likely to accrue from acceding to the child's refusal. While this obvious asymmetry between a competent child's ability to give but not refuse consent has been extensively criticised, it illustrates the law's struggle to reconcile its competing obligations to promote children's welfare and to respect their developing autonomy simultaneously.

Consent by a person with parental responsibility

A person with parental responsibility is permitted to give consent for medical treatment, and only consent from one person with parental responsibility is required. Consent is taken formally from this person when his/her child is incapable of giving consent for him/herself, or to authorise treatment when a competent child is refusing to give consent. In everyday practice, however it is a recognised professional requirement for doctors to enter into a partnership with the family, including the child and his/her parents in discussions about care planning and decision-making as appropriate given the circumstances of each case.

Consent by a court

The Children Act 1989 accords the High Court powers to make a 'specific issue' order for medical treatment to proceed, or the Court can authorise treatment or care arrangements separately under its inherent jurisdiction. Most commonly, consent is given by a court where there is irreconcilable dispute between the healthcare team and the parents and/or child about which the right course of treatment. Such disputes typically concern preferences for alternative therapies that have limited to no evidence to support their use in the child's case, or when doctors wish to withdraw life-sustaining treatment for babies or children with severely life-limiting conditions against the wishes of the parents. In such cases, the judge is entirely focused on determining, on the basis of the evidence, the course of action that will advance the child's welfare to the greatest extent. It is now well-established that, in some limited circumstances, a child's interests can be best served by being allowed to die.

Managing disagreements

In healthcare practice, it is not uncommon for conflicts between children and parents, between parents and doctors, or between individual parents to arise about whether the treatment in question should be authorised or not. Strictly speaking, the treatment of a child can proceed when that treatment advances the child's welfare and consent has been obtained from one person or institution who is legally permitted to give it.

But this is clearly not the end of the matter. The child's welfare is almost always likely to be served by resolving these kinds of conflicts, or in repairing the damage to interpersonal or professional care relationships when these have broken down over irresolvable conflicts about whether treatment should proceed. Involving children in decisions about their treatment, and including them as equal participants in the delivery of care, are likely to serve both their welfare and autonomy interests in the vast majority of clinical situations.

12 Reproduction

Figure 12.1 Judicial oversight of reproductive decision-making

(a)

(b)

(c)

Assisted reproductive techniques, the availability of donated gametes and surrogacy have extended the possible ways that people might have children. But should access to these forms of assistance be restricted? Should literally anyone be able to become a parent?

Obviously anyone can become a parent if they can produce a child without assistance. Should those who need assistance face barriers? If there should be barriers, who is to decide who can or cannot become a parent? And on what basis?

CASE STUDY: Re MB

Ms MB was in the late stages of labour and was told that she needed to have a Caesarean section, without which she and her child would die. Although she was willing to have the operation, she refused to consent to the necessary injection, due to a needle phobia. It was held that she lacked capacity to make the decision about the injection. She was in such a panic that she could not make a rational decision. The doctor was therefore authorised to make the decision which would promote her best interests – which was that the operation should be performed.

General ethical principles in reproduction

Reproductive autonomy is the principle that in matters of reproduction the state should not interfere in the reproductive choices that people make. For example, the state should not prevent someone from reproducing because they think their children will be disabled or bad for society. More controversially, some supporters of reproductive autonomy suggest that the state has a positive obligation to help people give effect to their reproductive choices: for example, that the state has an obligation to supply abortion on demand, or access to assisted reproduction to all who want it (Figures 12.1, 12.2, 12.3).

Supporters of reproductive autonomy argue that the right to autonomy requires respect for decisions that people make about reproduction because they are some of the most intimate and important decisions that people take. Forcing someone to have a child they do not want, or preventing them from having a child they do want, will be a major interference in a person's plans for how they would like to live their life. The most tyrannical regimes in history have sought to control people's reproduction. Supporters argue that the importance of respecting people's reproductive choices mean that the state should be obliged to provide resources to enable them to exercise their choice. Infertility, it has been suggested, should be seen like a disability, with the state being obliged to do what it can to limit the effect of that disability. As no fertile woman would be prevented by the state from having a child, so the state should not deny a woman needing fertility treatment access to that.

Opponents typically argue that although reproductive decisions are important for the adults involved, these decisions crucially impact on a third party: the child. When a person's reproductive decision will harm a child, that decision should not be respected. So, if a person who will be an unsuitable parent seeks access to assisted reproduction, they should be denied it. When a person wishes to end a pregnancy, the interests of the foetus might mean that the termination will not be justified.

Another principle is that of procreative beneficence. This principle espouses the argument that potential parents have an obligation to produce the best child they can. That might involve, for example, using assisted reproductive techniques to produce a number of embryos and then selecting the best to implant. Critics complain that the idea of creating the 'best' child carries great dangers. We should love our children unconditionally and not treat them as 'Grand Design' projects. Also, some see procreative beneficence as close to eugenics and attempts to create a 'master race', with history teaching us of the danger of this approach.

The status of the embryo and foetus

The law

The legal status of the embryo and foetus is ambiguous. It is clear that the foetus is not a person in the eyes of the law. It is at birth that personhood begins: when the baby is outside the mother and able to breathe independently. This means that in law killing a foetus is not killing a person and that legal proceedings cannot be brought on behalf of the foetus. However, it would not be true to say the foetus is 'nothing' or 'simply part of the mother'. The law does recognise that the foetus has interests that are to be protected. For example, the criminal law has an offence of procuring a miscarriage and a person can sue for injuries they suffered while they were a foetus. However, all attempts in the courts to prevent abortions taking place by relying on the interests of the foetus have failed.

Ethics

There is much debate over the moral status of the embryo. Here are three views:

1 The traditional 'pro-life' approach: This view states that the foetus has the moral status of a person from the moment of conception. It is then that the person's entire genetic make-up is determined. At that point, barring any intervention, the foetus will develop into a born person. There is no other point from then on at which one can draw a bright line to mark the start of personhood.

2 The capacity view: This argues that what gives someone the moral standing of personhood is the ability to think, be self-aware, interact with others and experience the world. These attributes are not fully apparent until birth, or sometime after.

3 The gradualist view: A middle approach, known as the 'gradualist' approach, argues that as the foetus develops it acquires more and more of the attributes of moral personhood and therefore has increasing moral significance. This view argues that we cannot pinpoint a particular time at which the foetus becomes a person, although we can say that at birth the foetus definitely is. There is no agreement on which view is correct, in part because much depends on what you think gives meaning to life.

Assisted reproduction

The law

Assisted reproduction is regulated by the Human Fertilisation and Embryology Acts of 1990 and 2008. The Human Fertilisation and Embryology Authority has the job of regulating clinics that engage in assisted reproduction. It does this through issuing guidance and inspections. Under the legislation there are certain activities that are prohibited (e.g. placing a human embryo in an animal). There are other activities that are only permitted under licence (e.g. the storage of an embryo).

There are some key principles that underpin the law on assisted reproduction:

• The principle of consent. A person's gametes cannot be used or stored without their consent. Similarly, an embryo cannot be stored without the consent of both gamete providers.
• The welfare of the child. Before a clinic offers a couple assisted reproduction, it must consider the welfare of any child who will be born as a result, including the need of the child for 'supportive parenting'. The clinic may, therefore, refuse to offer assisted reproductive treatment if it thinks that the child who will be produced will suffer.
• The right to know of your genetic origins. The law now recognises that children born using donated sperm or eggs have a right to know of their genetic origins. This means that children born after 1 April 2005 can, when they are adults, apply for information about their gamete donor, including their name, address and place of birth.

Parentage

• Who is the mother and father of a child born using reproductive assistance?
• The mother. The mother will be the woman who gives birth to the child. That is so even if she has used donated eggs to become pregnant.
• The father. The father will be the husband or partner of the woman who gives birth, even if donated sperm is used. The partner will need to show that he signed with the mother a notice that they consented to him being treated as the father.

• Other parent. If a woman attends a clinic with a female partner, she can become the 'other parent' of the child, although, oddly, not the mother.

A person who donates an egg or sperm for use in infertility treatment in a licensed clinic will not become a mother or father or any child born as a result.

Ethical issues in assisted reproduction

There are some ethicists who claim that assisted reproduction is immoral because it goes against the natural process of reproduction, but that is very much a minority view. More controversy surrounds the extent to which it is appropriate for the state to restrict access to reproductive services. To some, these services should be open to any who need assistance to produce a child. The state should not, and cannot, judge who will make a good parent. Others argue that if a clinic is to be involved in producing a child, it has a duty to ensure that the child will not be born into a undesirable environment.

There is also much debate over who should be regarded as the mother and father in cases of assisted reproduction. Some ethicists believe the law should respect the blood ties and state that the genetic parents are the parents in the eyes of the law. Other people suggest that what makes a person a parent is the role they carry out, not their genetic link. They will be much happier seeing, for example, the partner of the woman being treated as the father or mother of the child, even if they have no biological connection with the child.

Surrogacy

Surrogacy arrangements occur when one woman carries a child for a couple, intending to hand the child over at birth. The child may or may not be genetically related to the couple. The law is not supportive of surrogacy arrangements: commercial surrogacy contracts are prohibited and no surrogacy arrangement can be enforced. This means that if the woman who gives birth to the child decides to keep the baby, the courts will not intervene unless there is reason to believe she poses a risk to the child and so the child will be better off with the couple. However, if she decides to hand the baby over, the couple can apply for a parenting order or an adoption order and thereby become the parents of the child.

Ethicists are divided on the issue of surrogacy. Some argue that people should be allowed to do what they want with their bodies. If people want to enter a contract to carry a child, they should be able to and the law should enforce that contract. Others argue that surrogacy contracts involve the selling of a child and are contrary to the dignity of the child and of the surrogate mother.

Further reading

Herring, J. *Medical law*, 2011 (Oxford University Press), Chapter 6.

13 Termination of pregnancy

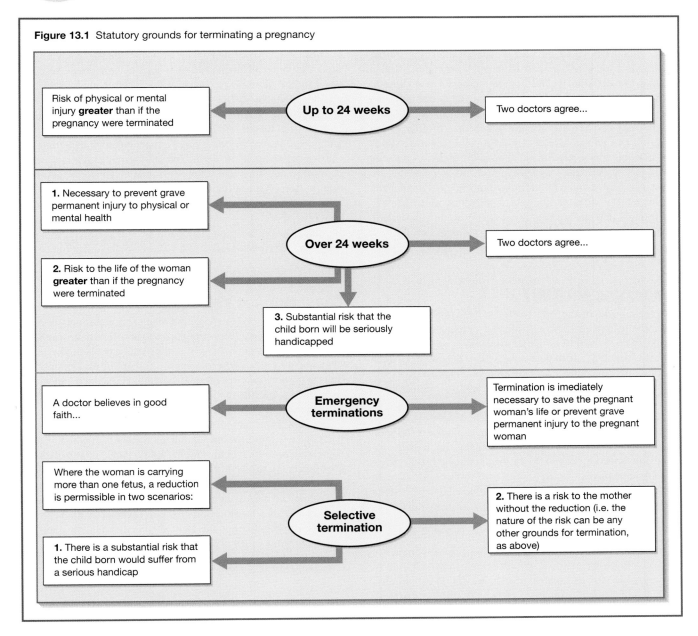

Figure 13.1 Statutory grounds for terminating a pregnancy

Up to 24 weeks
- Risk of physical or mental injury **greater** than if the pregnancy were terminated
- Two doctors agree...

Over 24 weeks
- **1.** Necessary to prevent grave permanent injury to physical or mental health
- **2.** Risk to the life of the woman **greater** than if the pregnancy were terminated
- **3.** Substantial risk that the child born will be seriously handicapped
- Two doctors agree...

Emergency terminations
- A doctor believes in good faith...
- Termination is imediately necessary to save the pregnant woman's life or prevent grave permanent injury to the pregnant woman

Selective termination
- Where the woman is carrying more than one fetus, a reduction is permissible in two scenarios:
- **1.** There is a substantial risk that the child born would suffer from a serious handicap
- **2.** There is a risk to the mother without the reduction (i.e. the nature of the risk can be any other grounds for termination, as above)

Medical Ethics, Law and Communication at a Glance, First Edition. Edited by Patrick Davey, Anna Rathmell, Michael Dunn, Charles Foster and Helen Salisbury.
© 2017 John Wiley & Sons, Ltd. Published 2017 by John Wiley & Sons, Ltd.

Introduction

Termination of pregnancy, or abortion, is the deliberate ending of a pregnancy with the destruction of a human embryo or foetus at any point before its birth. In the UK and the US, an average of one in three women chooses to terminate a pregnancy at some point during their reproductive years. Abortions can be carried out 'medically', with the use of drugs, or through surgery on the pregnant woman, the method being dependent on the number of weeks of gestation. As a medical procedure, abortion is often considered as somewhat set apart from other practices, because it involves the decision to end at least some form of human life, whether this life is believed to possess rights and interests or not. For the pregnant woman, the decision to terminate a pregnancy may also be a decision not to become a mother, or not to become a mother again. Hence, abortion also takes on a social significance that many other medical procedures do not possess. Abortion is an extremely delicate and controversial subject, which sparks impassioned opinions on both sides of the debate. Whatever ethical issues are thought to surround abortion, it is widely thought that ending a pregnancy is not simply like having a tonsillectomy, and the law governing abortion in the UK reflects this judgement.

The Abortion Act 1967

The starting point of the Abortion Act 1967 is that abortion is a criminal offence unless an available defence applies. It is particularly important to note that abortion is not considered a right in the UK, unlike in the US, where the famous Supreme Court decision *Roe* v *Wade* (1973) established the fundamental right to abortion in the first two trimesters of pregnancy as part of the constitutional right to privacy. The 1967 Act then proceeds to lay out the relevant defences. The general picture, set out in section 1, is that the more developed a pregnancy is, the stronger the defence or reason for termination must be (Figure 13.1). At all stages, the decision to terminate requires the support of two doctors, who agree that the relevant circumstances are made out. Up to 24 weeks of pregnancy, termination is permissible if continuing the pregnancy would create a risk of injury to the physical or mental health of the woman (or her existing children) that is **greater** than the risk created by continuing the pregnancy – a relatively low threshold. It is sometimes claimed that in early pregnancy the notion of 'mental health' is interpreted liberally, so that abortion is effectively available 'on demand' at this stage.

After 24 weeks, the conditions become stricter. Termination is permissible in three circumstances:

1 If the termination is judged to be necessary to prevent grave permanent injury to the physical or mental health of the pregnant woman.
2 If continuing the pregnancy would involve **risk to the life** of the pregnant woman, greater than if the pregnancy were terminated.
3 If there is a **substantial risk** that if the child was born it would suffer from a **serious mental or physical handicap**.

In these three circumstances there is no 24-week cut-off point, meaning that a termination for these reasons could be carried out at any point before birth. However, the conditions for late terminations are clearly harder to prove than for earlier ones. In 2009 (the latest figures released), only 1% of all abortions in the UK were carried out at 20 weeks or more of pregnancy.

Termination for foetal disability

Foetal disability is one of the more hotly contested grounds for termination. The terms 'substantial risk' and 'serious handicap' are clearly quite open-ended. In *Jepson* v *The Chief Constable of West Mercia Police Constabulary* (2003), a reverend learned of a case where a late abortion (post-24 weeks) had been carried out on the ground that the foetus suffered from a cleft lip. She sought judicial review of the Crown Prosecution's decision not to prosecute. The Crown Prosecution decided to reinvestigate the case but concluded that the doctors concerned had not acted in bad faith in the view that the child would be seriously handicapped. In 2010, the Department of Health released statistics which showed that 1% of abortions (2,085) carried out in 2009 cited the disability ground. Chromosomal abnormalities (such as Down's Syndrome) and congenital malformations (of the nervous system or cardiovascular system) were the most commonly reported handicaps. Termination for foetal anomaly clearly raises some difficult questions regarding the symbolic significance of such actions for disabled members of society, concerns about the welfare of the would-be child and heavy burdens placed on expectant parents. Advances in pre-natal screening have been a catalyst for these conflicts coming to the fore.

Conscientious objection

Section 4 of the 1967 Act exempts medical practitioners or their assistants who conscientiously object to abortion from any legal duty to participate in treatment authorised by the Act. The ambit of section 4 is currently very uncertain and politically contentious. The exemption does not remove the duty on the doctor to advise or to refer a patient requesting an abortion to another doctor. In *Janaway* v *Salford HA* (1988), it was held that a secretary at a health centre was not entitled to rely on section 4 in refusing to participate in typing work connected to abortion which, it was suggested, only applied to actually 'taking part' in the treatment. More recently, the Scottish High Court held that two Catholic midwives could not rely on section 4 to exempt themselves from managing and delegating staff on wards where terminations were carried out. This decision was, however, reversed in the Supreme Court, which held that the kind of participation in abortion treatment from which objectors are excused requires 'hands-on' involvement.

Regulation

Under section 1 of the Abortion Act 1967, all treatment connected with abortion has to be carried out at an NHS hospital or other registered clinic, under the authority of a registered medical practitioner. All terminations must be notified to the relevant authorities and certificates produced. Terminations after the 24th week of pregnancy can only be carried out in an NHS institution. Under section 1(4), the requirements of two supporting medical opinions and a registered venue can be waived in an emergency, where a doctor perceives that termination is 'immediately necessary' to save the life of the pregnant woman or prevent grave permanent physical or mental injury. Abortion is, nonetheless, more heavily regulated than any other medical procedure. In *British Pregnancy Advisory Service* v *Secretary of State for Health* (2011), the High Court declined an application by an abortion provider to permit women to take the second drug required for an early medical abortion at home, which would have rendered the process less burdensome. For those opposed to abortion, increased regulation has become a key tactic for restricting access or dissuading women from the decision to abort. In the UK, there have been recent calls to require women considering abortion to receive independent counselling from a body that is not an abortion provider. In the US, the battle often surrounds state funding of abortion clinics, and, more recently, the introduction of 'mandatory ultrasound' laws in many states, which require women requesting an abortion to undergo an ultrasound scan that projects an image of their foetus.

The Abortion Regulations 1991 provide the forms that need to be completed by practitioners providing abortion services. It is interesting to note that the format of the forms permits the two doctors to cite different grounds for termination. In practice, proving that a medically sanctioned abortion was illegal is extremely difficult, since section 1 of the 1967 Act only requires that the practitioners believe 'in good faith' that the grounds are made out, not that they actually were. It would therefore need to be shown that one of the doctors did not **believe** that a defence applied. One notable case in which a conviction was successfully upheld is *R* v *Smith* (1973). A doctor had carried out a private abortion, with evidence suggesting that he had made no internal examination of the patient and had not inquired into her personal history or situation. The only entry in his notes was that she was depressed, and it was moreover unclear whether the doctor who had provided the second opinion had examined the patient.

Abortion and contraception

At some point, the distinction between contraception and abortion may appear blurred. The 'morning-after pill', for example, sometimes forestalls pregnancy by preventing a fertilised egg (or 'zygote') from successfully implanting in the womb lining. When it works this way, is it a contraceptive or an abortifacient? In *R (John Smeaton on behalf of SPUC)* v *Secretary of State for Health*, it was held that the morning after pill fell within the classification 'contraceptive', notwithstanding that it works in some cases by preventing implantation, not only fertilisation. For many people, which side of the line the morning after pill falls down on will not be important. Whether its abortifacient function is relevant or not will depend on further beliefs about the moral significance of conception.

Actions to prevent abortion

It seems clear from the case law that there is no standing in the UK for a third party, such as the biological father, to seek an injunction against an abortion going ahead. In *Paton* v *British Pregnancy Advisory Service* (1978), it was held that a father had no right to prevent an abortion, or to be consulted or notified before it took place. The Paton ruling was followed in the later case *C* v *S* (1987) where the court rejected a man's attempt to represent the foetus in proceedings against its abortion. The case reached the European Court, which agreed with the decisions made by the English judiciary.

The ethical debate

Debate about abortion stands out for its intensity. In the USA, the issue has become heavily politicised, with government officials and Supreme Court Justices often being appointed on the basis of their views about abortion. This is probably because, for some, abortion entails something very close to the outright killing of human infants. For those who disagree, obstructing abortion options is to prevent women from controlling their own bodies and making private reproductive decisions that are theirs to make. Naturally, much will depend on how the foetus is viewed: as a member of our moral community, or not, or as something in between.

Conservatives point to the physiological similarity of a late foetus and a newborn, and to the alleged arbitrariness of birth as a dividing line for the right to life. They also draw attention to evidence of foetal sentience and the possibility of foetal pain in late pregnancy. Conversely, liberals underscore the vast dissimilarities between **early** foetuses and newborns, and argue that most foetuses are not yet developed enough to have interests in continued life. According to some religious perspectives, like that of the Catholic church, a foetus is a full moral person from conception, meaning that abortion is almost always morally impermissible. Finally, on some feminist views, even if a foetus is a full person with interests, it is still not entitled to the use of the pregnant woman's body for continued life when that is against her wishes, and when forcing continued gestation on women has profound implications for sex equality.

English law is clear that a human being is not considered to be a full person until birth, although there are some situations in which a foetus, or the child that it will become, has been recognised to have some legal status, for example by being identified as the beneficiary under a will. Failed abortions where the foetus is born alive present a uniquely difficult situation, since the foetus will then be deemed a child and doctors will be required to act in its best interests. Once born alive, killing the baby or failing to provide it with correct medical care could therefore amount to murder or manslaughter.

Many moderate thinkers about abortion hold to the view that later stage foetuses have more moral worth and right to protection than earlier ones (even if they are not full people) because of their more advanced development. This 'gradualist' or 'developmental' view, if correct, might imply that termination of pregnancy requires a stronger justification the later the pregnancy is, which in some ways broadly reflects the structure of the law.

Whether a purely medical procedure, a form of homicide or (as many people think) something quite different again, termination of a pregnancy almost always entails a difficult, and often emotional, personal decision on the part of the woman concerned. Moreover, abortion is something that now more than ever is about many things other than the disputed rights and interests of human foetuses and pregnant women. It is about our conceptions of personhood and personal identity, the role of women in contemporary society, family planning, politics, sex culture and sexual ethics, and religious beliefs.

14 Organ donation and transplantation

Figure 14.1 Potential organ donor population in the UK, 2014–2015

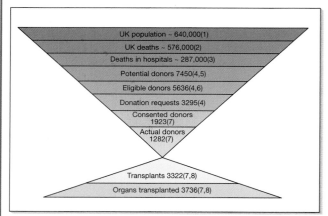

Figure 14.2 Sources of applicant registrations on the NHS organ donor register 2014–2015

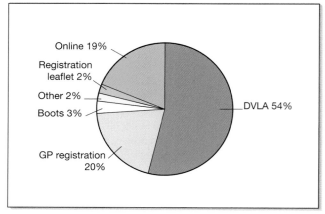

Figure 14.3 Age and gender of people on the NHS organ donor register by 31 March 2015

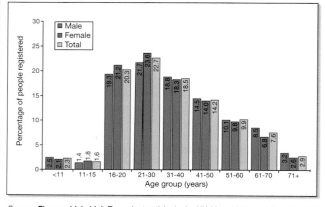

Figure 14.4 Deceased and living donor numbers and transplant numbers in the UK, 2005–2015

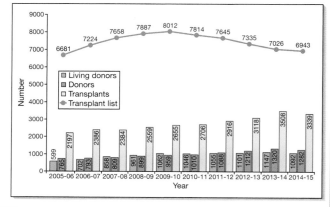

Source: **Figures 14.1–14.4** Transplant activity in the UK 2014-2015, NHS Blood and Transport.

Introduction

There is a chronic shortage of organs for transplantation in the UK. Thousands of people wait for suitable organs to become available. Transplants carried out include hearts, lungs, livers, kidneys, pancreas, intestines and corneas. Of these, the most common solid organs donated and transplanted are kidneys. Some gains have been made recently as the numbers of both deceased and living organ donations have generally increased (Figures 14.1, 14.2, 14.3, 14.4). Despite this, every year hundreds of patients die while on the waiting lists.

Organ donation and the law

In relation to the deceased, organ donation and transplantation is governed by the Human Tissue Act 2004 (England), the Human Tissue Act (Scotland) 2006, and the Human Transplantation (Wales) Act 2013. This note mainly deals with the law in England, but also briefly sets out the law in Scotland and Wales.

Human Tissue Act 2004

The Human Tissue Act 2004 enabled the creation of the Human Tissue Authority, which oversees and regulates all activities involving the use of human tissue (across the UK). In fulfilling this function, it has produced nine Codes of Practice to offer guidance on the use of human tissue, including two relating to organ donation and transplantation.

The bedrock of the 2004 Act is the idea of 'appropriate consent'. The Act governs the removal, storage, and use of organs and tissue from the deceased. Thus, the removal and use of an organ for transplant purposes will not be lawful unless appropriate consent has been provided. The focus of the Act is on the question of **who** is empowered to authorise the donation of an organ. While the Act does not set out an exact process for obtaining consent, it does set out in detail who can give it.

For deceased individuals, 'appropriate consent' is the consent of the person before their death or that of their 'nominated representative' if one was appointed prior to their death. When

Medical Ethics, Law and Communication at a Glance, First Edition. Edited by Patrick Davey, Anna Rathmell, Michael Dunn, Charles Foster and Helen Salisbury.
© 2017 John Wiley & Sons, Ltd. Published 2017 by John Wiley & Sons, Ltd.

a person dies without having given their consent or nominating someone to consent on their behalf, the consent of a person in a 'qualifying relationship' will be valid. There is a hierarchy of people who can give such consent:

1 spouse or partner;
2 parent or child;
3 brother or sister;
4 grandparent or grandchild;
5 nephew or niece;
6 step-parent;
7 half-brother or sister; and
8 friend of longstanding

While the 2004 Act governs the storage and use of organs or parts of organs from the living, the **removal** of these falls within the purview of the common law and the Mental Capacity Act 2005. In the case of the competent living adult, 'appropriate consent' means the consent of the person themselves. All cases involving a live donation must be assessed by an independent assessor from the Human Tissue Authority. In addition, when a person wants to make a donation to a non-specified person (see 'Living donation' below), they must be referred to a special panel that will look at the case.

When the living person lacks capacity, the case must be referred to the courts for approval in order for the donation to be lawful. Determinations of capacity will be done in accordance with the functional test for capacity set out in the Mental Capacity Act 2005.

The consent of a competent living child is deemed to be operationally valid. When a child is not deemed competent to consent, the person with parental responsibility may consent on their behalf. However, all donations by a child must have the approval of both the courts and the Human Tissue Authority, and will only be allowed to go ahead in exceptional circumstances.

Human Transplantation (Wales) Act 2013

Until recently deceased organ donation in Wales was also governed by the 2004 Act. However, the Welsh Act, which came into force at the end of 2015, changes the legislative default in Wales from an opt-in to an opt-out system of organ donation (see below). Wales now operates a system of 'deemed consent' in relation to deceased organ donation.

This means that, upon their deaths, persons ordinarily resident in Wales will be deemed to have consented to donate their organs for transplantation. They can record their wishes not to donate prior to their deaths or can appoint another person to make this decision for them after death.

Persons who were not resident in Wales in the 12 months leading up to their deaths are not captured by this law. Neither are those who lacked capacity for a significant time before their death. Living transplantation remains under the remit of the 2004 Act.

Human Tissue Act (Scotland) 2006

The Scottish Act uses the term 'authorisation' rather than 'appropriate consent'. Authorisation is required for the use of whole deceased bodies and the removal, use, and storage of tissue, including for transplant purposes. Similar to the English Act, it is the authorisation of individuals prior to death which is needed or of a relative after death. Again there is a hierarchy of those who can authorise the donation of the deceased's organs.

Living donation also falls within the purview of the Scottish Act. Specifically, the Human Organ and Tissue Live Transplants (Scotland) Regulations 2006 set out the conditions under which living transplantation is lawful.

The Scottish parliament recently considered and rejected proposals to move to an opt-out system of organ donation, although it is likely that the issue will be revisited in the future.

Ethical issues in transplantation

Given the chronic shortage of organs for transplantation, the pertinent question is how best to increase the numbers of organs available. Relevant strategies can be targeted at increasing either living or deceased donations, each of which raises a variety of ethical issues.

Living organ donation

In recent years, the number of living donors has been steadily increasing in comparison to the number of deceased donors. Live donations can include a kidney, liver lobe and lobe of a lung among others. Living donations account for over one third of all kidney donations. A live transplant is likely to have better long-term outcomes in terms of organ health and longevity than an organ from a deceased donor. As such, from the point of view of the recipient, an organ from a live donor could be considered preferable. However, as these are live donations, the donor undertakes risks that are not associated with deceased donations. In addition to potential long-term health complications, these risks include those associated with the retrieval operation itself plus any post-operative complications. The extent to which these arise is dependent on the type of donation taking place. For example, donations of a live lobe are inherently more risky than kidney donations.

Given the risks associated with live donations, questions could be raised about whether it is ethical to permit healthy persons to put themselves in harm's way purely for the benefit of another. Nonetheless, there are at least two interrelated reasons to think that live donations are ethical. First, those who are adequately informed make the decision to donate with full knowledge of the attendant risks. If we have cause to suppose that we ought to respect the autonomous decisions of competent people, then we might deem that being a live donor is within their legitimate sphere of decision making. Second, we generally think of doing something good for others not only as ethically permissible but morally praiseworthy. Indeed, the notion of altruism is seen by many as a fundamental principle that should underpin organ donation.

Despite this, we should be aware of challenges in assessing potential live donors. One issue that warrants special attention is whether or not the potential donors do in fact give free and informed consent. Some live kidney donors do not donate to a specified person: instead, they donate anonymously to the next suitable person on the waiting list (altruistic non-directed donation). Most live kidney donations, however, are to specific people, usually family members or someone with whom the donor has an emotional tie (directed donation). As such, there is a need to be mindful of the potential for familial pressure on the donor. While many would be happy to donate to a family member, we cannot assume that this is always the case. Given that there is likely to be greater pressure to donate to a family member than to an anonymous stranger, one could question why decisions regarding altruistic non-directed donors need the extra level of regulatory scrutiny that was noted earlier.

Deceased organ donation

Although living donation is on the increase, organs from deceased donors remain the mainstay of transplantation endeavours. Most of the UK currently operates an opt-in system of donation in which individuals must provide consent in order for their organs to be donated in the event of their death. Evidence of this consent can be gained from the Organ Donation Register (ODR) if the person actively registered during their lifetime. If their name does not appear on the ODR, the deceased's views regarding donation may be ascertained from their next of kin and other family members or close friends.

Although the Human Tissue Act 2004 takes the consent of the donors themselves to be paramount, transplant professionals are extremely reluctant to initiate donation against the express wishes of the family. This means that, practically speaking, families retain a veto in the organ donation process. Having said this, such situations are rare. It is more likely that relatives would refuse to donate either when the deceased expressed a wish not to donate or when they are unsure of the deceased's wishes.

Opt-in versus opt-out systems

In an opt-out system, unless a person takes active steps to opt out, they are considered to have consented to the donation of their organs after death. Different types of opt out are in operation among the countries that have such a system. Spain, for example, operates a 'soft opt out' whereby the deceased's relatives are consulted about the deceased's wishes even though they have not formally opted out. This is in contrast to countries such as Austria, which has a 'hard opt-out' system where relatives are not consulted.

Opt out is sometimes erroneously referred to as 'presumed consent' (or 'deemed consent' in Wales). If we consider the act of consenting to donation to be a way of expressing one's autonomy, it would seem to require the active engagement of the individual with the issue of organ donation. It is, therefore, difficult to see how it can be presumed. While consent cannot be simply be assumed from the fact that a person failed to formally object during their lifetime, the lack of active consent does not necessarily mean that opt-out systems are not ethical. The moral good done if extra lives are saved or a recipient's suffering is ameliorated may outweigh concerns regarding active consent. In addition, if the autonomous wishes of the deceased with regards to donation are paramount, then the current opt-in system also faces some ethical problems in this regard. Let us briefly see why.

One worry with opt-out systems of donation is that there will be some people whose organs will be donated who would not have wanted them to have been. One response to this might be to point out that if they had felt strongly enough about it they would have formally opted out. However, there might be reasons why people do not opt out even though they may want to. They may simply not be aware that this is the system of donation that is in place. They may intend to opt out, but, perhaps depending on what administrative hurdles are in place, they may not know how.

There therefore seems to be some reason to worry about organs being donated when this is not what the deceased would have wanted. Yet a similar concern is mirrored in the current opt-in system of donation: there may be people who would have wanted to donate their organs but, for a variety of reasons, this does not happen. They may not have made their wishes known to their nearest and dearest, or simple inertia may have prevented them from actually signing up to the ODR. If, therefore, we are troubled about the thwarting of a person's autonomous wishes, then we would seem to have cause for ethical concern in both opt-out and opt-in systems of donation. The reason for this is because it is not obvious that it is morally worse to donate a person's organs when they would not have wanted this than it is to not do so when they would have.

Other issues

One way to increase the numbers of organs available could be to offer monetary or non-monetary incentives to sign up to the ODR, for example a small financial or non-financial token, paying funeral costs or a tax break. One concern here is that individuals will agree to donate their organs when they otherwise would not have. Yet an incentive would not be needed if they were already willing to become donors. The key would be to ensure that any inducements offered were not 'undue': that is, not of a type or offered in a manner that leaves little real choice.

An alternative way to incentivise donation could be introduce a system of priority points, giving those who sign up to the organ donor register extra 'points' should they ever become in need of an organ themselves. Israel recently introduced the first such system. It is based on reciprocity: the idea that if you are willing to receive an organ, you ought to be willing to donate one. Although a reciprocity-based deceased donation system seems appealing, it should be noted that the reward is gained before any donation has taken place. This can be contrasted with the United Network of Organ Sharing in the USA where previous living donors are allocated extra points should they ever need an organ themselves.

Summary

Despite recent successes in increasing the number of organs for transplantation, every year people die while waiting for an organ to become available. No matter what system is adopted, not everyone is suitable to be an organ donor. This may be because of a pre-existing medical condition or because they die in circumstances that preclude donation. Different systems of donation, whether living or deceased, raise ethical issues that require careful consideration. Yet if changes are to be made to the current system in order to increase the numbers of organs donated, they must be evidence based.

Further reading

Farrell, A.M. and Quigley, M. 'Organ donation and transplantation'. In R. Chadwick (ed.). *Encyclopedia of applied ethics*, 2nd edn, Vol. 3, 2012. San Diego: Academic Press, pp. 288–296.

15 Mental health

Figure 15.1 Mental health

(a)

(b)

Introduction

How should a doctor respond when a patient affected by mental ill-health refuses treatment (Figure 15.1)? The challenge is to determine how much weight is appropriate to accord to a decision made in the context of delusional beliefs, cognitive impairment, addiction or obsessions. The symptoms of the illness may prevent the patient from evaluating the benefits of treatment that could alleviate those symptoms. A 2012 Court of Protection case (*A LA* v *E and others*) illustrates how complex the issues can be: E, a 32-year-old former medical student had a

long history of anorexia nervosa. During the course of the past 4 years, E's body mass index (BMI) remained well below 14. For the past 2 years or so, it had been in the region of 11 or 12. When BMI drops this low, people with anorexia nervosa are usually unable to evaluate the benefits of treatment, but unless treatment can be successfully administered to restore a healthier BMI, the ability to make a meaningful decision about treatment will not be restored. Despite repeated episodes of force-feeding, the team treating E could not bring about that level of recovery. She was being looked after in a community hospital under a palliative

Medical Ethics, Law and Communication at a Glance, First Edition. Edited by Patrick Davey, Anna Rathmell, Michael Dunn, Charles Foster and Helen Salisbury.
© 2017 John Wiley & Sons, Ltd. Published 2017 by John Wiley & Sons, Ltd.

care regime whose purpose was to allow her to die in comfort, in accordance with her expressed wishes. The court was required to decide whether this palliative treatment should continue, or whether prolonged invasive treatment to restore BMI to above 17 should be enforced. The judge had to consider the legal and ethical issues outlined in this chapter.

Treatment without consent

Chapter 11 outlines the general position on consent to medical treatment in England and Wales. However, there are some important exceptions that may apply when a patient needs psychiatric treatment. If someone is detained in hospital under sections 2 or 3 of the Mental Health Act 1983, amended in 2007 (MHA), most forms of treatment **for mental disorder** can be provided without consent, even if the patient retains decision-making capacity or has made an advance decision to refuse treatment. E received several episodes of treatment under section 3.

Detention under section 2 can last for up to 28 days and is for the purpose of assessment (which may include assessing response to compulsory medication). Detention under section 3 can last for up to 6 months (at which point it can be renewed) and is for the purpose of treatment. Before a patient can be detained under sections 2 or 3, two doctors (one of whom must have expertise in the diagnosis or treatment of mental disorders) and an approved mental health practitioner must make an assessment and agree that the following criteria apply:

- The patient must have a 'disorder or disability of the mind' (section 1(2)). However, addiction to drugs or alcohol does not justify detention. People with intellectual disabilities may not be detained unless they demonstrate 'abnormally aggressive or seriously irresponsible conduct'.
- For detention under section 2, the disorder must be 'of a nature or degree which warrants the detention of the patient in a hospital for assessment' and 'he ought to be so detained in the interests of his own health or safety or with a view to the protection of other persons'.
- For detention under section 3, the disorder must be 'of a nature or degree which makes it appropriate for him to receive treatment in hospital', 'it cannot be provided unless he is detained' (often, because the patient refuses the treatment due to lack of insight), 'appropriate medical treatment is available' and 'it is necessary for the health and safety of the patient or for the protection of other persons that he should receive such treatment'.

Section 7 defines medical treatment broadly, to include nursing, psychological interventions and specialist mental health rehabilitation.

Mental Health Act or Mental Capacity Act 2005?

Although they both provide a legal justification for providing treatment in the absence of consent, there are some important differences between the MHA and the Mental Capacity Act (MCA).

People detained under the MHA can appeal to relatively informal and accessible hearings and tribunals, whereas no such procedures exist for people being cared for or treated without their consent under the MCA. The courts have stated that the MCA must not be used to avoid the procedural safeguards associated with the MHA (*GJ v The Foundation Trust* [2009]).

Unlike the MCA, the MHA can only be used to justify the provision of treatment for **mental** disorder. This **can** include the treatment of a physical condition that is causing a mental disorder, such as hypothyroidism causing depression, and treatment of physical problems that are caused by mental disorder, such as starvation caused by anorexia nervosa. This is why E could be hospitalised and force-fed under section 3 of the MHA. It **cannot** be used to justify the treatment of a physical problem in someone who also happens to have a mental disorder, such as gangrene in someone who also has schizophrenia.

Whereas the MCA can justify any act that is in the **best interests** of the patient, the MHA can only be used when treatment is needed to protect the patient's **health** or **safety** interests so the scope is narrower. However, whereas the MCA can only justify an act that is in the best interests **of the patient**, the MHA can be used to provide treatment that is needed to protect **other people**. This aspect of the MHA could be thought of as being more utilitarian in its approach than the MCA: the focus is not simply on enabling the doctor to discharge their duty of care to people who may not be able to make their own treatment decisions, but also encompasses a form of 'police power', enabling the doctor to take action to safeguard the public.

Finally, it is also important to remember that the majority of people affected by mental ill-health will not meet the criteria for detention under the MHA and will also retain their capacity to make decisions about their care and treatment.

Assessing capacity in mental disorder

In E's case, the treating team had accepted that she had, in October 2011, the mental capacity to make an advance decision to refuse further active treatment, and had proceeded to offer palliative care. While accepting that they had reached this decision in good faith, the judge hearing the case in 2012 disagreed, and ordered that E be transferred for active re-feeding. This highlights the difficulties of assessing capacity in some forms of mental ill-health where the abilities to understand and retain relevant information are preserved. Despite retaining those abilities, people like E may have an extremely strong desire to avoid weight gain, or to no longer be alive, or an extremely strong fear of some aspect of the treatment. Such desires or fears may affect their ability to weigh up relevant information appropriately and reach a meaningful decision. As the judge stated, 'E's obsessive fear of weight gain makes her incapable of weighing the advantages and disadvantages of eating in any meaningful way.' The importance of conducting a detailed capacity assessment before accepting the decision of a person affected by mental ill-health to refuse life-saving treatment, and seeking the view of the Court of Protection in cases of doubt, cannot be overestimated.

Further reading

Hope, A., Savulescu, J. and Hendrick, J. *Medical ethics and the law. The core curriculum*, 2nd edn, 2008. Oxford: Elsevier, Chapter 11.

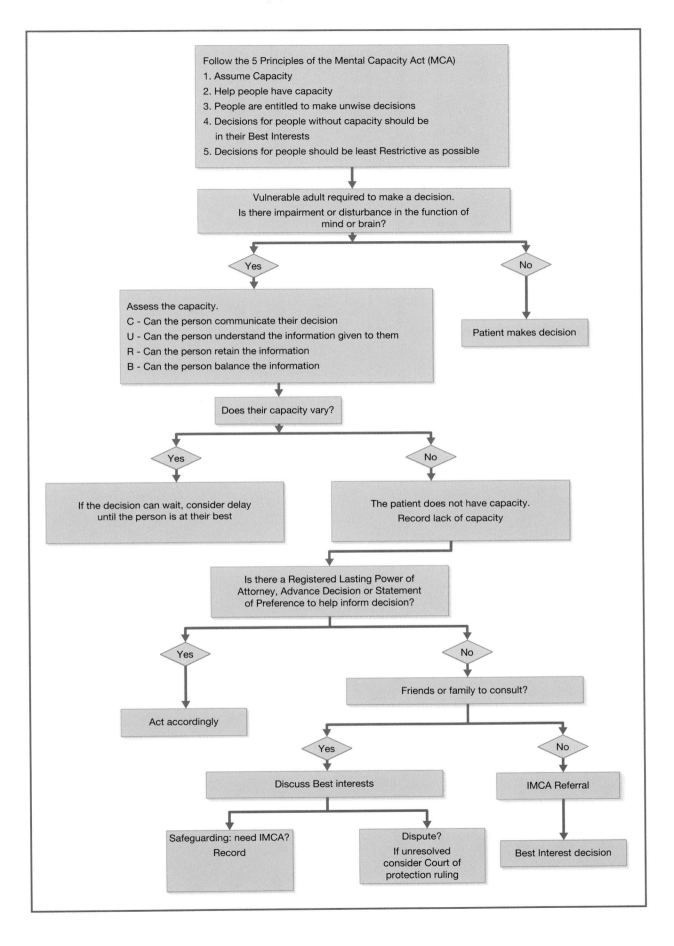

16 Safeguarding children and adults

Figure 16.1 Making decisions involving a child

Figure 16.2 Making decisions involving an adult

Nearly everyone agrees that someone suffering abuse should be protected by the law. But, what should the limits be? How badly must children be maltreated before it is appropriate to remove them from their parents? And, if the case involves an adult, what are we to do if they do not want to be protected from the abuse? These are questions that are fraught with difficulty and where the law must tread a delicate line.

Legal protections

There are a range of ways in which the law protects children and vulnerable adults.

Criminal proceedings

There are a wide range of criminal offences that protect children and vulnerable adults from abuse. There are aspects of the general law, such as the law on assaults and property crimes, and there are also some specific offences that are designed to protect vulnerable people. The Sexual Offences Act 2003, for example, contains a range of offences specifically designed to protect children or those with mental disorder from sexual abuse.

Normally in the criminal law, a person is not liable for failing to act. However, there are also specific offences of child neglect, neglect of a person lacking mental capacity, or neglect of a person who is being detained under the Mental Health Act 1983, amended in 2007 (MHA). These offences can be committed by people who have a responsibility to look after someone else and fail to do so.

Civil proceedings

Civil proceedings can be brought to protect a child or vulnerable adult from abuse. These can lead to the child or vulnerable adult being taken away from their families and into care (Figure 16.1).

Children

A local authority can apply for a care or supervision order in respect of a child who is suffering or is likely to suffer significant harm (Figure 16.2). The court will only make a care or supervision order if the significant harm is attributable to the level of care the parents are giving or are expected to give. Further, it must be shown that the care or supervision order will promote the welfare of the child. A supervision order will be appropriate if it is thought that the family needs the advice and assistance of a social worker, but that there is no need to remove the child. A care order will be appropriate if the local authority believe that the child needs to be taken away from the parents and placed with alternative carers.

Difficult cases can arise where the court is persuaded that the child is being abused, but it is not clear who is carrying out the abuse. If the court is persuaded that the abuse is definitely being carried out by a person caring for the child, even if it is not clear who it is, the court can still make a care order. However, if it is clear who is doing the abuse, the social workers may persuade the non-abusive parent to take the child away from the abuser.

Vulnerable adults

There is no statutory jurisdiction specifically dealing with the removal of a vulnerable adult from an abusive situation, but three main sources of law could be used if a local authority were concerned that a person was suffering abuse:

1 Under the Mental Capacity Act 2005, a court can make an order that will promote the best interests of a person who lacks mental capacity. It cannot be used in the case of a person who has capacity to make the decision, but decides to remain in the abusive circumstances. If force or restraint is required to give effect to a court order, there are special regulations that must be followed. These include a requirement that the force is necessary and there is no less forceful way of giving effect to the order. A court may decide not to make an order if it cannot be carried out without the use of force.

2 Under the MHA, a person suffering mental disorder can be detained ('sectioned' as it is commonly known). However, this can only be used in order to provide treatment for their mental disorder. It cannot be used simply to protect them.

3 The inherent jurisdiction can be used for those lacking capacity or who are deemed vulnerable adults. Vulnerable adults can include those who have capacity, but are acting under coercion or undue influence. That would include those living in an abusive relationship. The courts are still developing this jurisdiction, but under it a court will make orders to protect a person from abuse. It is unlikely that the court will be persuaded to use this jurisdiction unless there is a fear of serious abuse and the person either lacks capacity or is severely impaired in their ability to make decisions for themselves.

If an adult does not fall into any of these categories, they cannot be taken away from an abusive situation simply because that would be in their best interests. For example, a woman who is being beaten by her husband cannot be removed from the home without her consent, unless it is shown that she lacks the mental capacity to make her own decisions.

In 2014, the government introduced the Care Act, which included provisions to place adult safeguarding on a statutory footing. This legislation lays out the responsibilities that local authorities and NHS trusts have to develop adult safeguarding policies, but it does not include new legal powers of intervention.

Safeguarding children and adult policies

All NHS trusts and local authorities will have policies that are designed to protect children and vulnerable adults from abuse. The features of these will differ, but all must be compliant with the requirements of the Care Act 2014. They are likely to contain the following elements:

- All staff who are likely to have contact with children or vulnerable adults need to have appropriate Disclosure and Barring Service (DBS) checks and clearance.
- There is a clearly set procedure as to what should happen if there are concerns that a child has suffered or is likely to suffer harm as a result of abuse or neglect. This may well include procedures as to what should happen if a child misses an appointment or there are unexplained injuries.
- Staff should be trained to be aware of the signs of neglect or abuse.
- Positive steps are required to ensure that those cared for in a hospital or other healthcare settings have their welfare promoted.
- There are appropriate arrangements for sharing information with other agencies that may deal with children or vulnerable adults.
- Different agencies working with children or vulnerable adults should work together for their welfare.
- When allegations of abuse or neglect are made, they are to be taken seriously and investigated properly.

Under the Care Act 2014, the safeguarding procedures adopted by local authorities and NHS trusts must be aligned with 6 core principles: i) empowerment, ii) prevention, iii) proportionality, iv) protection, v) partnership, and vi) accountability.

17 Public health

Figure 17.1 Public health policy 'intervention ladder'

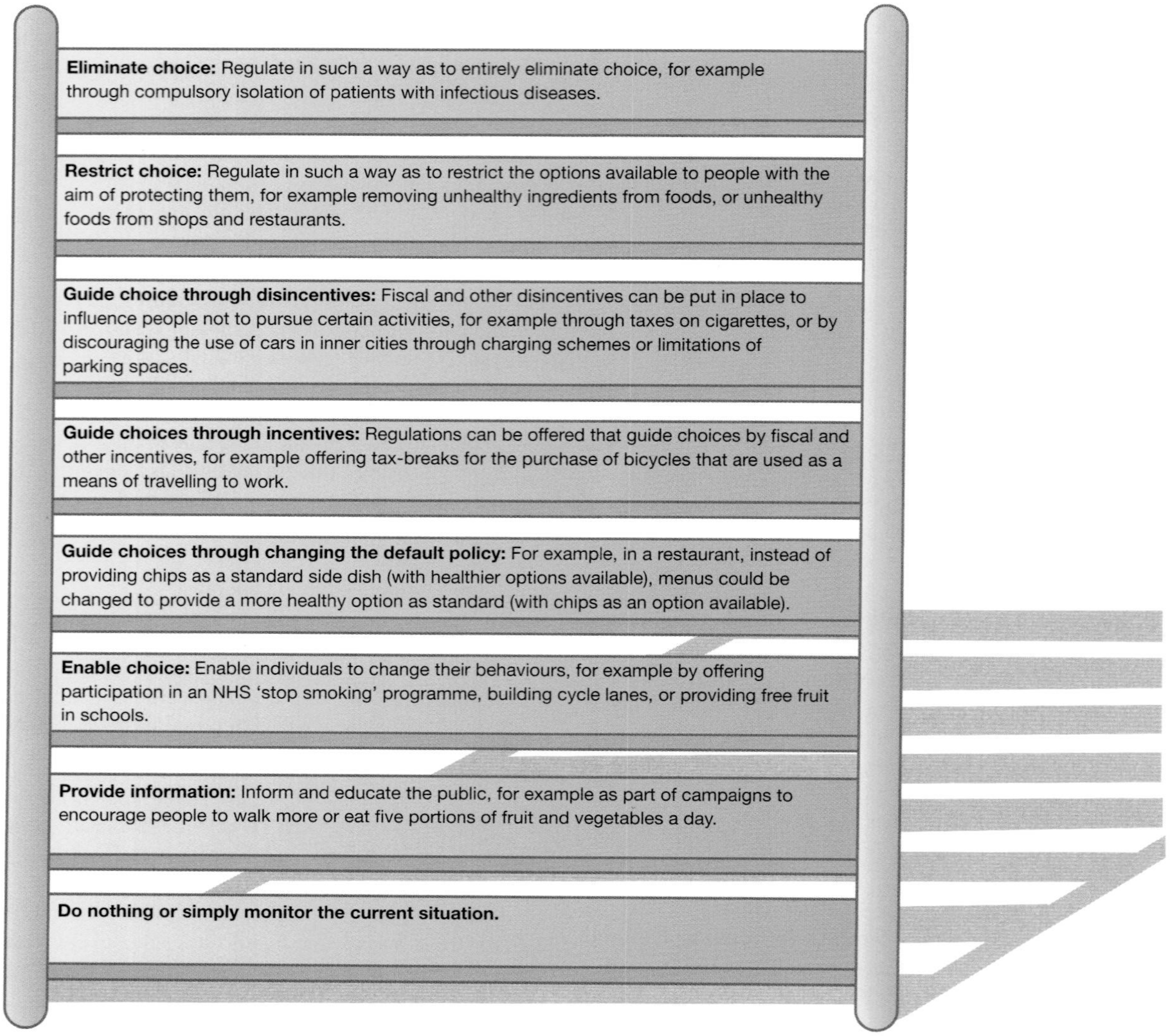

Eliminate choice: Regulate in such a way as to entirely eliminate choice, for example through compulsory isolation of patients with infectious diseases.

Restrict choice: Regulate in such a way as to restrict the options available to people with the aim of protecting them, for example removing unhealthy ingredients from foods, or unhealthy foods from shops and restaurants.

Guide choice through disincentives: Fiscal and other disincentives can be put in place to influence people not to pursue certain activities, for example through taxes on cigarettes, or by discouraging the use of cars in inner cities through charging schemes or limitations of parking spaces.

Guide choices through incentives: Regulations can be offered that guide choices by fiscal and other incentives, for example offering tax-breaks for the purchase of bicycles that are used as a means of travelling to work.

Guide choices through changing the default policy: For example, in a restaurant, instead of providing chips as a standard side dish (with healthier options available), menus could be changed to provide a more healthy option as standard (with chips as an option available).

Enable choice: Enable individuals to change their behaviours, for example by offering participation in an NHS 'stop smoking' programme, building cycle lanes, or providing free fruit in schools.

Provide information: Inform and educate the public, for example as part of campaigns to encourage people to walk more or eat five portions of fruit and vegetables a day.

Do nothing or simply monitor the current situation.

Note: The 'intervention ladder' aims to demonstrate the wide range of regulatory techniques that are available to advance public health agendas, recognising a need for proportionality. It exemplifies how different interventions may impact, with increasing constraint, on people's liberty to make choices that will harm their or other people's health.

Source: Data modified from *Nuffield Council on Bioethics*, 2007.

Medical Ethics, Law and Communication at a Glance, First Edition. Edited by Patrick Davey, Anna Rathmell, Michael Dunn, Charles Foster and Helen Salisbury.
© 2017 John Wiley & Sons, Ltd. Published 2017 by John Wiley & Sons, Ltd.

The idea of 'public health' raises questions that extend well beyond medicine, or even healthcare. This is apparent from what many see as public health's classic definition, denoting the organised efforts within a society to assure the conditions in which people can be healthy. Such efforts include the provision of a healthcare system, but extend to broad-ranging protective and preventive measures, such as sustaining a clean and safe environment, regulating to ensure the safety of food and drink, providing education regarding personal health and hygiene, protecting against potential health threats through preventive procedures such as vaccinations, and in extreme cases defending against severe health emergencies through the exercise of the state's coercive police powers (Figure 17.1).

Different meanings of public health

The term 'public health' is used to imply various, quite distinct, meanings (Coggon, 2012, chapter 3):

- **Public health as a political tool:** Sometimes public health is taken to describe a social mission or theory, and is thereby cited as the basis of a political imperative to act in certain ways to guarantee or promote people's good health. This idea is often expressed through the maxim 'the health of the people is the highest law'.
- **Public health as government business:** Some people use public health to denote the government's responsibility for protecting health. This may be limited just to the role of the Department of Health, or Public Health England and local authorities. Alternatively, it may extend across all governmental action that might bear on health, from road safety to agricultural policy to town planning to advertising standards.
- **Public health as the social infrastructure:** In some instances, public health is conceived more widely, to encompass both governmental and non-governmental responsibilities that are assumed for health. This could include, for example, voluntary measures taken by supermarkets to use a 'traffic light' labelling system on food products.
- **Public health as a professional enterprise:** Public health may refer to a profession, defined by its members' competences or expertise.
- **Public health as blind benefit or harm:** Many public health interventions can be proven to have a net effect across a population while it is impossible at the individual level to identify to a certainty who has benefited from them. In such instances, people talk of public health benefits or harms to describe a certain effect on health, even when it is not possible to identify this in individual detail.
- **Public health as conjoined beneficiaries:** Some argue that 'the public' is not just a collection of individuals, but a community with special characteristics beyond being simply the sum of its members. In such cases, public health is used to emphasise that 'no man is an island', and individual health benefits and harms are a morally shared concern, so that people have ethical reasons to care for their and others' health.
- **Public health as the population's health:** Sometimes public health relates to health data within or between populations, either in aggregate or by reference to distribution. It is used in this way to present facts about health within a specified group of people.

There is clearly a great variety among these different definitions. Often the term 'public health' is used to mean more than one thing even within the same document. It is helpful, therefore, to be able to distinguish its uses.

Public health, ethics, law, and practice

Within practical and professional ethics, many commentators distinguish public health ethics from clinical ethics. This is partly due to the distinct concerns of public health practitioners, who may be said to 'treat' populations rather than individual patients. The analytical approach of the 'population perspective', where facts about health are learned through observing groups of people, is often mirrored in practical policy responses, which are targeted through general means (e.g. through added taxes on tobacco products, or the banning of smoking in enclosed public spaces, to discourage smoking). While liberal values such as personal autonomy remain important, concerns for how these values should be respected when targeting populations prompt different questions from those found in individual clinical interactions between a doctor and a patient.

Given its population perspective, some consider public health to be an inherently utilitarian enterprise, directed to gaining the greatest aggregate good. However, blunt utilitarianism is not a sound way for public health practitioners to approach their work: both the law and ethical theories of political liberalism demand that limits be placed on what can be done in the name of public health.

An alternative idea that many see as underpinning public health implies that practitioners have a mandate to encourage wide-scale social changes to produce better health across the population, with a profound concern too for social justice and equity in health outcomes. Such an agenda must be viewed within a wider political and legal frame.

The regulation of health-affecting behaviours can provide a good example here. Public health practitioners are able to provide clear evidence of the harmful effects of the consumption of products such as foods with high sugar content, tobacco and alcohol. Evidence of the harms they cause, especially where these compound social inequities, indicate to many a need to 'regulate against' unhealthy options: for example, by using taxes to discourage consumers from buying drinks that contain a lot of sugar, prohibiting smoking in cars or placing minimum prices on alcohol. As reflected by the current and previous government's engagement with the Behavioural Insights Team (its 'Nudge Unit'), and its commitment to the Public Health Responsibility Deal, there may be side-constraints against 'coercive healthism', meaning that sub-optimal health outcomes are preferred in order to protect individual liberty. Thus, while the government may institute measures that tend towards healthier lifestyles, individual choices conducive to ill-health will remain.

Ultimately, such questions will be decided given the dominant political culture. Thus, while there is an important role for public health practitioners, concerns other than protection or promotion of health come into play. In some instances, however, there is a clearer mandate for coercive public health measures. This is perhaps most strikingly the case in regard to legislated mandates to control and contain diseases. In such instances, many presumptive liberties of citizens may be set aside in order to assure the protection of the population's health.

Further reading

Coggon, J. *What makes health public?* 2012. Cambridge: Cambridge University Press.

Coggon, J, Syrett, K. and Viens, A.M. *Public health law*, forthcoming 2016. Abingdon: Routledge.

Gostin, L.O. *Public health law and ethics – A reader*, 2nd edn, 2010. Berkley: University of California Press.

Gostin, L.O. and Wiley, L.F. *Public health law – Power, duty, restraint*, 3rd edn, 2016. Berkley: University of California Press.

Rose, G. 'Sick individuals and sick populations.' *International Journal of Epidemiology* 1985; 14:1, 32–38.

Winslow, C-E. A. 'The untilled fields of public health.' *Science* 1920; 51:1306, 23–33.

18 Allocation of resources

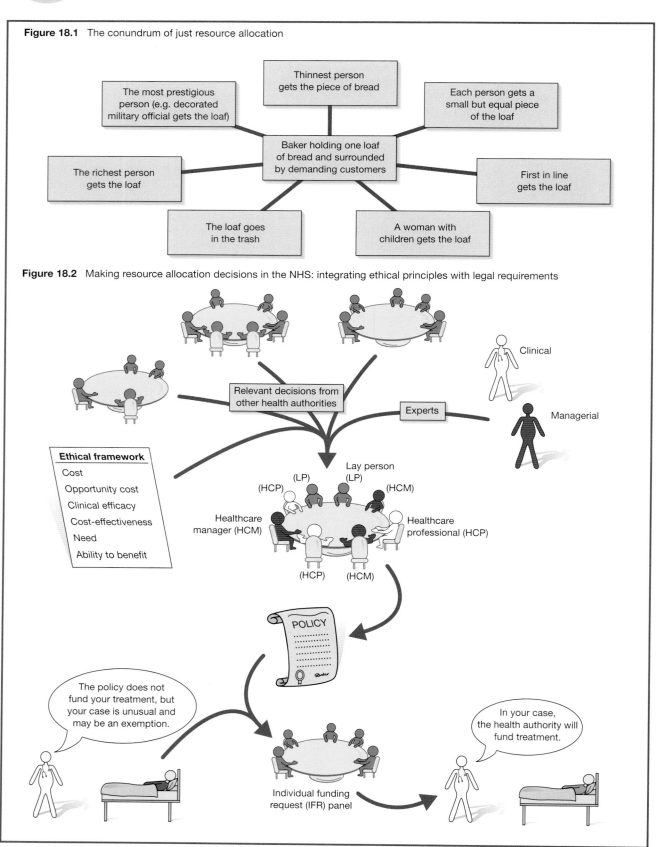

Figure 18.1 The conundrum of just resource allocation

The most prestigious person (e.g. decorated military official gets the loaf)

Thinnest person gets the piece of bread

Each person gets a small but equal piece of the loaf

The richest person gets the loaf

Baker holding one loaf of bread and surrounded by demanding customers

First in line gets the loaf

The loaf goes in the trash

A woman with children gets the loaf

Figure 18.2 Making resource allocation decisions in the NHS: integrating ethical principles with legal requirements

Clinical

Managerial

Relevant decisions from other health authorities

Experts

Ethical framework
- Cost
- Opportunity cost
- Clinical efficacy
- Cost-effectiveness
- Need
- Ability to benefit

Lay person (LP)

(LP)

(HCP)

(HCM)

Healthcare manager (HCM)

Healthcare professional (HCP)

(HCP)

(HCM)

POLICY

The policy does not fund your treatment, but your case is unusual and may be an exemption.

In your case, the health authority will fund treatment.

Individual funding request (IFR) panel

Medical Ethics, Law and Communication at a Glance, First Edition. Edited by Patrick Davey, Anna Rathmell, Michael Dunn, Charles Foster and Helen Salisbury.
© 2017 John Wiley & Sons, Ltd. Published 2017 by John Wiley & Sons, Ltd.

Ethics and resource allocation

The UK National Health Service (NHS) was founded to provide 'comprehensive' healthcare to all, free at the point of delivery, a lofty pursuit that must be carried out on a fixed budget. The fact of finite resources inevitably means that at times it must decide to deny some services, because funding is insufficient to provide the very best care for all people all the time. At the heart of such decisions lie the ethical considerations that must be contemplated in order to achieve the just allocation of this essential yet finite resource (Figure 18.1).

Equality and fairness

The NHS must ensure that individuals are treated equally, fairly and consistently. This can be construed in several ways. In one approach, **equality of outcome**, cost-effectiveness is typically prioritised, so as to bring the greatest overall benefit to the population. It suggests that two treatments that have the same outcome should be resourced to the same extent. However, (leaving cost aside) if treatment A has a better outcome than treatment B, then A should be prioritised over B. In the other approach, **equality of opportunity**, the intrinsic value of individuals is prioritised such that each person should be afforded the same opportunity to attain the best health possible for themselves. This ideology suggests that an individual who requires extensive resources should be allocated these on the basis of his equal moral right to health.

These two approaches at times prioritise opposing courses of action. For instance, expensive acute care for one individual can be markedly less cost-effective than cheaper services for many. Such competing demands can muddy where one is to draw the line in decisions of healthcare allocation. Thus, to be ethically robust in its decision making, the NHS must contemplate the following relevant factors at play, and it must do so by means of a fair process (Figure 18.2).

Factors to consider

• Cost: The cost of a service obviously impacts on a fixed budget. Some items on the healthcare agenda that would otherwise be accepted may be unaffordable given finite resources, especially as yet unidentified situations may arise requiring funding later in the year. Thus it would be ill-advised to have already spent a large portion of the budget on an arbitrary first come, first served basis rather than on a more rational approach.
• Opportunity cost: Opportunity cost refers to the benefits you forego by choosing to spend funds on a specific treatment rather than an alternate treatment. Thus one must consider not only what one is planning to allocate, but which treatments will now not be allotted as a result of this decision.
• Clinical efficacy: Clinical efficacy must be considered in resource allocation to ensure that individuals are indeed benefiting from the resource, and that funds are not being wasted on futile endeavours.
• Cost-effectiveness: Cost-effectiveness is a key consideration in order to bring the most benefit to a population per unit of resource. This can be evaluated by means of the QALY (quality-adjusted life year). A QALY regards a year of healthy life expectancy to be worth 1, but a year of unhealthy life expectancy to be worth less than 1; the worse the quality of life of the unhealthy person, the lower the value. The **QALY theory** asserts that the lower the cost per QALY of a specific healthcare service, the higher its priority. Therefore, such a theory when applied to a population maximises the quantity and quality of life of its constituents. Arguments against QALYs point to the ambiguity involved in calculating quality of life, the limited scope it attributes to healthcare's purpose, and the lack of any weight with respect to the distribution of QALYs.
• Need: Prioritizing need means first allocating resources to those who most need them, regardless of cost. Such prioritisation means that those individuals in greater need of treatment take precedence in decisions regarding the allocation of healthcare. The concept rests on the idea that justice is achieved by the worst-off groups being maximally well off: for example, the theory would favour treating a smaller group of sick people rather a larger group of relatively healthier individuals.
• Ability to benefit: The ability of the patient to benefit is related to but distinct from consideration of need. It takes into account the extent to which an individual can benefit from a specific therapeutic option.

Fair process in making decisions

The factors described above are relevant to balancing the sometimes competing needs of the individual with society at large. Explicit procedures are required to reach decisions in a fair and practical manner. The following four conditions were set forth to guide the process, rather than the content, of making such decisions (Daniels and Sabin, 1997)

1 Publicity: 'Decisions regarding coverage for new technologies (and other limit-setting decisions) and their rationales must be publicly accessible.'
2 Reasonableness: 'The rationales for coverage decisions should aim to provide a reasonable construal of how the organisation should provide "value for money" in meeting the varied health needs of a defined population under reasonable resource constraints. Specifically, a construal will be "reasonable" if it appeals to reasons and principles that are accepted as relevant by people who are disposed to finding terms of cooperation that are mutually justifiable.'
3 Appeals: 'There is a mechanism for challenge and dispute resolution regarding limit-setting decisions, including the opportunity for revising decisions in light of further evidence or arguments.'
4 Enforcement: 'There is either voluntary or public regulation of the process to ensure that conditions 1–3 are met.'

Sub-principles

In consideration of the four principles set forth to guide fair process in decision making (i.e. those of i) publicity, ii) reasonableness, iii) appeals and (iv) enforcement) the following sub-principles can be extracted to assist the decision making of health authorities:

• Expertise: The appropriate range of expertise, both clinical and managerial, should be involved in the process of considering the reasons and evidence for and against each decision. This will promote the realisation of the most authoritative outcome.
• Representation: Decisions should be relevant to the clinical context as well as to the range of stakeholders. To this end, fair process should include representatives from a range of healthcare professionals and managers as well as lay representatives.
• Provision for exceptions: It is reasonable for patients with unique circumstances to expect that their situations will be treated differently from others. A decision-making process needs methods for dealing systematically with exceptional cases, providing flexibility within the system to care for individuals with extending circumstances. The need for this allowance follows from the principle for appeals, as mentioned in (iv) above.

Decision makers must attend to the process by which they make their decisions as well as to the decisions themselves. This model allows for the systematic consideration of those factors that affect decisions of resource allocation.

Legal and policy considerations

As outlined above, there are a range of considerations that contribute to the final decision in the allocation of healthcare resources. Stakeholders may differ in the weight they give to each factor. The search is not for the one 'correct' answer, in which all other options are 'incorrect', for often there will be multiple valid positions, all with their pros and cons. Instead, the NHS must consider the full range of reasons that different individuals value and use a rigorous systematic method of evaluation to reach reasonable decisions that can be agreed on as legitimate when held under the lens of moral scrutiny. This regard for methodology and rationality is reflected in the **NHS Constitution**, and new statutory regulations, which state:

> You [the patient] have the right to expect local decisions on funding of other drugs and treatments [i.e., other than those recommended in NICE guidance] to be made rationally following a proper consideration of the evidence. If the local NHS decides not to fund a drug or treatment you and your doctor feel would be right for you, they will explain that decision to you (NHS Constitution).

and:

> … each Clinical Commissioning Group (CCG) must have in place arrangements for making decisions and adopting policies on whether a particular healthcare intervention is to be made available for patients whom [it] has responsibility …
>
> … [and] must compile information in writing describing the arrangements it has made (The National Health Service Commissioning Board and Clinical Commissioning Groups [Responsibilities and Standing Rules] Regulations 2012).

Procedural requirements in the NHS

The courts have ruled that a number of basic principles need be applied to decisions of resource allocation. Policies and procedures must be in place within the NHS that demonstrate a fair and consistent methodology for proper priority setting. Basic principles to be considered include the following:

• Framework: Decision makers require an overarching ethical framework that they can apply to decisions of resource allocation regardless of the content of each case. Having a framework in place that requires the consideration of all relevant factors and that can be applied consistently between patients encourages a fair process. Currently, NHS England adopts an Interim Ethical Framework are designed to inform local resource allocation decisions by CCG.

• Consistency: The weight of priorities and the outcomes of decisions as determined by different health authorities may vary. However, significant variations between regional health authorities require justification. Decisions in a particular postal code that are eccentric and inconsistent with practice elsewhere may appear irrational. Thus decisions should be made with consideration of the norms and procedures of health authorities elsewhere, encouraging learning from the experience of others and an atmosphere of collaboration.

• Communication: A doctor may recommend a treatment for their patient, but that does not mean the health authority is obliged to pay the cost of that treatment (see 'Case report: gender reassignment surgery' further on). If it decides against providing support, the health authority must be able to explain its reasoning. The health authority must provide that individual with a written statement of its reasons for that decision. This may include explaining the larger ethical framework governing the authority's approach to the question and/or referring the patient to the limitations of the specific treatment policy governing their condition.

• Exceptions: Any blanket ban on therapies will be subjected to close scrutiny. The health authority's commissioning policy must allow for funding in rare cases due to an individual's exceptional circumstances. Again, NHS England provides national guidance for CCGs on how Individual Funding Requests (IFRs) should be managed so that the process is consistent across England.

Case report: gender reassignment surgery

North West Lancashire Health Authority introduced a blanket ban on funding gender reassignment surgeries. This was contested by three patients in 1998. The Court of Appeal ruled the health authority's ban to be unlawful. The patients were described as females trapped in male bodies and living in a 'distressed mental and physical state.' The health authority argued that it was constrained by 'scarce resources' and it had the right to refuse funding. The court confirmed that it was not duty-bound to support all treatments and was entitled to have a system of priority setting. However, a blanket ban was irrational for preventing the health authority from examining all the relevant circumstances of the claim, especially the particular needs of these applicants. The case was referred back to the health authority to be reconsidered (and funding was granted). As a result, health authorities are now obliged to have in place general systems for priority setting and particular systems for considering claims for 'exceptionality'. These duties are endorsed by the NHS Constitution.

Further reading

Daniels, N. and Sabin, J. Limits to health care: Fair procedures, democratic deliberation, and the legitimacy problem for insurers. *Philosophy and Public Affairs* 1997;26 (4):303–350.

Newdick, C. *Who should we treat? Rights, rationing, and resources in the NHS*, 2005. Oxford University Press.

Sheehan, M. and Hope, A. 'Allocating healthcare resources in the UK: Putting principles into practice'. In R.Rhodes, M.Battin and A.Silvers (eds). *Medicine and social justice: Essays on the distribution of healthcare*, 2002. Oxford University Press, pp. 219–230.

19 Clinical genetics

Figure 19.1 Case example: genetic counselling for familial breast cancer

(a) Family history

> Your GP sent you to genetic services to talk to us about breast cancer. Can you tell me who in your family has had cancer, and what kind?

> Well I wrote it down...my sister had breast cancer, and my aunt died of ovarian cancer.

(b) Information gathering

> So, can you tell me what you know about breast cancer that runs in the family? It's OK if you haven't heard much about it, lots of people haven't.

> I know that my family seems to get cancer a lot, and my GP wanted me to see if I had the gene that causes it.

(c) Information provision

> Having the 'breast cancer gene' doesn't guarantee you'll get cancer. If you do get the test and you are positive for a gene mutation, then you'll have a higher risk of getting breast and ovarian cancer. But we can't tell for sure if you will get cancer or not.

> That's right.

> Oh, I see. So I'm not definitely going to get cancer.

(d) Decision-making and follow-up

> Given what we've talked about, how are you feeling about whether you'd like to consider genetic testing?

> I'm not sure...I think I need to talk to my sister and mother first for advice.

> Completely reasonable. What points might you bring up with your family when you talk about it?

Figure 19.2 Case example: Fragile X syndrome sharing information within families

(a)

> Genetic testing confirms your son has Fragile X syndrome (FXS), and you are a carrier.

(b)

> My nephew has autism, low muscle tone, and seizures, so my doctor recommended I come to the genetics clinic. I might terminate my pregnancy if my child could be similarly affected.

> She doesn't know her sister has been to see me and is a carrier for FXS. It would be difficult testing her for FXS without citing her sister and her nephew's history.

(c)

> I know my sister is pregnant and her child could be affected. I haven't talked to her... we aren't on speaking terms right now, and I disagree with her on pregnancy termination anyway. Please don't tell her anything about me or my son.

(d)

> I've asked my first patient to speak to her sister about the FSX, but she won't. I've asked if I can share her information with her sister, but she won't give me permission to do that either.

> Who has control of shared information? How do I provide good care to both sisters and their children for a serious condition? What can I do?

Medical Ethics, Law and Communication at a Glance, First Edition. Edited by Patrick Davey, Anna Rathmell, Michael Dunn, Charles Foster and Helen Salisbury.
© 2017 John Wiley & Sons, Ltd. Published 2017 by John Wiley & Sons, Ltd.

Introduction

Clinical genetics is a multidisciplinary medical specialty that serves patients and families who are affected by, or at risk of, genetic disorders. These services are anchored around regional centres, which are staffed by clinical geneticists (both consultants and junior doctors), genetic counsellors and laboratory scientists. Additionally, clinical genetics services frequently have close relationships with general practitioners and also interface with other specialties such as obstetrics, paediatrics, neurology, cardiology and oncology.

Patient pathways and experiences in genetics services

A patient's experience in clinical genetics can be impacted by the kind of referral they receive to the service. Once in clinic, they will receive genetic counselling, during which the appropriateness of any genetic testing will be explored.

Referrals

A 'consultand', or patient attending genetic counselling, typically comes to a clinical genetics service through one of three ways: as a 'proband', through a family member referral, or through a de facto referral. A proband is the first member of a family who presents to the clinical genetics service because they are considered at risk for, or are affected by, a genetic disorder. This referral might result from either a clinician noticing symptoms or risk factors consistent with an inherited condition; or the patient's expression of concern due to family history of a disorder and questions about related implications.

The other two kinds of referrals logically follow from the provision of information to a consultand's family members. A family member referral usually occurs when a proband shares information with relatives potentially affected by the information. If this sharing seems unlikely to take place and the genetics service thinks the benefits of disclosure outweigh the harms of failing to disclose, the service may also choose to contact these relatives' general practitioners, or even to attempt to personally contact the at-risk relatives themselves. A de facto referral occurs when a patient is accompanied to a consultation by a potentially affected family member, and thus that family member becomes another patient.

Genetic counselling

Genetic information is not necessarily more sensitive or inherently different from other kinds of medical information, but it involves a complicated set of ethical and social implications for patients, family members and health professionals alike. Genetic counselling is a communication-intensive process designed to help patients and their families think through these implications. It is also non-directive and value-neutral, meaning that the clinician facilitates discussion and provision of appropriate information without imparting their own opinion or declaring patients' decisions to be 'right' or 'wrong'. Genetic counselling will sometimes, but not always, lead to genetic testing. However, genetic counselling should always be considered part of the consent process for genetic testing.

As part of an initial genetic counselling visit, a patient will be asked to provide a detailed family history. This enables the clinician to construct a family pedigree, which will be used to estimate the risks of the consultand and their family members having a certain inherited disorder. A typical session will also involve one or more of the following stages:

- Information gathering – ascertaining the patient's knowledge and expectations about the particular genetic disorder;
- Information provision – correcting the patient's misconceptions and providing details about genetic testing, disorders and diseases, and treatments;
- Decision making and follow-up – discussing who will help make a decision and how it will be made, as well as possible psychological, social, financial and familial issues in response to testing outcomes.

An example of each of these stages can be seen in Figure 19.1, which depicts snapshots of a genetic counselling session for familial breast cancer.

Genetic testing

During the process of genetic counselling, a patient may decide to proceed with genetic testing. This involves taking a blood, skin, hair, amniotic fluid or other tissue sample; sending it to a regional genetics laboratory; and feeding back the results to the patient in person, over the phone or in a letter.

Genetic testing has many functions, ranging from newborn screening to paternity determination. One particularly important distinction to make is between diagnostic and predictive testing:

- Diagnostic testing is used to confirm or disconfirm a diagnosis of a suspected inherited condition in a symptomatic patient.
- Predictive testing is provided to an asymptomatic patient with a family history of an inherited condition. A positive presymptomatic result means a patient is guaranteed to develop an inherited condition, whereas a positive predispositional result means a patient is at increased risk for an inherited condition but not guaranteed to develop it.

Impact of evolving technologies

Rapidly evolving technologies have further complicated genetic testing, with the advent of direct-to-consumer genetic testing (DTC-GT) and research studies involving new microarray and sequencing methods. DTC-GT, which involves patients purchasing genetic tests directly from a company, raises questions about the quality of informed consent, the adequacy of data protection, the regulation of testing performed in non-clinical settings, and the pathway by which DTC-GT results are integrated into clinical care. Studies such as the UK-based 'Deciphering developmental disorders' project have had to incorporate frameworks to deal with incidental findings (results that are unintentionally discovered and do not relate to the disorder being studied), such as misattributed paternity or harmful breast cancer gene mutations, as well as protocols for feeding information back to participants and providing open access to data.

On the clinical side, 'mainstreaming' has become both a source of optimism and concern, as non-genetics professionals are increasingly encouraged to order genetic tests, particularly for cancer patients, to increase efficiency of care. The main potential problem is miscommunication between provider and patient: for example, a lack of informed consent prior to testing or incorrectly interpreted test results. Better education for non-genetics professionals and increased communication between genetics services and other providers are two potential safeguards.

Common ethical issues encountered in clinical genetics

The Genethics Club, a national forum at which ethical issues in clinical genetics practice are discussed, has identified three types of issues arising most frequently in meetings: sharing information with family members, genetic testing of children and reproductive decision-making. Cases often touch on multiple issues, such as the example of a family with a history of Fragile X syndrome in Figure 19.2 that covers both reproductive decision making and sharing information with family members.

Sharing information with family members

As with other kinds of medical information, clinicians have an ethical obligation to keep genetic information confidential. In most medical contexts, confidentiality may be described via the 'personal account model': information belongs to the patient in front of the clinician, and must only be shared without the patient's consent when there is risk of death or serious harm to another individual.

However, confidentiality in the context of genetic information can raise tensions between the duty to the patient in front of the clinician and a duty to the patient's family members. One way of thinking of this is the 'joint account model', in which genetic information shared between family members might be thought of as analogous to bank account information shared jointly between account members. On this model, family members should have access to the shared genetic information unless there is a compelling reason for them to be excluded. The GMC's revised 2009 guidelines on confidentiality also support the idea that genetic information can sometimes be considered 'shared information'.

The 'right not to know'

Closely related is the 'right not to know', which refers to a person's right to refuse a test or information about their health. In clinical genetics, the right not to know has implications for both the patient in front of the clinician and the patient's family members. For example, if an identical twin with a grandparent who had Huntington's disease requests genetic testing in clinic, then a test on the consultand would also be a test on her twin sister. The sister may not wish to know whether she has inherited a deadly, incurable disease and may lack adequate preparation to deal with the consequences of the information, particularly if she has not attended genetic counselling. Furthermore, a test on the consultand would equally be a test on their potentially affected parent: a positive predictive test would automatically mean that the autosomal dominant gene mutation had been passed from the grandparent to the parent to the twins.

Even in cases where the information would not be used maliciously, it may slip out in a family argument or even normal discussion. This is why genetics services strongly urge patients considering genetic testing to also consider the effect that such a test may have on their families, and to speak to their families accordingly.

On the other hand, when a consultand chooses not to know, there may also be serious individual and familial repercussions. The consultand cannot seek treatment if it is available (e.g. prophylactic surgery if found to have a CDH1 [gastric cancer] mutation). Nor can they prepare for potentially poor outcomes in non-medical ways (e.g. by making lifestyle choices or setting financial affairs in order if they test positive for Huntington's disease). This inability to plan extends to any family members potentially affected by the same condition, who may not be able to consider genetic testing without the consultand's result.

Genetic testing of children

The 2010 British Society for Human Genetics (BSHG) report on genetic testing of children advises that the primary consideration in the decision to test should be the child's best interests. When a test could lead to different clinical management during childhood, it will generally be considered appropriate. One such case would be with an inherited cancer like familial adenomatous polyposis (FAP), which may have an early age of onset and carries a near-certain risk of developing colon cancer unless treated.

If a test concerns an adult-onset disease or future reproductive risks, then testing should likely be delayed until the child can make their own decision, unless there are compelling reasons to think otherwise. Conditions that fall under this category include genetic predispositions for Alzheimer's disease and breast and ovarian cancer (e.g. BRCA1 and BRCA2).

Overall, the BSHG report recommends that any decision to test a child should proceed cautiously whenever possible, with an emphasis on open discussion and consideration of timing so that the child can be involved in the process.

Reproductive decisions

Reproductive decisions often combine elements of sharing information with family and genetic testing of children, in addition to unique issues such as pre-implantation genetic diagnosis (PGD). Relative to other clinical situations, genetic counsellors may particularly emphasise patient autonomy in reproductive decision-making cases because of the personal nature of the decision and its long-lasting effects on the woman's life. This emphasis can be complicated when a consultand considers termination of pregnancy because of a 'minor' condition such as Triple X Syndrome – which is not considered a disorder that seriously impacts the future child – as the counsellor may believe termination of pregnancy on the basis of minor conditions to be inappropriate.

Similar to the guidelines for testing in children, prenatal testing for adult-onset disease is generally discouraged, as is testing for genetically linked traits. But prenatal testing is recommended for some serious child-onset diseases so that parents can decide whether to use assistive reproductive technologies, terminate the pregnancy or plan how they will care for a severely ill child.

One increasingly popular assistive reproductive technology is PGD, or genetic testing carried out on embryos prior to their implantation through in vitro fertilisation (IVF). PGD is nationally regulated by the Human Fertilisation and Embryology Authority (HFEA), which determines which genetic conditions are serious enough to warrant testing. With regards to sex selection, the HFEA only considers it justifiable if done for medical reasons, such as selecting against embryos at risk for a sex-linked disorder like Duchenne muscular dystrophy.

Further reading

Harper, P.S. *Practical genetic counselling*, 7th edn, 2010. Oxford: CRC Press.

Parker, M. *Ethical problems and genetics practice*, 2012. Cambridge University Press.

Rose, P. and Lucassen, A. *Practical genetics for primary care*, 1999. Oxford University Press.

20 Human research

Figure 20.1 Human research

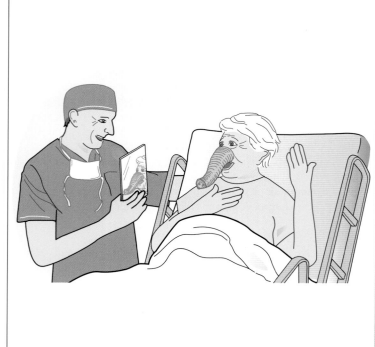

If you are thinking of undertaking medical research involving human participants you should...
- Produce an information sheet
- Explain the purpose of the research study
- Explain why the patient has been chosen
- Tell the patient to ask questions if he/she is not clear or wants further information
- Explain that participation is entirely voluntary
- Explain that the patient can withdraw at any time
- Explain that a decision not to take part or to withdraw will not affect the standard of care the patient receives
- Explain what will happen to the patient if he/she takes part and what they will have to do
- Explain the alternatives for diagnosis or treatment
- Explain the side effects of any treatment, the risks and benefits of taking part
- Explain that the patient will be informed if new information becomes available during the research
- Explain what happens when the research stops or if something goes wrong
- Explain that the information collected will be kept strictly confidential
- Explain what will happen to the results of the study, as well as who is organising and funding it
- Provide a contact for further information
- Provide the patient with a copy of the information sheet and signed consent form to keep

In order for medical practice to progress, there will inevitably be studies and research involving human subjects. Such research is necessary in order to understand the causes and effects of diseases and to enable preventative, diagnostic and therapeutic interventions to evolve. Invariably such research will also involve risks, and the law has to strike a balance between allowing new or existing techniques or treatments to develop and safeguarding the health of those taking part (Figure 20.1).

Regulation and ethical considerations

While issues relating to consent to medical treatment regularly come before the courts, specific principles governing practices for research subjects are generally to be found in national and international ethical codes or have become the subject of statutory or regulatory control. Examples are the World Medical Association's *Declaration of Helsinki* (as amended), the Royal College of Physicians' *Guidelines on the practice of ethics committees in medical research involving human subjects*, the Medicines for Human Use (Clinical Trials) Regulations 2004 and the Human Fertilisation and Embryology Act 1990.

The *Declaration of Helsinki* starts with the principle that 'it is the duty of physicians who participate in such research to protect the life, health, dignity, integrity, right to self-determination, privacy and confidentiality of personal information of research subjects.' It goes on to state that each research study involving human subjects must be clearly described in a research protocol which should contain a statement of the ethical considerations involved and indicate how the principles in the *Declaration* have been addressed. It should be approved by an independent ethics committee before the study begins and be conducted only by individuals with appropriate scientific training and qualifications. It should be registered publicly and the physicians should not participate unless they are confident that the risks involved have been adequately assessed and can be satisfactorily managed. The importance of the objective must outweigh the inherent risks and burdens to the research subjects. Participation by competent individuals must be voluntary and privacy protected. Each human subject must be adequately informed of the aims, methods, sources of funding, any possible conflicts of interest, institutional affiliations of the researcher, the anticipated benefits and potential risks of the study, and the discomfort it may entail, as well as the right to refuse to participate or to withdraw consent at any time without reprisal. If the subject is incompetent, the physician must seek informed consent from the legally authorised representative.

Medical Ethics, Law and Communication at a Glance, First Edition. Edited by Patrick Davey, Anna Rathmell, Michael Dunn, Charles Foster and Helen Salisbury.
© 2017 John Wiley & Sons, Ltd. Published 2017 by John Wiley & Sons, Ltd.

Therapeutic research

Research involving human subjects is normally divided into two broad categories – namely, therapeutic research and non-therapeutic research. The former involves patients who are suffering from an illness or disability and in whom it is hoped that taking part in the medical trial will result in a therapeutic as well as a research benefit. The latter generally involves healthy volunteers who are not patients. When it comes to the advice that should be given to patients in either context, many consider the distinction as wholly unwarranted and artificial, because patients in both forms of research need to be provided with similar levels of information disclosure for their consent to be valid. A study labelled 'therapeutic' might carry far more risk than one labelled 'non-therapeutic' and have a vanishingly small chance of benefit, and yet be more readily accepted by the patient.

Therapeutic research most commonly takes place in the context of a clinical trial. Typically, a doctor may wish to test the efficacy of a new treatment where none had previously been available; or to test the efficacy of a new treatment or existing treatments against other established forms of treatment. It goes without saying that if new treatment is being tested, the doctor must have investigated fully all the existing literature and studies before conducting research on human subjects. Those in the control group must receive the best available established treatment and the trial must have an appropriate mechanism for being discontinued if the new treatment proves less beneficial than established treatment or vice versa. They must be given the opportunity to understand the objectives, risks and inconveniences of the trial.

As therapeutic research involves medical treatment of a patient's illness or disability, the requirements for effective consent by the patient and the doctor's duty to disclose information about the risks of any procedure are the same as for any medical treatment (see Chapter 11). However, where the consent concerns therapeutic research, the doctor should be particularly cautious if the patient is in a dependent relationship with the doctor (e.g. the patient might fear that should they decline the new therapeutic treatment, they would not be given the best available treatment). For that reason, it is recommended that consent is obtained by a doctor who is not engaged in the research and is completely independent of this relationship. In addition, in the context of therapeutic research, it has also been suggested that for the consent to be valid, the patient should be informed that they may refuse to participate or withdraw at any time from the research without adverse consequences in terms of the treatment they will receive; that they may be a member of a control group with periodic view; and that it is a randomised controlled trial if that is the case.

In the context of clinical trials on medicinal products for human use, the general principles outlined are given statutory force by the Medicines for Human Use (Clinical Trials) Regulations 2004 which cover all such trials and the circumstances in which both minors and incapacitated adults can take part in such trials. The latter can only take part if it can be demonstrated that the pharmaceutical product will either produce a benefit to the subject outweighing the risks, or produce no risk at all. Furthermore, the trial must relate directly to a life-threatening or debilitating clinical condition.

Non-therapeutic research

All the principles outlined above apply equally to healthy volunteers. However, whereas the withholding of information about potential risks can sometimes be justified to patients on the basis that it is in their 'best interests', that cannot be the case in non-therapeutic research because such volunteers do not need the treatment for treatment of any medical condition. They are entitled to a full and frank disclosure of all the known or potential risks associated with the research before giving their consent.

If a potential research subject lacks the capacity to give valid consent, the question then arises as to whether they should ever be able to take part in non-therapeutic research because it could not be shown to offer benefit to them. The position is now governed by Sections 30 to 34 of the Mental Capacity Act 2005 and the Regulations made under this Act. Such research will be unlawful unless approved by an authorised research ethics committee or in accordance with other Regulations relating to clinical trials. The committee itself may only approve such research if it is in connection with an impairing condition affecting the person or its treatment. and the statutory provisions impose rigorous risk–benefit requirements. In the context of medicinal products, non-therapeutic research on an adult lacking capacity could not be authorised under the Human Use (Clinical Trials) Regulations 2004 because it could not be demonstrated that it would benefit the subject or produce no risk at all.

In the context of children, the general view has been that non-therapeutic research cannot be justified as the research by definition is not in the interests of the child and may expose them to some risk, however, small.

21 Care of older adults

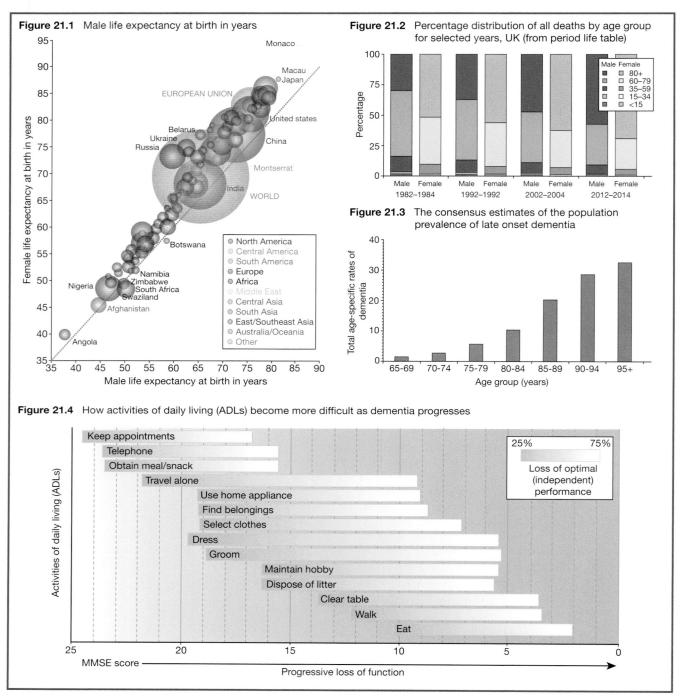

Figure 21.1 Male life expectancy at birth in years

Figure 21.2 Percentage distribution of all deaths by age group for selected years, UK (from period life table)

Figure 21.3 The consensus estimates of the population prevalence of late onset dementia

Figure 21.4 How activities of daily living (ADLs) become more difficult as dementia progresses

Medical Ethics, Law and Communication at a Glance, First Edition. Edited by Patrick Davey, Anna Rathmell, Michael Dunn, Charles Foster and Helen Salisbury.
© 2017 John Wiley & Sons, Ltd. Published 2017 by John Wiley & Sons, Ltd.

Introduction

Life expectancy in the Western world is now well over 80 years (Figures 21.1, 21.2). People expect to live long, happy, healthy and productive lives. But, unfortunately, old age and disability have not yet been cured. As we age chronologically, our bodies age biologically. Understanding the aging process is fundamental to understanding how to deal with disease in older patients. Making decisions around treatment options, balancing good against harm, symptom control and secondary prevention, quality versus quantity of life all make caring for older people both challenging and rewarding.

Over the next 40 years, the number of people over 65 is predicted to increase from 10 million today to 19 million, of whom 8 million will be over 80 years old. Many of these people will lead healthy independent lives well into their 80s and 90s, but with this increasingly old population comes a new pandemic – dementia. Twenty per cent of over-80s suffer from dementia, costing UK society today £17bn. This is predicted to rise to £50bn by 2050 (Figures 21.3, 21.4). As well as significant cost to society, dementia brings a whole set of moral challenges as to how we care for patients who are unable to participate fully in the medical decision-making process.

Resolving ethical dilemmas in practice

The same moral values: respecting autonomy, fairness, doing good and avoiding harm, the same virtues: compassion, trustworthiness, conscientiousness, integrity and discernment, and the same professional duties: promoting health, respecting confidentiality, gaining informed consent and treating patients with dignity all still apply. However, interpreting and balancing conflicting values or duties can be difficult. Specific challenges can arise frequently in the care of older adults, and these challenges will be the focus of this chapter.

Justice, fairness, and rationing

The health service has finite resources, and the challenges associated with resource allocation are discussed elsewhere in this book (see Chapter 18). Deciding where and how this money should be spent is the role of government and healthcare commissioners but it is also every doctor's responsibility. This is not something medical practitioners can dodge, however much they might wish to. If money is spent on cancer drugs, then less is available for maternity or dementia care. It is commonly thought that justice requires fair access to treatment, acknowledging the intrinsic and equal value of each human life regardless of age, disability or gender. In this view, the starting point at least should be that older people have access to the same range of treatments as younger patients, including renal replacement therapy, cardiac surgery and intensive care. In any given case, it is important to establish the potential cost-effectiveness of the proposed treatment. A fit 80-year–old man with pneumonia and respiratory failure is more likely to benefit from intensive care than a 60-year-old with severe chronic obstructive pulmonary disease (COPD) and respiratory failure, for example.

Comorbidities and frailty must both be taken into account. Two patients of the same age and with the same medical problem may not necessarily benefit from the same treatment. For example, two patients have severe aortic stenosis: Mr Jones requires a Zimmer frame to walk and has help with personal care every day, but Mr Adams still rides a bicycle and is fully independent at home. The risks of surgical complications are higher for Mr Jones than for Mr Adams, and the benefits of surgery for physically active Mr Adams are potentially greater. The best way of avoiding the accusation of ageism in situations like these is to be able to provide clear reasons for the decisions made, and to communicate openly and honestly with the patient and their family.

Confidentiality and communication

The successful therapeutic doctor–patient relationship is based on trust. The duty of confidentiality forms a central part of this relationship, and is discussed at length in Chapter 10. While this duty is not absolute, there is a clear expectation that unless there are overriding public considerations, the patient's information belongs to them and should only be used with their permission [implied or explicit].

When the patient is able to make their own decisions, this is relatively easy. If the patient does not want anyone else to know, then that choice should be respected in most cases. But what if the patient is not able to understand the decision or appears confused? For example, a patient with memory and cognitive impairment might refuse to see their GP or have any contact with healthcare services. In these situations, it is very important to see the patient within their social setting in order to make ethical judgements about how to proceed. Care must also be taken to ascertain what role in this process should be given to family caregivers. Relatives of patients with dementia often complain that they feel excluded from medical decision making and that they are not given enough information about their health problems. They complain that they are not listened to when they try to get help for a relative who is dependent on them but who cannot or will not ask for help for themselves.

Consider Mr Brown who has dementia and was hospitalised with pneumonia but is now well enough to return home to live with his wife. The nurses report he is disorientated but he can wash and dress and mobilises independently on the ward. The ward clerk phones Mrs Brown to tell her Mr Brown is coming home. Mrs Brown is very angry – she has phoned the ward every day for a week and been given very little information, and yet today without warning her husband is coming home. Mrs Brown cares for her husband at home and she cannot do this without information about him. We would not expect nurses or doctors to care for patients without access to their medical records and yet we forget that informal carers need this information too. In this situation, the patient may retain capacity for decision making but he may need our help to understand that it is important for us to discuss his healthcare needs and keep his family fully informed of his progress.

Consent, capacity and best interests

The Mental Capacity Act 2005 is an important and useful piece of statute law, and is discussed in Chapter 11. While this law has been well received in healthcare, a number of issues can arise in caring for older adults that concern inadequate understanding about how the law should be applied in practice, or for which the law provides no easy answers:

• Despite the assumption in favour of capacity, professionals often seek to assess a patient's capacity without first considering whether they have an impairment of, or disturbance in, the functioning of mind or brain.
• Capacity is still talked about in generality, rather than being connected to specific decisions.

- Capacity is much less likely to be questioned if a patient gives consent to treatment, for example when an older patient happily agrees to have surgery for a broken hip.
- The speed at which decisions need to be made does not allow sufficient time for capacity to be regained: for example, patients suffering from delirium are often discharged from hospital before their delirium has cleared.
- Doctors are still asked to make capacity decisions for areas outside their expertise, and for which they are not the decision maker: for example, in relation to social care planning. More of these decisions should be made collaboratively with different professionals – social workers, occupational therapists and doctors – working together.
- Decisions about the best interests of older patients who lack capacity need to be carefully documented in the medical record. If there is disagreement on best interests within the team or with the family, it is very helpful to go through each element and explain how they have been weighed up. Here, again, good communication is the key to resolving differences. It is particularly important to explain that doctors have a duty to take into account the current wishes and behaviour of the patient who lacks capacity and to choose the least restrictive option, because this will help families to understand why risks that seem unacceptable to them are appropriate.
- The capacity of patients with dementia fluctuates and this is particularly difficult, not least because it is often associated with fluctuating safety awareness. Consider Mrs White who suffers from dementia with marked variability in her cognition. When she is alert and orientated, she understands the problem, demonstrates awareness of the risks of her behaviour and passes stage 2 of the test for capacity. But when she becomes more confused, she forgets how to maintain her own safety. Compromise is usually the best solution here. We try to persuade Mrs White to accept some safety measures – for example, a recorded message that plays if she tries to leave her home at night – while maintaining her independence.

'Do not attempt cardiopulmonary resuscitation', advance care planning and care planning

It is important to understand the differences between 'do not attempt cardiopulmonary resuscitation' (DNACPR) decisions, advance care planning and care planning.

DNACPR decisions can be initiated by the patient or the medical team. However, neither the patient nor their relative can insist on resuscitation if the medical team feel it would not constitute appropriate medical care. The patient's or family's (if the patient lacks capacity) opinion should only be sought if there is a chance that CPR could be successful. It is very important to communicate clearly and compassionately with patients and their families, but it is not fair to pretend that they have a choice about a treatment that will not work, or, if it does

work, will not reverse the underlying condition from which the patient is dying.

Advance care planning is a process or dialogue between a healthcare professional and a patient about future anticipated healthcare needs and options for care. It should be offered to all patients suffering from chronic, potentially life-threatening diseases, particularly if the capacity to make contemporaneous healthcare decisions is likely to be lost (e.g. in the cases of Huntington's disease, dementia and Parkinson's disease). Many older patients find the prospect of filling in forms very daunting. Even with the help of motivated family members, few wish to make advance decisions to refuse treatment or to appoint lasting powers of attorney. However, many patients will express preferences about their future care which, although not legally binding, are very helpful to the clinical team if they are clearly documented in the medical records.

Care planning addresses current health needs. It can be done with patients who have capacity to make medical decisions, or on behalf of patients who have lost such capacity as part of the process of determining their best interests. Frail elderly patients with multiple medical problems have a shorter life expectancy than many patients with cancer but are much less likely to have a clear healthcare plan for the immediate future. Unfortunately, the lack of advance care planning often leads to emergency admission to hospital in crisis, or when death is a near certainty.

Artificial nutrition and hydration

The provision of artificial nutrition and hydration (ANH) raises a number of ethical issues that are considered in Chapter 22. Specific practical issues arise commonly in the care of older adults.

If the patient has capacity to make medical decisions, then they will decide if they want ANH started or stopped. When patients lack capacity, as is often the case, decisions are made within clinical teams, with doctors having ultimate responsibility for the decision made. Usually, however, it is the nurses, carers and family who will carry out the plan – ascertaining whether putting the previously made decision into action is appropriate given the patient's current circumstances – and therefore everyone's views must be heard and acknowledged before decisions are made. If there is still disagreement, a second opinion should be sought.

Consider Mrs Green who suffers from vascular dementia. Recently she has been choking on liquids and eating very little. She has lost 2 stone in weight. Her family are upset and want her to have a feeding tube installed. Should such a tube be installed? The answer to this question will depend on the specific details of the case. Does the patient have capacity to be involved in the decision? What are the medical facts? It is particularly important, when a patient has dementia and cannot give a clear history, to think of all the possible causes, not just the most common. Does she have obstructive dysphagia or neuromuscular dysphagia? Are her dentures loose or lost? What other feeding options might be better options?

22 End of life care

Figure 22.1 A dilemma at the end of life

Figure 22.2 End of life care decision making flowchart

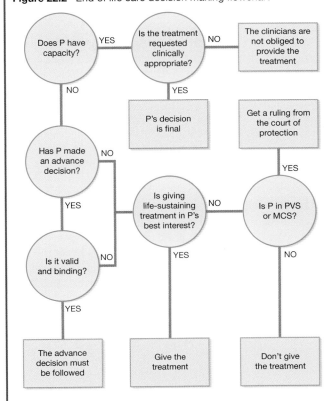

Box 22.1 Key English law rulings on life-sustaining treatment

- Withdrawal of artificial nutrition and hydration (ANH) from a patient in PVS approved: *Airedale NHS Trust* v *Bland* [1993] AC 789
- Withdrawal of ANH from a patient with some but not all features of PVS approved: *Re D (Adult: Medical Treatment)* [1998] 1 FCR 498
- Lawful to discontinue ventilation and renal support of an elderly terminally-ill patient who was conscious and able to respond to questions: An *NHS Trust* v *A and SA* [2005] EWCA Civ 1145
- Doctors authorised to withhold ventilation if a 2-year-old child born 14 weeks prematurely with chronic respiratory and kidney problems and profound brain damage suffered an infection that might lead to a collapsed lung: *Portsmouth Hospitals NHS Trust* v *Wyatt* [2005] EWCA Civ 1181
- Application to withdraw ventilation refused when an 18-month-old child had a very severe and degenerating form of spinal muscular atrophy, was suffering pain and discomfort from medical procedures, had a short life expectancy but was aware of his surroundings. However, a decision to withhold CPR and intravenous antibiotics was approved: An *NHS Trust* v *MB (a Child)* [2006] EWHC 507 (Fam)
- Doctors authorised to withdraw parenteral nutrition from a 6-month-old child born prematurely with a severe neuromuscular disorder. Parenteral nutrition was likely to lead to liver failure at around 1 year of age. The child had some appreciation of what went on around her and suffered regular discomfort and distress: *Re K (Medical Treatment: Declaration)* [2006] EWHC 1007 (Fam)
- Withdrawal of ANR from a patient in minimally conscious state (MCS) refused, but DNR order approved: *W* v *M and others* [2011] EWHC 2443 (Fam)
- The UK's ban on assisted suicide is formally compatible with the European Convention on Human Rights. It is therefore not currently a violation of a patient's right to respect for private life that he cannot be helped by a doctor to die when he is unable to take his own steps to end his own life due to physical impairment.
- However, the Court expects Parliament to debate legislation about whether those involved in this case should be permitted to end their own life. If not, a declaration of incompatibility may follow: *R (Nicklinson)* v *Ministry of Justice*; *R(AM)* v *Director of Public Prosecutions* [2014] UKSC 38.

Medical Ethics, Law and Communication at a Glance, First Edition. Edited by Patrick Davey, Anna Rathmell, Michael Dunn, Charles Foster and Helen Salisbury.
© 2017 John Wiley & Sons, Ltd. Published 2017 by John Wiley & Sons, Ltd.

Treating patients who are at or nearing the end of their lives throws up some of the most challenging medical and ethical decisions facing healthcare professionals (Figure 22.1).

What is end of life care?

Patients requiring 'end of life' treatment are not just the elderly and the terminally ill. The GMC's guidance, 'Treatment and care towards the end of life: Good practice in decision making', refers to patients who are 'approaching the end of their life', which it defines as 'likely to die within the next 12 months'. Those patients will include:

- those who will die imminently;
- those with advanced, progressive and incurable conditions;
- those with chronic conditions who are at risk of death from a sudden acute crisis in their condition;
- those whose general poor state of health means they are expected to die within 12 months; and
- Extremely premature neonates with very poor prospects of survival.

This definition also includes patients who are stable, but who are being kept alive artificially, such as patients in a persistent vegetative state (PVS) or a minimally conscious state (MCS).

Providing life-sustaining treatment

In general terms, the approach to the treatment of end of life patients is no different from the approach to the treatment of any other patient: treatment must only be given with the patient's consent if they have the capacity to provide it, and otherwise in their best interests, and the same approach applies whether the issue is starting treatment or withdrawing it. The complicating factor, medically, emotionally, ethically and legally is that decisions about treatment at the end of a patient's life will often determine whether or not a patient lives or dies and, if they die, how and when they die.

The rest of this chapter develops the legal dimensions of consent laid out in Chapter 12 as they relate to end of life care (Box 22.1). The general law relating to patient confidentiality, outlined in Chapter 11, also applies to patients at the end of their lives. A clinician has no more right to give other people details of the condition of a terminally ill person then they do of any other patient.

Patients with capacity

When a patient has capacity to make decisions about their own medical treatment, it remains the case at the end of their life, just as it does at any other time, that they have an absolute and inalienable right to decide whether or not to receive treatment, even if the refusal of treatment will lead to their death. Equally, a terminally ill patient who has capacity may request treatment that is clinically inappropriate in the hope that it will keep them alive (Figure 22.2). Just as at any other time, a doctor is not obliged to provide clinically inappropriate treatment.

When a patient has capacity, a clinician must not disclose any details of their medical condition or treatment to anybody else without their consent.

Also a clinician must not keep from a patient with capacity information necessary to make a decision about treatment unless giving that information would cause serious harm, which means more than being upset or refusing the treatment. Conversely, a terminally ill patient who has capacity may not want to be fully informed about their condition and may want others to make treatment decisions for them. A patient with capacity can choose not to be fully informed about their condition, but they cannot delegate decisions about their treatment.

Patients without capacity

Patients without capacity must be treated in accordance with their best interests, and the law recognises that it may be in a patient's best interests not to receive treatment which is necessary to keep them alive. This may be because:

- the patient has no life to speak of, for example because they are in PVS;
- treatment would be futile;
- the chance of treatment being successful is outweighed by the burden on the patient of receiving that treatment or the likelihood that, if successful, it will cause significant harm of another kind, for example brain damage; and
- treatment will only prolong an inevitable death and will cause additional distress in the meantime.

Treatment in this context includes the provision of ANH, and decisions about whether to provide or continue ANH are made in the same way as any other treatment decisions.

Advance decisions

There is no need to make a decision about what is in the patient's best interests if they have made a valid and binding advance decision. Sections 24 to 26 of the Mental Capacity Act 2005 enable an adult with capacity ('P') to make an advance decision to refuse a particular treatment at a future time when they no longer have capacity. When that treatment is life-sustaining, in order to be valid, the decision must be in writing and it must contain a statement that it applies even if P's life is at risk. Furthermore, the decision and the statement must also be signed by P, or by another person in P's presence and at P's direction, in the presence of a witness who has also signed the decision and the statement.

Even then, the decision will not be binding if the treatment in question is not the precise treatment specified in the decision, any circumstances specified in the decision are absent, or there are reasonable grounds for believing that circumstances exist which the patient did not anticipate at the time of the advance decision and which would have affected their decision had they anticipated them. However, if the decision is binding, then it must be followed. If there is doubt about whether the decision is valid or binding, the Court of Protection can be asked to rule on it.

No advance decision

When there is no valid and binding advance decision, the patient's treating clinicians must make an assessment of what is in their best interests. Although a key consideration will be the patient's diagnosis and prognosis without treatment and the benefits and risks of the treatment proposed, this is not simply a medical question. The decision must take into account everything that is known about the patient, including their religious and other beliefs. A doctor should be wary of making value judgements about the patient's quality of life. If the patient has previously expressed views about their future treatment that are not binding, that is nevertheless relevant, although a view expressed in very different circumstances may carry little weight. The patient's family and others close to them, such as carers, will also have relevant views. However, the decision is in the end the clinician's and it is to be made objectively: it is not a question of what the patient would have decided if they had capacity.

The courts have sometimes said that, before life-sustaining treatment can be withdrawn from a patient, the circumstances must be intolerable to them. It is now clear that this is not a specific requirement that must be satisfied before treatment can be withdrawn, but it may be a helpful consideration when weighing up what is in the patient's best interests.

The Code of Conduct accompanying the Mental Capacity Act 2005 provides specific guidance on how to weigh up the advantages and disadvantages of life-sustaining treatment. It makes clear that it will generally be in a patient's best interests to receive life-sustaining treatment. However, it acknowledges that that may not be the case and that, if it is not in a patient's best interests to receive treatment, a doctor is not obliged to provide it, even if the patient's death is a foreseeable result. However, even if the patient's death is inevitable, the decision to withdraw or withhold treatment must not be motivated by a desire to bring about the patient's death.

Involving the court

If there is doubt or disagreement (e.g. between the clinicians and the patient's family) about what is in the patient's best interests, a ruling can be sought from the Court of Protection. The Court will presume that life-sustaining treatment should be provided and the burden is on the party who wants it withheld or withdrawn to prove that that course is in the patient's best interests. Except in cases of PVS (discussed in more detail further on), the court will draw up a 'balance sheet' with the pros and cons of giving and withholding treatment in each column. Only if the side favouring withdrawal of treatment is substantially 'in credit' will the court conclude that that is in the patient's best interests.

PVS and MCS

In England and Wales, it is mandatory to seek a ruling from the Court of Protection before withdrawing life-sustaining treatment from a patient in PVS or MCS.

When a patient is established to be in PVS, the court does not conduct any sort of balancing exercise. The House of Lords decided in *Airedale NHS Trust* v *Bland* [1993] AC 789 that a person in PVS has no life to speak of and that it will always be in their best interests to withdraw ANH. The purpose of seeking a court ruling is to ensure that there is no dispute about the diagnosis and to protect the clinicians from any criminal liability resulting from a decision with the only purpose of ending the patient's life.

When a patient is in MCS, the court will undertake the same balancing exercise that it does in other best interests decisions. In *W* v *M and others* [2011] EWHC 2443 (Fam), a judge rejected an argument that it would never be in the best interests of a patient with MCS to withdraw ANH. In that case an application to withdraw ANH was refused, even though it was supported by the patient's family and treating doctors, after hearing evidence from the patient's day-to-day carers.

'Do not resuscitate' orders

It may be appropriate to decide in advance of a medical emergency arising that, if such an emergency does arise, the patient should not receive life-saving treatment such as CPR or antibiotics. This will be so if it can be said in advance that administering that treatment would not be in the patient's best interests. That question is approached in the same way as it is

in any other circumstances. If it is highly unlikely that CPR would be successful or that, if successful, it would inevitably be accompanied by brain damage that would erase the patient's quality of life, then making a DNR order can allow the patient to die in comfort and with dignity. As with any other treatment, the appropriateness of a DNR order can be ruled on by the Court of Protection.

If a patient without capacity suffers a cardiac arrest and there is no DNR order in place, GMC guidance states that CPR should be attempted, unless there is time to make a proper assessment of the risks and benefits of undertaking it.

Equally, if a patient with capacity wants CPR to be attempted whatever the likely outcome, then, unless it is clinically inappropriate to do so, this must be done.

Euthanasia and assisted suicide

Assisted suicide involves helping another person to commit suicide. Euthanasia involves the killing of another person for their own good. If a doctor decides to give a patient who is in extreme pain a syringe of lethal medication, which the patient administers in order to end their life, this is assisted suicide. If the doctor administers the injection themselves in order to end the patient's suffering by killing them, this is euthanasia. In the UK, both are criminal acts. Euthanasia has no special legal status on the grounds that the doctor is seeking to act compassionately in the patient's interests: it is simply murder. Aiding or abetting suicide is an offence under section 2 of the Suicide Act 1961, and recent attempts to permit doctors to assist patients to end their own lives in certain circumstances have all failed in Parliament.

Difficulties arise when a doctor gives pain-relieving medication with the intention of relieving suffering, but in the knowledge that it will hasten death. At an ethical level, the doctor could assert doctrine of 'double effect': in broad terms, it is ethically acceptable to aim to do good, even if the good act will have foreseen but unintended bad consequences, provided i) the bad consequence is not a means to achieve the good intention, and ii) the bad consequence can be justified by the seriousness of the situation. However, this ethical principle is not necessarily reflected in the criminal law. To be guilty of murder, a person must have intended to cause death, or serious injury, and a defendant may be taken by a jury to have intended what is, to the defendant's knowledge, virtually certain to result from his actions (*R* v *Woollin* [1991] 1 AC 82). Thus, the doctor who administers an almost certainly lethal dose of painkillers with the intention only of relieving pain, is at risk of a conviction for murder.

In practice, juries tend not to convict those whom they consider to have acted ethically, whether doctors or relatives of patients who have been helped to die, and the case may never reach a jury at all if the prosecutor decides that a prosecution is not in the public interest. There is now formal guidance from the Director of Public Prosecutions on when to prosecute cases of assisted suicide, but it might be thought that the state of the law is unsatisfactory if such important decisions are left to the discretion of prosecutors and the common sense of juries. On the other hand, it may be impossible to legislate for the multiplicity of situations in which a life will end, and perhaps trust in the machinery of justice is the least worst option.

Palliative care

Even if it is has been decided that it is in a patient's interests to be allowed to die, they must still be made as comfortable as possible.

This means that food and drink must be provided if the patient can eat and drink safely, and that pain relief must be provided if necessary. However, a patient with capacity who has decided to refuse treatment may also refuse food, drink and pain relief.

Ethical considerations

Except insofar as objections may be raised to suicide per se, no ethical difficulties arise for clinicians in the case of an adult patient with capacity refusing life-saving or preserving treatment. However, a clinician who becomes an active participant in a patient's death, or has to make a decision about the treatment of a patient without capacity, is entering very difficult ethical territory.

Where euthanasia and assisted suicide are concerned, the justification for what would otherwise be a morally wrong act is that the immorality of involvement in the death of another is outweighed by the need to respect the autonomy of the patient. However, that justification is harder to make if one believes – as many do – that a precondition of acceptable euthanasia or assisted suicide should be that the patient is terminally ill or otherwise intolerably incapacitated. In holding that view, one is saying that to live or to die is not an entirely personal choice, or, rather, that the right to die at will should only be afforded to those physically and mentally able to undertake the task by themselves.

Opponents of euthanasia and assisted suicide often express the fear of the slippery slope that leads to doctors having universal power or life and death, sorting their patients into those worth saving and those for the scrapheap. However, doctors already have to make such decisions. It hardly needs saying that the mere concept of its being in a patient's best interests to be dead rather than alive is a hugely difficult one. Whether or not one believes that could ever be said of a person will depend on their cultural and religious beliefs about what life is or should be, and what might be expected to come after it. It might be thought that the strong presumption in favour of preserving life maximises the morality of such decision taking, but there are plenty of people who believe that a life of pain and suffering is no life at all – a belief that might be shared by the very patient whose life the doctor is, with the best of intentions, prolonging.

23 Health management

Figure 23.1 Key reports into the NHS

Porritt Report 1962

Farquharson-Lang Report 1966

Salmon Report 1966

Cogwheel Report 1967

King's Fund/Institute of Hospital Administrators Joint Working Party 1967

The Grey Book 1972

NHS Reorganisation Act 1973

Royal Commission 1979

Health Services Act 1980

Griffiths Report 1983

Working for Patients 1989 and the NHS and Community Care Act 1990

Managing the New NHS 1993 and the Health Authorities Act 1995

Health Act 1999

The NHS Plan 2000

NHS Next Stage Review 2008

Liberating the NHS 2010

Figure 23.3 The management multihat machine

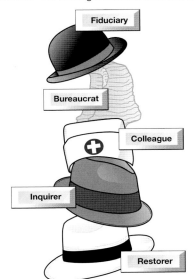

Fiduciary

Bureaucrat

Colleague

Inquirer

Restorer

Figure 23.2 The clinical leadership competency framework

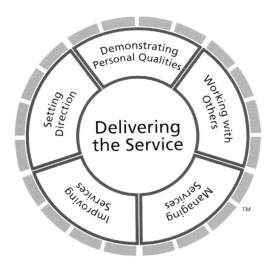

Setting Direction

Demonstrating Personal Qualities

Working with Others

Delivering the Service

Managing Services

Improving Services

TM

1. Demonstrating Personal Qualities
• 1.1 Developing self awareness
• 1.2 Managing yourself
• 1.3 Continuing personal development
• 1.4 Acting with integrity

2. Working with Others
• 2.1 Developing networks
• 2.2 Building and maintaining relationships
• 2.3 Encouraging contribution
• 2.4 Working within teams

3. Managing Services
• 3.1 Planning
• 3.2 Managing resources
• 3.3 Managing people
• 3.4 Managing performance

4. Improving Services
• 4.1 Ensuring patient safety
• 4.2 Critically evaluating
• 4.3 Encouraging improvement and innovation
• 4.4 Facilitating transformation

5. Setting Direction
• 5.1 Identifying the contexts for change
• 5.2 Applying knowledge and evidence
• 5.3 Making decisions
• 5.4 Evaluating impact

Medical Ethics, Law and Communication at a Glance, First Edition. Edited by Patrick Davey, Anna Rathmell, Michael Dunn, Charles Foster and Helen Salisbury.
© 2017 John Wiley & Sons, Ltd. Published 2017 by John Wiley & Sons, Ltd.

All clinicians manage

All clinicians do health management, whether they like it or not. They manage their time, they manage clinical teams, they manage waiting lists, they manage trainees, they design care pathways. Many consultants will lead large-scale hospital changes, and many GPs manage their own businesses. Here we discuss some of the ethical dimensions of health management (Figures 23.1, 23.2).

It is often said that there is a basic difference between clinical work and health management: clinical work focuses on doing the best for individual patients, while health management focuses on doing the best for groups of patients as a whole. There is some truth in this.

We don't have to look too deeply to see how the entirely proper aim of meeting the specific needs of an individual patient can come into conflict with the equally proper aim of meeting the overall needs of a whole group of patients. For example, responsible doctors will want to prescribe whatever drugs might improve or extend the life of their patient. From the perspective of doing the best by an individual patient, it is self-evidently right to prescribe the drug the patient needs, irrespective of cost. On the other hand, responsible health managers will want to make sure that the group of patients they serve get the greatest overall benefit from a limited pharmacy budget. From the perspective of doing the best by a group of patients, it is self-evidently right to consider the cost of all the prescriptions and gauge whether everyone's needs can be met from the available budget. If they cannot, and assuming the budget cannot be increased, then some form of rationing is necessary.

Championing the rights of individual patients is a principled position, and championing the collective interests of the group is also a principled position. The moral tension between the two positions sometimes translates into moral battles, and may be present in unspoken moral disagreement between clinicians and managers. However, while it is true that clinical care tends to focus on individual needs and management tends to focus on group needs, there is a significant overlap. Clinicians also manage. So the moral tension between clinical care and management is not just a source of tension between clinicians and managers: it is also a moral tension inbuilt into clinical roles.

A framework for understanding clinical management

This section offers a framework for thinking about the demands of everyday clinical management, and how these create moral difficulty (Figure 23.3).

1 Acting as a fiduciary on behalf of patients
A 'fiduciary' is a person who is trusted by someone else to act on that someone's behalf. The idea of a fiduciary relationship is found in both ethics and law. It is evident in professional codes that expect clinicians to make patients' interests their primary concern. The law is even more clear on the nature of the fiduciary relationship. It expects the fiduciary always to act so as to benefit the person for whom they act, and always to put the other person's interests ahead of their own.

In clinical management, the fiduciary role implies that you must speak up for patients in all the managerial contexts in which patients are not present to speak for themselves. This, of course, means pretty much everywhere. Taken to an extreme, the fiduciary relationship would mean putting patients' interests ahead of everyone else's all the time: ahead of those of clinical staff, managers, board members, clinical commissioners,

national and regional authorities, regulators and so on. Clearly this is impossible, because others have human needs and legitimate roles that require consideration too. Clinicians, for instance, need time to rest and to train. If you are managing a rota, you will sometimes place needs for time off and training ahead of patients' need for continuity of care. Boards need information to carry out their role, and the clinical time required to generate it is obviously time not spent on direct care for patients. The ethical challenge is thus to balance the fiduciary imperative with other legitimate management considerations. We will keep returning to this requirement for balance as the chapter proceeds.

2 Using collective resources fairly and efficiently
Clinical management sometimes means acting as a bureaucrat. Few people profess any affection for bureaucracy, but antipathy towards it tends to conceal its genuine value. The noble purpose underpinning bureaucratic administration is efficient and equitable use of collectively owned resources. A good bureaucracy minimises waste (of time, money and energy), avoids favouritism (so everyone's reasonable needs receive equal consideration) and serves the collective good (managers' personal goals are set aside in favour of common ends). Rules are the bureaucrat's favoured tool. This is because rules bind everyone, promoting consistency of action and equal treatment. Well-designed rules benefit and constrain us all. They set direction and underpin equality. However, we tend to chafe when they get in the way of our preferences.

The bureaucratic aspects of clinical management, as well as their ethical implications, permeate every level of activity. They are visible in clinical commissioning (weighing the claims of older peoples' services against, say, fertility treatment); team management (ensuring, for instance, that both service and educational needs are being met); or when implementing service policies that do not benefit a specific patient (such as a rule against admission to intensive care when a patient has too low a probability of recovery).

These examples suggest that the moral tension between clinical care and management that we noted earlier in the chapter is partly a tension between being a 'fiduciary' and being a 'bureaucrat'.

3 Being collegial
Good care is provided when people work supportively together, and much professional activity is managed by collegial consensus. Being collegial means helping out when colleagues need it, repaying the favour when they help you, supporting each other through difficulties, contributing to professional organisations such as medical Royal Colleges, and so on. Colleges play an important role in developing educational curricula, providing training for their members, setting standards of good practice through clinical guidance, promoting outcome measurement, and providing peer review of services and individual practice. Clinical management is clearly heavily dependent on collegiality. Collegiality supports good patient care by sustaining relationships between colleagues and encouraging everyone to 'go the extra mile'.

However, the strong bonds of collegiality sometimes result in colleagues' interests being put before those of patients (what George Bernard Shaw memorably called a 'conspiracy against the laity'). The most common example of this misplaced loyalty is reluctance to act on concerns about a colleague's competence or probity. Patients continue to be killed, injured and abused by clinicians known by their colleagues to be providing poor care. In this case, the habit of loyalty to colleagues gets in the way of the fiduciary duty to patients. This is less a moral dilemma than a conflict between emotion and duty.

4 Investigating quality and dealing with harm

Most clinical professionals are constantly striving to improve the quality of what they do. This means they must understand what produces good- and poor-quality care in organisations. In addition, medicine is inherently risky. Patients will – however hard clinicians work to prevent it – suffer harm from errors and complications. Improving care quality, preventing harm and dealing with harm after it has occurred calls for investigative skills. This 'inquisitorial' aspect of clinical management comes to the fore in practices such as audit, mortality and morbidity meetings, and investigations carried out after serious incidents. A major inquisitorial role will rarely fall to junior clinical staff, but clinical management tasks such as organising an audit project or raising and responding to concerns commonly do.

Inquiring into quality requires sensitive management of patients and staff. Patients may not want to hear that services are not as good as they hoped, or that treatment they thought was over has left them damaged in some way. Bureaucratic (organisational) loyalties sometimes lead people into thinking it is better to cover up trouble than risk damaging an organisation's reputation. Collegial loyalty may make it difficult to ask searching questions of another's practice.

5 Restoring trust and confidence

We often hear the question 'What should we do for the best?' in ethics. But the question 'What should we do now that things have gone horribly wrong?' is just as important. When things go horribly wrong for patients, the people affected – patients, their families and clinical colleagues – all need support. Lessons have to be learned, and trust and confidence have to be rebuilt. It is fair to say that care organisations have not managed this very well in the past. But it is increasingly widely recognised that the task of clinical management includes taking steps to restore trust with patients and communities, disseminating the learning from poor care or errors, and supporting colleagues who suffer distress after unintentionally harming a patient.

Clinical management thus includes mastering restorative ethical practices such as acknowledgement of complaints, supportive disclosure when patients are harmed and effective apology.

Behaviours for ethical healthcare management

It is a popular misconception that ethics is about decisions. Frankly, who cares what you think? What is ultimately important is how you – and those you influence – act.

You may rather like the idea of yourself as a fiduciary. Being a fiduciary licenses assertive behaviour on behalf of patients. Speaking up strongly for patients' interests (in planning meetings, for example) gives many clinicians a warm altruistic glow. But acting as a fiduciary can be challenging. For instance, when it first appeared, AIDS was talked about as a 'gay plague'. People feared they would catch it by shaking hands, and shunned AIDS sufferers. Clinical leaders made their fiduciary commitment visible. They demonstrated by their own behaviour that AIDS patients deserved respect, were entitled to research into their condition and should expect compassionate clinical care.

You may be less enamoured of the idea of being a bureaucrat. The word is loaded with negative connotations, such as 'boring', 'obstructive' and 'spineless'. But we saw how health systems rely on good bureaucrats. Good bureaucrats are conscientious, open, impartial and willing to be held to account for their decisions. They allocate resources fairly, organise efficiently and avoid waste. They don't allow personal moral beliefs, such as that abortion is wrong, to get in the way of providing good service to the public.

Collegial behaviours are congenial to many clinicians, who enjoy the camaraderie of medicine. But collegiality can be demanding. For instance, ethical clinical management calls for equal treatment for all one's colleagues: notwithstanding sex, gender, ethnicity, religion, culture, age, etc. These factors can affect job planning, rotas, appointments and promotions, and need scrupulous attention to fairness. Or, you may find yourself working in teams where one or more of your colleagues is experiencing performance difficulties. Here your fiduciary duty is to ensure that patients are safe, while collegiality demands you be helpful and fair to your colleague.

Adequate audit and just inquiry into harm rest upon disinterested analysis of all the relevant evidence. Inquisitorial behaviours are those we associate with the law at its best, and include objectivity, neutrality, 'hearing the other side' and independent judgement.

Finally, restorative behaviours are all to do with acknowledgement. They entail really listening to people who feel that there has been some breach of trust. When people experience poor care or harm, they need acknowledgement that it occurred, that it is unacceptable and that steps will be taken to prevent the same thing happening again. Some familiar restorative behaviours include genuinely listening to distressed patients or relatives, and giving a sincere apology.

We have seen above how the demands of ethical healthcare management can pull in different directions. Ethical clinical managers are aware of the scope for conflict between equally important goals or behaviours, and they strive to maintain a balance between them.

24 Primary care

Figure 24.1 An example of the 'ordinary' ethics of primary care

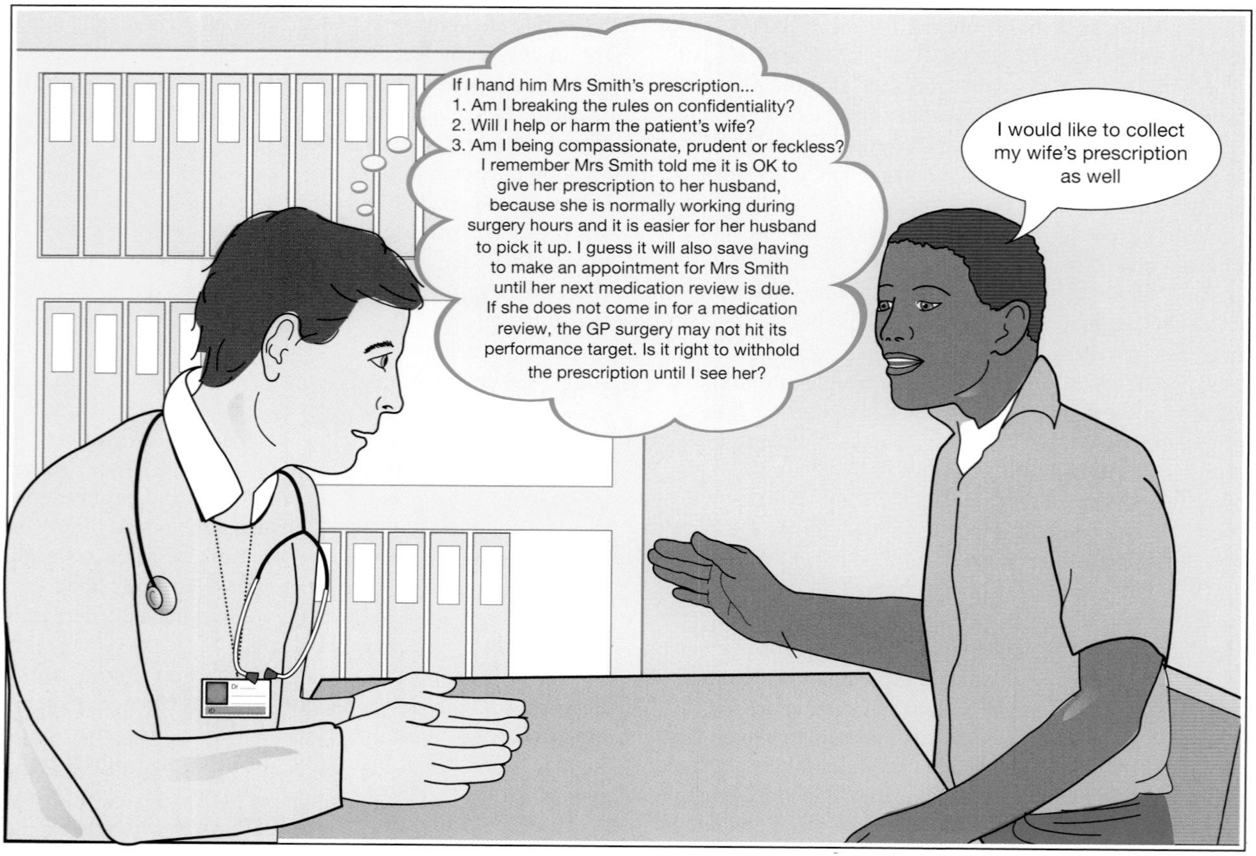

Introduction

When one thinks about ethics in primary health care, the focus might be taken to be the ethical issues that face GPs. However, primary care includes a variety of clinicians (e.g. pharmacists, nurses, health visitors, community physiotherapists, occupational therapists, counsellors and dentists) and non-clinicians (e.g. social workers, practice managers, receptionists, cleaners and even voluntary workers).

Although the ethical decisions made in primary care may appear less dramatic than those in hospital medicine, most healthcare encounters take place in primary care. As primary care is often the first step on the patient's journey through health services, decisions can also have an impact on the care that patients receive in the future. Patients in primary care are (relatively) more likely to be able to make autonomous decisions by usually (although not always) being less ill and having more control over their choice of healthcare provider.

Ethical frameworks in general practice

The Royal College of General Practitioners (RCGP) in the UK has as its motto, 'Scientia cum caritas', which means 'Science with caring'. General practice training in the UK prioritises the psycho-social aspects of medicine as well the biomedical aspects. Many centres of medical ethics in the UK have their origins in departments of general practice.

UK GPs may be influenced by various ethical approaches. The GMC's code of conduct, *Good medical practice*, and the RCGP's *Good medical practice for general practitioners* are essentially deontological, founded on the duties of a doctor. The quality and outcomes framework of the GP contract is utilitarian, based on evidence of what promotes the greatest cost effectiveness and therefore the greatest good for the greatest number. Vocational training is still rooted in concepts of professional growth and development, aimed at producing lifelong learners; arguably rooted in virtue ethics. More

Medical Ethics, Law and Communication at a Glance, First Edition. Edited by Patrick Davey, Anna Rathmell, Michael Dunn, Charles Foster and Helen Salisbury.

recently, the RCGP recommended values-based approaches as essential reading for its trainees.

Ethical and legal aspects of primary care

Gatekeeping and therapeutic parsimony

In the UK, patients generally see specialists after a referral from a GP, a system that restricts access to secondary care in both the NHS and private health insurance schemes. This potentially benefits both individual patients and the healthcare system. Individual patients benefit from having a personal doctor who can view their problems together with them rather than in isolation, and who can protect them from over-investigation and over-treatment.

Patients as a whole benefit because the system ensures that expensive secondary care resources are spent on those who have the greatest need (therapeutic parsimony). However, gatekeeping may also damage the doctor–patient relationship, because the doctor cannot act solely in the interests of the individual patient. This possible conflict of interests may be influenced by the personal, professional and financial incentives for or against referral. Primary care clinicians may also influence the choice between self-care and professional care.

GPs and other primary care clinicians working in the UK's NHS are encouraged to prescribe the cheapest effective treatment rather than the newest most effective. If the decision to refer or not refer, and treat or not treat, is based on factors other than clinical need alone, this is arguably a form of rationing. GP appointments are often very short (5 or 10 minutes) and time may often be rationed according to patients' need (Figure 24.1).

Families and communities

A characteristic feature of primary care is that doctors often care for several patients who are related to each other. They also often care for a number of individuals and families who live or work in close proximity, and whose lives are intimately related to each other. Particularly in rural areas, the same applies to primary healthcare staff. This can be a considerable strength of primary care, since clinicians gain a fuller understanding of the social context in which patients live and become ill. It can also pose ethical problems, however, particularly in conflicts between duties to different individuals – family members, employers and employees, and even between friends, when the illness of one has an impact on the life or health of another. The duty to respect confidentiality can also give rise to specific problems, because patients may not always understand or accept that information given to the doctor by one family member may not be divulged to others. Respect for confidentiality, and maintaining confidence among patients that confidentiality is respected, can be difficult.

Continuity of care

The ongoing professional relationships that GPs and other primary care staff have with patients means that they can develop a deeper understanding of their patients' choices and values. This can make respecting autonomy more complicated than in secondary care, where obtaining consent for procedures may take place in a single consultation and a patient's refusal to accept treatment can end the clinical relationship. By contrast, a GP might revisit a patient's decision on a number of occasions: for example, whether the patient wants help to quit smoking.

Commissioning and healthcare resource allocation

In the past few decades, GPs have had varying control over how local healthcare budgets are spent. Recently, the Health and Social Care Act 2012 in England calls for some GPs to be involved in the local commissioning of healthcare services. On the one hand, there is an argument that such decisions should be made by GPs who know the local area and population well. On the other hand, there is the argument that being a patient advocate as well as a commissioner is itself a conflict of interests. There may also be a wide variation in population needs over quite a small geographical distance – making a fair decision more difficult.

Everyday decision making

The day-to-day activities of those working in primary care raise ethical and legal issues that parallel other healthcare settings, and that have been discussed in detail in previous chapters.

As GPs look after the main electronic record of patients and have unrivalled ability to access patient information, the protection of data and the requirements of the Data Protection Act 1998 are particularly salient. The primary care team, including nurses, other clinicians and receptionists may have similar levels of access in practice without patients necessarily being aware of it.

Concerns about patients' decision-making capacity, advance care planning and substitute decision making mentioned elsewhere (see Chapters 11 and 21) will arise frequently in primary care because many people who are frail because of illness or disability, age or dementia reside in the community, and GPs will often be their first port of call with regard to health matters. Often GPs will also have responsibility for looking after residential and nursing care homes, and may become actively involved in social care decisions about place of residence or family contact.

With regards to the care of children, GPs, health visitors and others in primary care may be able to identify abuse or neglect long before a child presents in secondary care. The Education Act provides guidance on benefits for children who have special educational needs. The Sexual Offences Act 2003 also clarifies that clinicians will not be prosecuted as accessories to a crime if they give contraception or sexual health advice to a child below the legal age of consent, provided that the child has decision-making capacity, is likely to have sex even without the advice, and refuses to involve their parents.

Further reading

Bowman, D. and Spicer, J. (eds), *Primary care ethics*, 2007. Abingdon: Radcliffe Publishing.

Papanikitas, A. and Toon, P. 'Primary care ethics: A body of literature and a community of scholars?', 2011, *Journal of the Royal Society of Medicine* 104(3): 94–96.

Rogers, W.A. 1997, 'A systematic review of empirical research into ethics in general practice', *British Journal of General Practice* 47, 733–737.

Rogers, W. and Braunack-Mayer, A, *Practical ethics for general practice*, 2nd edn, 2010. Oxford University Press.

Communication

Chapters

25 The importance of good communication   72
26 The patient-centred consultation   74
27 Building the relationship   75
28 Listening and questioning   76
29 Explanations   78
30 Explaining procedures   80
31 The computer in the consultation   81
32 Shared decision making   82
33 Communication of risk   84
34 Talking about lifestyle changes   86

35 Breaking bad news   88
36 Bad news: patients' reactions   90
37 Dealing with anger and aggression   92
38 Talking about sex   94
39 Communicating across cultures   96
40 Communicating with people with disabilities   98
41 Communicating with colleagues   100
42 Professionalism   102
43 Feedback   104
44 Looking after yourself   106
45 Kindness   108

25 The importance of good communication

Figure 25.1 The importance of good communication

(a) Good practice

(b) Bad practice

Medical Ethics, Law and Communication at a Glance, First Edition. Edited by Patrick Davey, Anna Rathmell, Michael Dunn, Charles Foster and Helen Salisbury.
© 2017 John Wiley & Sons, Ltd. Published 2017 by John Wiley & Sons, Ltd.

Good communication is key to being an effective doctor. Detailed scientific knowledge and diagnostic acumen will only be put to good use when coupled with the skills to listen carefully and convey ideas accurately to patients and colleagues (Figure 25.1).

Making a diagnosis

Most of our work as doctors begins with a patient who has symptoms and we start by taking a history. An accurate history is the key to a sound diagnosis. Very basic skills such as listening attentively and not interrupting until the patient has finished their opening statement will set the tone for the rest of the consultation. How comfortable the patient feels to tell us their story will depend on these skills and the rapport we have been able to build with them. Whether or not difficult or embarrassing symptoms are brought up may depend on the patient's initial reading of how sympathetic, kind or non-judgemental the doctor appears. Our sensitivity to what may be difficult to discuss and the empathy shown in exploring these areas will determine the information we garner, and how interested we appear will determine how much detail is revealed. We also need skills of clarification to ensure that we have an accurate picture of the history. Many clues to diagnosis will come from the patient's own ideas about what may be wrong, informed by their own past history, family history or research they have already done. Asking patients what they think is the cause of their symptoms not only demonstrates an interest in their ideas but will very often add to your own thinking.

Providing treatment that works

Once a diagnosis has been successfully made, treatment of some sort is usually prescribed but research has shown that only about half the medication we prescribe is taken as the doctor intended. How likely the patient is to follow the suggested (or preferably agreed) management plan will depend on a number of factors that include understanding about what is going on and belief that the treatment will help. If patients understand why it is important to control blood pressure, they are more likely to take antihypertensives as prescribed. If you can explain something of the risks of antibiotic resistance, they are less likely to demand them for a viral infection or stop taking them after a few doses. Similarly, the patient's belief in and commitment to a programme of treatment will depend to a degree on their trust in you and confidence in your skills. This in turn will be based on whether you appear knowledgeable and trustworthy, and whether you seem to care about them. In addition, the placebo effect plays a large part in the success of many treatments: the doctor is part of the cure and the treatment is more likely to work if the patient believes in it and in you.

Relieving worry and fear

Patients are troubled by symptoms of pain or disability but also by worry about what those symptoms might represent, and fear about what the future may hold as a consequence. One major role of the doctor is to explore those worries and fears and, where possible, allay them. Even when it is not possible to reassure a patient, having a chance to voice those fears may be therapeutic in itself. If a patient attends with a symptom that they are worried may be a sign of something serious but there is no place in the consultation to voice that worry, there is a risk that they may still be worried when they leave. 'Is there anything particular you were worried this might be?' is a useful question and sometimes brings forth quite surprising answers about which you can confidently reassure the patient. Some worries are so common that it may be worth reassuring the patient even before they have been expressed: for example, many patients presenting with a headache are worried that they may have a brain tumour, but may be scared of seeming foolish if they mention it. A technique called normalisation may be useful here:

Doctor: Was there anything you were worried might be causing the headaches?

Patient: No, not really, I just wanted to be sure it wasn't anything serious …

Doctor: Many people who have headaches worry about the possibility of a brain tumour. I don't know if you have been worrying but, from the symptoms you've told me about, I'm very confident that you don't have one.

Not getting sued

Poor communication is a very common theme in complaints against doctors, in fact much more common than problems with diagnostic accuracy or technical skills. Taking care to listen to your patients will make you less likely to make errors. Apologising swiftly when you do make mistakes will make it much less likely that legal action will follow. An American study has shown that qualifying doctors who failed in communication skills assessments were statistically more likely to be sued for malpractice in later professional life.

Communicating with colleagues

Doctors work in teams with a range of health professionals and patient safety relies on clear spoken and written communication between team members. There are formalised ways of communicating medical information, such as the presentation of a medical history, which have been developed over many years to be time-efficient ways of conveying the important parts of a patient's story. In other situations, such as handover at the end of a shift, the form is often less defined and it depends on individual doctors to ensure that they have communicated clearly what needs to be done. Structured communication tools such as SBAR (Situation, Background, Assessment, Recommendation; see Chapter 41) can be useful in communicating with colleagues, especially across a hierarchy or when asking for assistance.

26 The patient-centred consultation

Figure 26.1 The patient-centred consultation

atient-centred medicine is not easy to define and is often understood by reference to what it is not: doctor centred, hospital centred, technology centred or disease centred. Research shows that patients want care that focuses on their main reason for attending, their need for information and their concerns. They want their doctor to see them as a whole person and to make an attempt to understand their world. Putting the patient at the centre of the consultation improves patient satisfaction and leads to better health outcomes (Figure 26.1).

One way of understanding patient centredness is to consider the following model:
The two-agenda model of the consultation

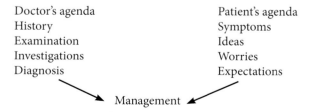

Doctor's agenda	Patient's agenda
History	Symptoms
Examination	Ideas
Investigations	Worries
Diagnosis	Expectations

Management

When meeting a patient, the doctor usually has an agenda or mind map of the consultation ahead. The patient is likely to have one too but it probably looks quite different. If the desired outcome of the consultation is a shared management plan, something that the patient and doctor agree on, attention will need to be paid to both agendas. How much attention you give to the patient's agenda will go a long way to determining how patient centred you are and also how likely the patient is to follow through on the plan you have devised. This applies both to taking prescribed medicines – only about half the medicines we prescribe are taken according to their prescription (and many not at all) – and even more to other aspects of self-care such as exercise, diet and smoking.

Some doctors prefer to leave the exploration of patients' ideas, worries and expectations to the very end of their history taking, but, for patients, the distinction between symptoms and thoughts about symptoms may not be clear-cut, so you are likely to be presented with these intertwined. You may miss important elements of the history if you do not follow up the cues relating to ideas and worries that are offered during the opening stages of the history. Sometimes patients may be so worried about their symptoms that their anxiety may interfere with their ability to give a clear account. In these cases, you will have to stop and ask about what is worrying the patient before you address your own agenda. You will often not be able to reassure the patient until you have much more information (and maybe not even then), but just expressing their fears and knowing that they have been heard may be enough to enable your patient to continue.

Being patient centred also means putting the patient's needs before your own or that of your organisation, or, as the General Medical Council (GMC) puts it, you must 'make the care of your patients your first concern'. Finding out what would be easiest for the patient and organising your services for their benefit should be a first step in patient-centred care.

Medical Ethics, Law and Communication at a Glance, First Edition. Edited by Patrick Davey, Anna Rathmell, Michael Dunn, Charles Foster and Helen Salisbury.
© 2017 John Wiley & Sons, Ltd. Published 2017 by John Wiley & Sons, Ltd.

27 Building the relationship

Figure 27.1 Building the relationship

Relationships between doctors and patients vary from the short encounter in A&E to many consultations over decades between GPs and the families they look after. Different patients and different clinical situations may call for different types of relationship, and doctors will vary too in how much of themselves they are willing to share. Here, however, are some basic do's and don't's of building a relationship with a patient that is likely to work for both patient and doctor (Figure 27.1).

Looking the part

We all make judgements about people from the moment we meet them: patients will have expectations about what a doctor is like and it helps in building the relationship if we do not confound those expectations too much. In practice, this means dressing the part, looking clean, neat and professional.

Preparation

In a clinic, make sure you have finished writing the notes for the previous patient before calling the next one, so that you can give them your full attention the minute they come into your consulting room. When possible, take a minute to look at the patient's record, note long-term diagnoses and catch up with the last few entries.

Greeting

How you greet the patient will set the tone for the subsequent consultation. If you are stressed and running late, which for many doctors is very often the case, try not to show this in your body language: slow your walk as you reach the waiting room, relax your shoulders and smile as you say hello to your patient. Apologise for any delay. Check you have got the name right and, if unsure, ask the patient how it should be said or how they would like to be addressed.

There is not time in a busy medical day to make a lot of small talk, but a moment taken to put the patient at their ease will be well spent. This may be achieved by an enquiry about how they are, or their journey to the clinic.

Maintaining rapport

Patients want a doctor who is interested in them as a person and who cares about what they are experiencing, rather than viewing them purely as a diagnostic challenge. Listening attentively and asking about the effect of a condition on the patient's life demonstrates this interest, as well as revealing very useful clinical information. Throughout the consultation, be aware of your patient's physical comfort or lack of it, especially during examination.

Boundaries

While striving to be friendly, a degree of formality is very important in medicine. Unlike a conversation between friends, the consultation does not involve an equal sharing of personal information and is focused entirely on the patient. Most doctors will choose to deflect personal questions about themselves. As doctors, we hear many sensitive and otherwise private facts about our patients and see their bodies uncovered. This is possible because there is a clearly defined clinical relationship and medical purpose to our questions and our examinations. Patients may become very uncomfortable if they are not sure that these boundaries are in place. For example, if they are unsure about why the answer to a question about their sex life is relevant, or the purpose of an intimate examination, they may misunderstand our motives. This can be avoided by explaining your questions and your examinations, and by offering a chaperone.

Medical Ethics, Law and Communication at a Glance, First Edition. Edited by Patrick Davey, Anna Rathmell, Michael Dunn, Charles Foster and Helen Salisbury.
© 2017 John Wiley & Sons, Ltd. Published 2017 by John Wiley & Sons, Ltd.

28 Listening and questioning

Figure 28.1 Listening and questioning

How much a patient tells you depends on the quality of your listening. Most medical students are great listeners at the start of their studies, but it is a natural skill that can get crowded out by so much medical knowledge and may need to be consciously nurtured. To do this, you need to become aware of what verbal and non-verbal signals you are sending out, which tell the patient that they have your full attention (or that they don't). Many patients think long and hard about what they want to tell the doctor and will have prepared their story, so, if you can find the right open question to trigger the narrative and then listen well, you may be told many of the details you want to know, thus reducing the number of questions you need to ask. Doctors tend to interrupt, but research shows that most patients will finish their initial account within 90 seconds. There are various ways you can encourage your patient to talk.

Non-verbal skills

• Body language – Sitting in an attentive posture, leaning towards the patient. If the patient is in bed, pull up a chair so that you can be at the same level, not standing looking down.
• Eye contact – Stay focused on the patient, avoid looking at your computer, notes, shoes, watch, etc. (If you do need to take notes, it is worth waiting until the patient stops and then saying, 'I'm just going to write a few notes.')
• Stillness – Try not to fiddle.
• Nodding – As if to say 'Go on' (this can easily be overdone – if in doubt ask for feedback on this from a colleague).
• Non-verbal encouraging noises – 'mm's.
• Smile (when appropriate to what is being said).
• Tone of voice and pace of questions – These can convey that you have time to listen (or that you don't).

Questioning skills

If you listen to a skilled doctor taking a history, one question seems to flow from the answer to the previous one and there appears to be a logical progression from the presenting complaint to the conclusion. What you hear is a conversation, with the patient doing most of the talking, being prompted by the doctor. In contrast, some medical interviews can sound like a grilling from the secret police, a barrage of questions given monosyllabic answers. The following tools should help

• Open questions – 'Can you tell about what's been happening right from the beginning?
• Verbal encouragement – 'Do go on', 'What happened next?'
• Reflection – this is a useful technique whereby you repeat some of what a patient has just said as a way of encouraging them to elaborate. It can be used to help you steer the narrative towards the elements you are most interested in without interrupting too much:

    Patient: 'Well doctor, I'm that stressed I'm not sleeping, I'm not coping at work, I sometimes feel I don't think I can go on.'

    Doctor: (if you want to explore what's underlying this): 'You're very stressed …?', or

                 (if you want to explore suicide risk): 'You can't go on …?'

• Clarification – words for symptoms do not have clear or constant meanings so it is worth exploring what a patient means when they use a word like 'dizzy' (vertiginous? light-headed?

As if they might faint?) or 'sick' (nausea? vomiting? general malaise?). Similarly, you may need to pin down time periods or quantities ('When you say a bit of blood, was that a drop, a teaspoonful, an eggcupful?').
• Cues – these are things that may be only half-said or hinted at, but may be crucial in understanding the patient's thoughts or fears about their condition. For example, in relating an experience of chest pain, a patient might say, 'Well at first I thought it was probably indigestion but then it got so much worse …' The doctor could respond with: 'And how severe was that?' Did it spread anywhere?', or, picking up on the ideas cue, 'What did you think then?' Clearly these are not 'either/or' because you will want to establish both the clinical detail and the patient's thoughts and fears, and at each stage of a history there will be multiple cues you could pick up. However, in terms of building rapport, it is often useful to pick up the ideas cues early in the consultation because it is easy to forget them once they have passed.

Summary

Summary is a really useful technique, particularly at the end of the initial patient narrative. It serves several purposes: it shows the patient that you have been listening; it gives the patient an opportunity to correct you, or to add important details they missed the first time; and it serves as a useful framing device, giving structure to your consultation. It can be a useful tool with patients who have a complicated, confusing or long-winded history ('Can I just stop you there and summarise what I've understood so far …?) Having summarised the history of the presenting complaint back to the patient, and addressed any omissions or mistakes, you are then in a good position to move on to asking about their past medical history.

Structure

A consultation should be structured to take account of the needs of both the doctor and the patient. The patient needs to tell their story, and to be sure that the doctor has heard and understands what it meant and why it is important. You need to gather an accurate account of the symptoms and events leading up to the presentation to enable them to make a correct diagnosis. If your questions appear to come out of the blue, having no obvious connection to what went before, the patient may be confused or wonder if you have understood what they have just said. Additionally, if you ask a question that the patient thinks they have already answered, they may feel you have not been listening.

Framing

Explicit framing can be a useful way of providing structure to your consultation. This might happen at the beginning: 'First I'd like to find out what you have already been told about the condition, and then I'll fill in any gaps. After that, we can go through possible treatments and talk about what happens next.' It can also be used in the middle of a consultation when you want to change the subject ('Now I'd just like to ask you a few questions about the rest of your health.'). Explicit framing is often necessary when taking a full history because, for the patient, there is no logical connection between one set of questions (e.g. on past medical history) and the next (a systems enquiry).

29 Explanations

Figure 29.1 Listening and Questioning

(a) Convey the right attitude

(b) Use appropriate language

(c) Visual aids

(d) Check understanding and invite questions

Medical Ethics, Law and Communication at a Glance, First Edition. Edited by Patrick Davey, Anna Rathmell, Michael Dunn, Charles Foster and Helen Salisbury.
© 2017 John Wiley & Sons, Ltd. Published 2017 by John Wiley & Sons, Ltd.

Most doctors spend a lot of time explaining things to patients. Diagnosis, aetiology, treatment, management options, risk, prognosis ... the list goes on and on. Being able to give a good explanation that the patient understands is a core skill (Figure 29.1).

Foundations

Attitude

In earlier days, the model of medicine was a paternalistic one: doctors made decisions in the best interests of patients and it really did not matter if the patients did not understand what was going on. Nowadays we are expected (by the GMC and by patients) to work in partnership with patients, sharing decisions with them. For this to happen, patients need to understand what is going on and what the options are for treatment. Understanding is also a really important step towards patients taking responsibility for their own care and for concordance with treatment plans jointly developed.

Before you can explain something, you need to understand it yourself, and there is nothing like trying to teach someone else to make you realise the gaps in your knowledge. However, most of the time you will have adequate knowledge for the task or know where to find it.

Time

Doctors often say 'There just isn't time' to explain things to patients. If you are resuscitating someone in A&E, this may well be true, but in most other situations explanations do not have to take a long time and are likely to save time in the long run because patients who understand their treatment plan are more likely to follow it.

What makes a good explanation?

Explanations need to start with whatever the patient already knows on a topic and there is no way of knowing this without asking them. Sometimes what the patient 'knows' may be inaccurate and it is important to clear up existing misconceptions before you try to build on shaky foundations. Listening to what the patient already knows will also give you a clue about what language to use in your explanation. Asking 'How much has been explained to you so far about what is going on?' can be a good way of finding out what the patient knows without it seeming like a test.

Language

Many explanations fail because the words used are unfamiliar to the patient. After a few years in medicine, it is often difficult to remember what counts as lay language: monitor your words closely for traces of jargon ('hypertension' instead of high blood pressure, 'catheter' instead of tube) and observe your patient closely to pick up clues that you are not being understood. Most patients will not interrupt if you use a word they don't understand: they may feel that they ought to know and don't want to appear ignorant. Analogies are sometimes useful but be careful both that the example you use makes sense to the patient and that you do not stretch the analogy further than it will logically go.

Framing your explanation

If you have several things to explain in a consultation, it is very helpful to patients to signpost this at the beginning. ('First I'd like to explain to you what exactly the tests have shown, then we could talk about possible treatments').

Chunking and checking

Break up your explanation into short sections and check at each stage that you have been understood. There are a number of ways of doing this but the crucial point is that the patient should feel that you are checking how well you have explained, rather than how clever they have been in understanding. If you keep your eyes on the patient's face while you are explaining, you should be able to spot the point at which they glaze over or look anxious because you have lost them in your explanation. In between your chunks of information, phrases like 'Am I making sense so far?' or inviting questions will help you know if you are pitching it right.

Sometimes, particularly if the explanation has been complex and it is crucial that the patient has a clear understanding (e.g. if they need to make a difficult decision between treatment options), it may be appropriate to check understanding by asking the patient to explain back to you. Phrases like 'Just to make sure I've been clear enough in my explanation, would you mind just telling me what you've understood so far?' can be useful here.

Using diagrams and models

Drawing a picture can be a very useful way of communicating with a patient. Some concepts are much easier to explain pictorially, particularly anatomical knowledge – it may be very difficult for a patient to understand what is going on in biliary colic, for example, if they do not have a mental image of where the gall bladder is and what it does. Do not be put off by your lack of artistic ability as the picture just needs to convey the concepts, not faithfully reproduce an anatomy textbook. Drawing a picture for a patient is a very good way of building rapport because it demonstrates that you are taking the time and trouble to explain to them personally. It often gives the patient an opportunity to ask questions. Even if they do not have the right words for something, they can point at the relevant part of the picture and ask.

Models can often help too – many doctors have models of hearts or joints or even whole skeletons on their desks to aid their explanations.

Repetition and summary

Don't be afraid of repeating yourself: recapping the main points at the end of an explanation can be very useful in emphasising what you think are the most important issues.

Inviting questions

At the end of an explanation, it may be helpful to invite questions ('Is there anything you'd like me to go over again?', or 'Is there anything else you would like me to explain?').

30 Explaining procedures

Figure 30.1 Patient-centered explanations of procedures

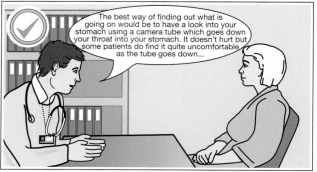

Patients undergo all sorts of procedures in hospital from the relatively trivial and self-explanatory, such as having blood taken, to the really quite complicated and scary-sounding endoscopic retrograde cholangio-pancreatogram. Consent is a clear prerequisite for any investigation or treatment but tends to be only formally sought and signed for on a form when the patient is having some sort of anaesthetic or a very invasive procedure. In other situations, the fact that a patient does not object is often taken to signal consent, and filling in a consent form every time you took blood or requested an X-ray would clearly be cumbersome. However, it is good practice to ask every time you are going to do something to a patient, 'Is it ok if …?'

Of course consent is only valid if it is informed consent, so we need to think about how we explain procedures to patients (Figure 30.1). Think about what the patient might want to know:

- Why am I having this procedure?
- What might you find?
- Where will it happen?
- How long will it take?
- Will it hurt?
- Does it ever go wrong?
- Will I need to stay in hospital?
- Can I go straight back to work?

If the procedure is something that involves needles or tubes (e.g. cannula, nasogastric tube, urinary catheter), show the patient the materials as part of the explanation. These things are often less alarming in reality than in the imagination.

If a procedure is painful or uncomfortable, make sure that you warn the patient about this. There is a wide variation in patients' reactions to procedures and it is worth including phrases such as 'Most people find this just slightly uncomfortable but occasionally some may find it painful, although it is over quite quickly.' If you fail to warn patients that a procedure may be painful, or falsely reassure them, they are likely to worry that something has gone wrong when it does hurt.

Try to frame your explanation in terms of what the patient will experience rather than what you will do to the patient, and think about what you would want to know if you were in the patient's shoes (or bed). Be careful about the language you use to describe the procedure: avoid aggressive-sounding verbs like 'poke' and 'stick' and think of ways to describe the materials that will used that will be least alarming (e.g. a catheter as a 'thin, soft, flexible tube').

As with all explanations, watch and listen to patients so that you can pick up cues they may give you that they do not understand or are worried. Go slowly, checking that your patient understands at each stage. Diagrams can be useful to make your explanation clearer and remember to invite questions at the end of your explanation. Patients occasionally refuse investigations, which of course they have every right to do, and this is most likely to occur if you have either scared the patient with your description or failed to explain the purpose of the test adequately.

Medical Ethics, Law and Communication at a Glance, First Edition. Edited by Patrick Davey, Anna Rathmell, Michael Dunn, Charles Foster and Helen Salisbury.
© 2017 John Wiley & Sons, Ltd. Published 2017 by John Wiley & Sons, Ltd.

31 The computer in the consultation

Figure 31.1 The computer in the consultation

Over the last 30 years, paper medical records have been replaced with the electronic patient record in many hospitals and clinics. There are clear advantages – it doesn't get lost, it can be accessed from multiple sites, it can be searched and you don't need to read anyone else's handwriting. However, if not used well, the computer can be a barrier to a good consultation, and sometimes it even seems to take over with an agenda of its own ('The computer says I need to check your smoking status.'). If we want to keep our consultations patient-centred, we must make sure we use the computer as the useful tool it is and avoid it becoming the focus of the consultation (Figure 31.1).

Tips for success

• Think about the room set-up: make sure the computer does not literally come between you and the patient.
• Consult the record before the patient comes in – catch up with what happened at their last visit, what medication they are on, any important investigations whose results you need to know.
• Ignore the computer completely at the beginning of the consultation while the patient is explaining to you why they have come to see you. Offer eye contact to the patient, not the screen.
• When you do need to record something, explain what you are doing as you turn to the keyboard ('Bear with me a minute while I just make a note of that.').
• Share the screen – this is the patient's record. Explain results, show graphs or diagrams. Demonstrate useful patient information websites.

Work out the best way of documenting the consultation so that you don't have an awkward few minutes while you are typing and the patient is sitting waiting (or tries to tell you about a different problem). If your memory is good enough, you can wait until the patient has left the room and then type up your notes. Alternatively, you can use your typing as a way of summarising and checking – the patient can correct you and you also end with an agreed note of the consultation:

Doctor: So, let's just make a record of that. (typing) You've had 3 days of loose stool and vomited twice …
Patient: (interrupting) actually it was three times …
Doctor: Ok – vomited three times and …

Templates

Some electronic patient records have a lot of room for free text, but some are constructed around templates with lots of boxes to tick. Try to begin your consultation (e.g. an asthma review) with questions about how the condition is affecting the patient, and only turn to the template when you have established rapport and gained some understanding. If it is a short template that you use repeatedly, you may be able to internalise the questions and ask them as part of your normal history taking (e.g. standard questions in an asthma review about sleep disturbance, inhaler use and limitations on activities), filling in the tick boxes later. If it is a complex template, try sharing it with the patient.

Ward rounds

Computers on wheels (COWs) are becoming a regular feature of some ward rounds and some of these points also apply to ward work. Remember the patient is your focus.

32 Shared decision making

Figure 32.1 Shared decision making

Medical Ethics, Law and Communication at a Glance, First Edition. Edited by Patrick Davey, Anna Rathmell, Michael Dunn, Charles Foster and Helen Salisbury.
© 2017 John Wiley & Sons, Ltd. Published 2017 by John Wiley & Sons, Ltd.

Shared decision making can be defined as:

the conversation that happens between a patient and their healthcare professional to reach a healthcare choice together. This conversation needs patients and professionals to understand what is important to the other person when choosing a treatment. (Definition from NHS shared decision making)

It is a model of consultation whereby the views and knowledge of both the doctor and the patient can be explored together, in order to make informed choices about treatment. This process can be applied to choosing tests, treatment options, or making decisions about lifestyle or behavioural changes (Figure 32.1).

Shared decision making fits well with the aspiration of working with patients in partnership, set out as one of the duties of a doctor by the General Medical Council (GMC; *Good medical practice*, 2013), where they state that as a doctor 'You must work in partnership with patients, sharing with them the information they will need to make decisions about their care, and 'You must listen to patients, take account of their views and respond honestly to their questions.'

It is also thought that when patients are involved in making decisions about their health, they are better informed and more likely to act in concordance with the medical advice or treatment.

To share a decision needs the engagement and commitment of at least two parties – the healthcare team member and the patient, but sometimes other people (e.g. members of the patient's family) may also be involved. Traditionally, it was felt that the doctor brought their medical knowledge, expertise and experience to the conversation, while the patient brought their concerns, beliefs and personal values. In reality, patients also bring their knowledge: for example, from research they have done on the internet, or from experience they have gained through having their illness. For many long-term conditions, patients develop a store of knowledge, expertise and experiences of treatments that have worked (or not worked) for them. Both parties can also share their hopes of treatment and patients can explain what their priorities are.

Shared decision making is important when there is more than one option that could be reasonably chosen clinically. This is referred to as 'clinical equipoise'. In reality this is true of most decisions, unless there is very clearly only one choice that is undisputedly best for everyone. Decisions where there is more than one option are known as 'preference-sensitive choices' and much of the work on supporting shared decision making comes from looking at these. A good clinical example would be considering anticoagulation choices in atrial fibrillation.

Consider the case of a woman attending a doctor who wishes to start contraception. There are a number of good options available. The decision will need to have a medical component: the doctor must find out if there are any options that would be medically unsuitable or contra-indicated (e.g. offering oestrogen-containing pills to a woman who has migraine with focal aura). Once the doctor has established what options are medically available for the patient, the decision needs to take account of the woman's priorities and circumstances (e.g. Does she also want treatment for acne? Does she have concerns about weight gain? Does she want to avoid taking tablets because she may be concerned about swallowing or remembering pills?). This cannot be known by the clinician without asking and discussing the issues with the woman.

Making decisions in partnership enables choices that accommodate the patient's personal situation. For example, if someone taking medicine for well-controlled epilepsy would not be able to accept a risk of seizure because it would affect their right to hold a driving licence, then they might choose not to try making changes to their medication. This might not be a relevant factor for another individual facing the same decision about the same medication.

One type of resource that is used to support shared decision making is the decision aid. There are a number of types of these, such as option grids, or web-based toolkits (e.g. the NHS shared decision-making support tools). These can be reviewed together by the patient and doctor in a consultation, or looked at separately, with the discussion happening at a later meeting. They are designed to show information about the pros and cons of different options. They have been shown to improve patients' knowledge, risk understanding and health involvement. They are available for a number of clinical situations and provide a starting point for discussion. This can also allow exploration of the patient's priorities, which may not be what the doctor would have guessed or known. Whatever the method used, it is essential to make sure that the person has received and understood enough information about all the options to make a truly informed choice.

One way of thinking about shared decision making is the 'Ask three questions' message. This is designed to encourage and empower patients to ask the questions they need in order to be involved in their healthcare choices. The questions are:

1 What are my options?
2 What are the possible benefits and risks of those options?
3 How likely are the possible benefits and risks of each option to occur? And how do I get support to make this decision?

It is helpful to make sure that the patient has had the chance to ask all these questions, or to consider whether they have been answered in dialogue.

Sometimes people may choose not to be involved in shared decision making. This may be their choice consistently in healthcare decisions, or may just be about a particular decision at a particular time. For example, making decisions in the face of a new or serious diagnosis may feel overwhelming for some people. It is important that this is respected as a valid choice. However, it is also important to keep the door open, so that they can review or change their choice at any future time if wished. Many decisions do not have to be made instantly, and it is sometimes worth allowing time (or deferring the decision) so people can consider their choices and involvement. It can be useful to offer a follow-up discussion to review whether both parties are still comfortable with the decision made and with the process, or whether there are any new questions or concerns that have arisen.

33 Communication of risk

Figure 33.1 Communication of risk

Figure 33.2 Cates plot of the effects of stopping smoking

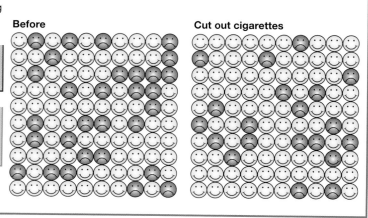

Before: If we didn't do anything differently your current risk of having a heart attack or stroke before your 60th birthday would be three in ten.

Cut out the cigarettes: We can now change a few things and see how it affects the diagram. This is what would happen if you took up the challenge and stopped smoking. Your risk would be dropped by a third, down to two in ten.

With a growing emphasis on preventative medicine across all specialties, we spend more time than ever treating risk, not illness. This can be a difficult concept for doctors to communicate and therefore for patients to understand. The overall goal is to inform the patient about their options and help them to make a decision based on their values. By modifying the way we discuss risk, we can improve our patients' understanding and engagement with behavioural modifications, and increase compliance with treatment.

When discussing risk, it is necessary to adapt the way we communicate to one that patient understands. To motivate a patient to engage with a management plan takes more than just than just a purely rational level of understanding: the information must also be processed on an emotional level (Figure 33.1).

First of all, check that the patient wants to have a discussion about the proposed topic. This serves a dual purpose of signposting the discussion and allowing an opportunity to address any concerns that the patient has.

Linguistic communication of risk

The English language has a wide variety of words that convey various amounts of risk. The advantage of communicating risk linguistically is that no knowledge of statistics is required and the conversation flows naturally. Additionally, linguistic communication of risk is more emotionally engaging than numerical communication of risk, and therefore more likely to motivate the patient to engage with managing their risk.

Modifier	Root
Somewhat	Likely
Equally	Possible
Almost	Certainly
Highly	Probably
Very	Rarely

The wide variation in interpretation of words can be a barrier to a precise understanding of risk. One patient's 'possibly' may be the next patient's 'likely'. Also, the lack of precision makes the conversation feel vague and, at times, frustrating (for both patient and doctor). The use of modifying words may be helpful to decrease misunderstanding and improve the accuracy of risk communication. For example:

> …because you have had … in the past, you are very likely to have another … However, if you take your medication every day, it will greatly reduce your chances of another … In fact, the vast majority of people on this medication are never bothered by … Given that the medication is so effective, how would you feel about taking it?

Numerical communication of risk

Studies show patients often prefer to receive information in numeric form. The precision gives a scientific air to the conversation and helps to instil trust in the advice given. However, numerical information is not very good at engaging patients on the emotional level that drives behavioural change. Additionally, patients may not be able to understand and apply the required mathematical concepts. Many patients will get lost or overwhelmed by the numbers.

A general principle is that the more time and effort patients spend doing mental maths, the less time they spend thinking about what the numbers mean for their health, or how they can modify them. Here are some simple rules to help minimise the amount of mental arithmetic that is needed on behalf of the patient:

- Stick to the same format of numerical expression throughout the consultation. If you start using frequencies, use them for any information that will be directly compared. If you use fractions, carry on using fractions.
- A surprising number of patients do not understand percentages: frequencies are more easily grasped – thus 'one in ten' rather than '10%'.
- Don't be afraid to round numbers: the slight inaccuracy is an acceptable trade-off for the patient actually being able to follow the conversation.
- Avoid putting the patient in a situation where they try to perform mental arithmetic on their own. It is better to talk through the calculation, or provide the answer.

To inform the patient about their choices, it is important that they first understand their absolute risk. For this to work, patients and doctors need to have a shared reference point. For example, if the patient thinks that 50% is the standard risk of having a heart attack over the next 5 years, you may have trouble agreeing on the seriousness of their 30% risk. It is therefore important to provide some context for the patient's absolute risk by comparing it with the average for their age/gender/ethnicity, or by comparing it with an everyday event (e.g. car crash). Allow some time for this information to be processed, work at the pace of your patient and check understanding as the conversation progresses.

The next step is to establish how the risk changes with a particular intervention (e.g. lifestyle modification, having an operation, taking medication). This is best communicated by discussing both relative risk reduction and absolute risk reduction at the same time:

> At the moment you are taking aspirin to stop the blood from clotting. This may be helping but your chances of having a stroke are still quite high; in fact, they are one in ten. However, if you had the operation on the artery in your neck, it would halve to one in twenty… What are your thoughts on that?

Visual communication of risk

There are many different computer programs that have been built to calculate individual risk for specific conditions (e.g. QRisk2, Adjuvant! Online). Many of these calculators have built-in tools for generating images to facilitate the communication of risk. Graphs and diagrams are more likely to hold a patient's attention than prolonged discussions with numerous facts or statistics.

Additionally, many complex statistical calculations can just be 'seen' instead of needing to be calculated by the patient. As well as being more intuitive, pictorial representation may be more persuasive. Potential disadvantages are that patients may focus on trends rather than relating the image to their current situation.

When communicating with diagrams, try to stick to the ones that have been specifically designed for use with patients. It is important to talk through what the images represent. For example, in the Cates plot (Figure 33.2) yellow smiley faces represent positive outcomes whereas blue sad faces represent negative outcomes.

34 Talking about lifestyle changes

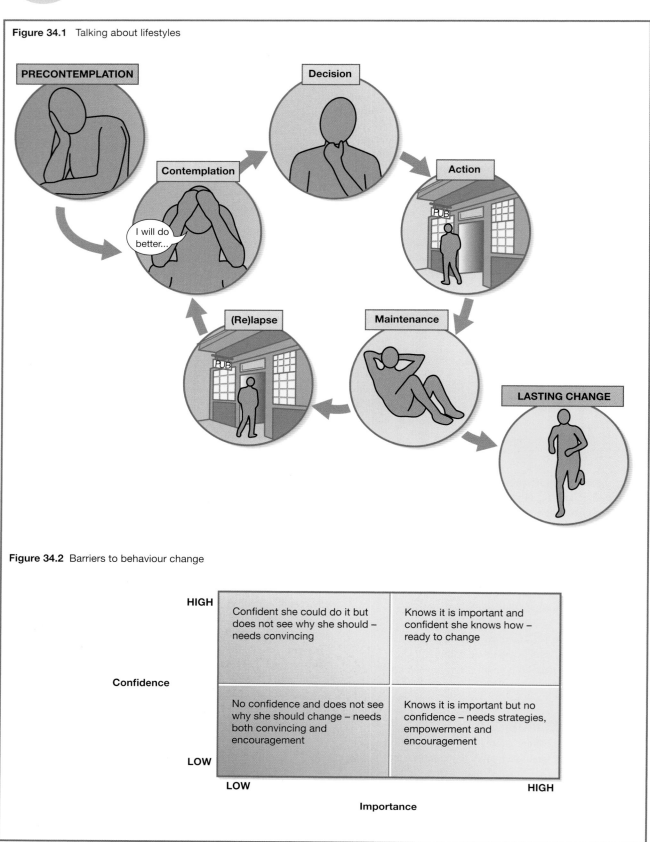

Figure 34.1 Talking about lifestyles

Figure 34.2 Barriers to behaviour change

Medicines can have powerful effects on health but these are dwarfed by the effects of patients' own behaviour. We all know, and mostly our patients know too, about the harmful effects of tobacco and obesity, and the benefits of exercise and a good diet. When faced with an overweight, diabetic patient with arthritis and cardiovascular disease who continues to smoke, it can hard to know where to start with lifestyle advice. However, there is good evidence that advice from doctors can be an important factor in people's decisions to make lifestyle changes such as stopping smoking.

Is the patient ready to change?

There are many theoretical models of change management or readiness to change. In essence, change takes time and if the patient has not even started to think about losing weight or stopping smoking, it will probably take more than one consultation to get to the stage where action can be taken. The most well-known model is called the transtheoretical model of change and originated in work by Prochaska and DiClemente.

The model (Figure 34.1) consists of several phases the person may pass through on the way to changing their behaviour:

- **Pre-contemplation** phase – the patient has not accepted that a problem exists. They have not yet started to think about change.
- **Contemplation** – the patient has started to think about changing but has not yet made a decision.
- **Decision** – the patient is preparing and planning for change.
- **Action** – making the change.
- **Maintenance** – the change has been made but support may still be needed.
- **Lapse** is a temporary return to previous behaviour.
- **Relapse** is a full return to the behaviour.

Lapse and relapse do not imply failure – they simply show that change is difficult, and it is unreasonable to expect anyone to be able to change a behaviour perfectly without any slips. When relapse occurs, several trips through the stages may be necessary to make lasting changes.

A note of caution: although this model is widely taught, there is a lack of good evidence that following these steps in a consultation makes a difference to how likely the patient is to change their behaviour.

In practice, when you talk to a patient about losing weight or giving up smoking, you need to start with a general question, for example: 'Are you thinking about giving up smoking?' to gauge what stage a patient is at, before offering advice about how to change. There is evidence that lifestyle change undertaken as part of a group, for example weight loss groups, is more likely to be successful that an individual working on their own.

Another useful way of approaching lifestyle factors is to think about the barriers to behaviour change for a patient. Some patients carry on smoking because they do not really believe that anything bad will happen to them as a result. They feel they could change if they wanted to, but see no reason to do so.

Other patients are already really scared that they are damaging their health but, often having tried and failed, they have no confidence that they can give up. It is useful to make a diagnosis before you start offering advice – do they need more confidence that they can change their behaviour, or more convincing that they need to?

This is also a useful way of thinking about any task that is not being attended to: is it because you are not convinced it is important (in which case it is worth stopping to think whether you should just cross it off your to-do list altogether) or is it because you do not know how to tackle it (in which case you should think about where to get some advice).

Many people feel bad about the habits they have which are harmful, and the ways in which people talk about smoking, excessive eating, alcohol and other drug use often add to this feeling of self-blame. If we are to help people to make changes, we need to avoid being judgemental: it is very common for patients to switch off if they feel they are being nagged rather than encouraged. Patients are very much more likely to change their behaviour if they have arrived at the decision themselves, rather than being told they must or should change. The most productive way forward, therefore, usually involves questions and exploration:

> Do you want to give up smoking? What happened when you tried before? What are the pros and cons of continuing? What makes it difficult? How could you tackle those barriers? What sort of support would be useful to you?

Using this technique, it is often possible to help people towards making the changes they need for their health, always bearing in mind that it may take more than one consultation to achieve lasting change.

Although it is important that you address lifestyle issues in your consultations, you probably will not have the time and may not have the skills to support patients through major lifestyle change. It is very useful to find out what the local provision for smoking cessation, exercise on referral, weight management, and drugs and alcohol support are where you are working, so that when you have opened the topic you will have something to offer the patient. Some doctors also attend specific coaching classes to learn the skills needed to help patients to change their behaviour.

A word of caution: doctors are encouraged to carry out health promotion at every opportunity but beware of raising sensitive issues inappropriately. If a patient has come to see you about a urinary tract infection, it may damage any rapport you have built if you raise the issue of her weight uninvited.

Further reading

Prochaska, J.Q., and DiClemente, C.C. Stages and Processes of Self-Change of Smoking: Toward An Integrative Model of Change. *Journal of Consulting and Clinical Psychology* 1983;51;1,390–395.

35 Breaking bad news

Figure 35.1 Breaking bad news

What counts as bad news will vary hugely from one patient to another. Some news is likely always to be bad, such as a diagnosis of cancer, and some will depend on context, such as the news that a patient is pregnant. What is more certain is that from your first days as a junior doctor you will be the one breaking the bad news: you are likely to know the patient best and be the doctor on the ward when the scan results come back or the relatives visit wanting news. You can never make it a pleasant experience to receive bad news but you can make it least worse by the way you do it. Patients usually remember with great clarity the life-changing moment when they heard the news, and in particular they remember the warmth and humanity of the doctor and whether they seemed to care (Figure 35.1).

Preparation

If you know in advance that there is bad news coming, it is very helpful to prepare.

Think about the environment: is there a quiet room you can go to? A box of tissues? If you can't move the patient from the ward, pull the curtains round for some semblance of privacy.

Avoid interruptions: hand your bleep to a colleague or one of the ward staff, pin a notice to the door, let nursing staff know what you are doing and that you should not be interrupted.

Who should be there? If this is planned, you may be able to ask the patient whom they would like to be present ('Mr Simpson, we need to talk about where your treatment is going. Would you like your wife/son/daughter to be with you when we do?'). Otherwise, it may be appropriate to have a nurse there, either someone who has been looking after your patient up to now or a specialist nurse who may be able to stay with the patient to support and answer questions when you have to leave. Whoever is there, make sure that you introduce yourself and your role and that everyone knows who everyone else is.

Prepare yourself with as much information as possible so you can answer anticipated questions about the news and what happens next. Think about the exact words and phrases you will use in delivering the news: they may be remembered by the patient for the rest of their life.

You will not always have the opportunity to prepare but you should always make an effort to get the environment right. If you are asked at the nursing station for an update on your patient's condition and the news is bad, take the patient or relative to a side room before launching in. The change of venue serves to prepare the recipient that bad news is coming and also ensures privacy.

Sometimes you will be asked for news about which you are unsure: it may be appropriate to refer the patient to one of your seniors, especially if there is an imminent ward round where there will be a chance to talk, but sometimes it will be kinder to go and seek out the information. Waiting and uncertainty are some of the most unpleasant aspects of being a patient.

What does the patient know already?

What happens next depends hugely on what the patient already knows or suspects. It may be that you have already had a conversation with the patient about what you are looking for with a certain test or scan, in which case you can pick up from where you left off. However, very often you will need to find out using questions like 'What has been explained to you so far about what the problem might be?' or 'Do you know what we were looking for with this test?' Sometimes the appropriate question is not just 'What have you been told?' but also 'What have you been thinking yourself about what might be causing your symptoms?'

If a patient has had no previous warning that the news might be bad, you may need to start a few steps further back in your explanation.

How much does the patient want to know?

Some patients want to know about their condition and its treatment in great detail and some would really rather not. Sometimes it may be appropriate to ask exactly this question: 'Are you the sort of person who likes to know all the details of what is going on?', but often you will gather this from the patient's cues, from the questions they ask and their responses to your offers of information.

Giving the news

Getting the pace right in delivering bad news is very important: if you go very slowly, the patient may become uncomfortable wondering what you are leading up to. However, diving straight in with no warning can appear blunt, abrupt or unkind. An opening phrase such as 'I'm afraid I've some bad news for you' will orientate the listener to the likely tone and topic of the conversation.

Use clear, unambiguous language. Patients surprisingly often do not hear the news that is given because the words used do not make any sense to them. If the news is about cancer, use that word, rather than mass, tumour, neoplastic lesion or any of the other euphemisms that exist. Similarly, if there are metastases, talk about spread of the cancer to other parts of the body.

Leave plenty of time for the patient to absorb the information. Stop after you have given the news and wait for cues from the patient before you go on. Silence, while the patient absorbs what you have just said, and an expression of empathy will probably be most appropriate. If you are giving news about a serious diagnosis or terminal prognosis, it is not unusual for a patient to fail to register very much at all after your initial statement. It is vitally important to follow the patient's cues about how much information they want and can take on board in that consultation.

- Prepare the environment
- What does the patient already know?
- How much do they want to know?
- Use clear language
- Go slowly
- Respond to emotions
- Plan ahead.

36 Bad news: patients' reactions

Figure 36.1 Bad news: patient reactions

(a) Denial

(b) Distress

(c) Anger

(d) Stoicism

Medical Ethics, Law and Communication at a Glance, First Edition. Edited by Patrick Davey, Anna Rathmell, Michael Dunn, Charles Foster and Helen Salisbury.
© 2017 John Wiley & Sons, Ltd. Published 2017 by John Wiley & Sons, Ltd.

Responding to emotions

Patients react in a number of ways to bad news. You need to be prepared to respond to a wide variety of reactions and emotions (Figure 36.1).

Denial

Some patients may find it very difficult to believe the news that is being given. Such patients are often late to present to medical services even when they seem to have clear and serious symptoms. They may look for reasons not to believe the news – perhaps there has been a mistake in the lab? Are we sure the scan has not been misreported? Rather than argue with the patient in denial about the facts of the case, it is often useful to respond to the underlying emotion. Acknowledging the denial openly may be helpful ('I can see this is very difficult to take in.'). Beware of being in a rush to get on with the consultation: if the patient has not yet taken in the diagnosis, they probably will not be able to focus on any plans you are trying to make with them.

Anger

There are lots of reasons why patients may be angry when they receive bad news and that anger may be directed at you yourself, at other doctors, at God, or fate or the person who caused the accident. Try as much as possible to allow the patient to express their anger as this may be helpful to them. Often you will hear of the inadequacies of other members of the profession that have led to the current catastrophe. It can be helpful to empathise ('That sounds like a very upsetting experience.') without necessarily accepting blame on their behalf – as you were not there, you only have one side of the story so it is impossible to make a judgement.

Grief and fear

Many patients will be very distressed when they hear bad news. With unequivocally bad news there is little you can say to make it better, but a simple 'I'm so sorry' may help. Be prepared to sit a while not saying anything, with a box of tissues to offer until the patient is ready to go on. Sometimes mixed in with the grief is fear, especially if the bad news is a cancer diagnosis. If your patient is scared, it is worth finding out exactly what they are scared of. Cancer means different things to different people and the fear may be of pain, of chemotherapy, of losing one's hair, of having to tell the family or of death itself. You will not necessarily be able to reassure the patient completely, but sometimes anatomising the fear can make it more manageable. Sometimes the fears may be groundless, in which case you can reassure the patient. Questions like 'Is there any specific aspect of the diagnosis that is frightening?' can be helpful.

Stoicism

Some patients may be entirely matter-of-fact when they receive bad news, preferring to keep their emotions well hidden. In some ways, this makes life much easier for the doctor but be careful not to assume that, just because emotions are not expressed, they are not there. When a patient asks, 'So what are my chances?', they may not be asking for percentage 5-year survival figures, but looking for reassurance. Some patients really do want to know the facts and figures, and it is right to answer these questions as accurately as you are able. Again, it is worth thinking about both the emotional and the literal meanings of such a question, the need for comfort and reassurance and the need for information, and working out on what level to respond.

Planning ahead

Bearing in mind that the patient may have taken in very little of what you have said after the headline bad news, it is important that they go away from the consultation with a clear idea of what happens next. This might be in the form of an appointment for a scan or another consultation, or the contact details for a specialist nurse whom they can ring.

Who else needs to know?

If you have given a life-changing diagnosis to a patient, think about who else might need to know. Do you need to offer to explain to other members of the family? Are there other teams in the hospital looking after this patient whose treatment will be affected by this change in circumstances? Think also about communication with the patient's GP. Clinic letters are often held up and discharge summaries will not arrive until after the patient has left hospital. In the meantime, the GP may consult with the patient or a member of the family, and it is really helpful for them to have accurate information if that happens.

Housekeeping

Housekeeping refers to looking after your own emotions. Telling someone something they really don't want to hear and being with them through their grief or anger can be emotionally wearing. In many other caring professions, there are formal support structures to enable practitioners to debrief and reflect on their own feelings about a charged encounter but this is rare in medicine. Finding a time to think about what you did well and what you could do better next time is important. It is also useful to be able to offload and talk about your own feelings to a colleague or close friend (always bearing patient confidentiality in mind). Many medical students worry that they will care too much and others that there must be something missing as they never get upset. In reality, what matters to the patient is that you remain in control of your emotions during the consultation, and can be gentle and empathetic when you give bad news.

37 Dealing with anger and aggression

Figure 37.1 Dealing with anger and aggression

Do: Empathise

Don't: Transfer blame

Medical Ethics, Law and Communication at a Glance, First Edition. Edited by Patrick Davey, Anna Rathmell, Michael Dunn, Charles Foster and Helen Salisbury.
© 2017 John Wiley & Sons, Ltd. Published 2017 by John Wiley & Sons, Ltd.

There are many reasons why anger is commonly expressed in hospitals and other healthcare settings. Negative experiences, such as being kept waiting, or feeling insufficiently informed about what is going on, are common causes of anger and these are often exacerbated by the presence of other emotions such as fear or guilt. A variety of medical states may also make it more likely that the anger will be expressed as shouting or aggression: alcohol and other drugs (or withdrawal from them) hypoglycaemia, pain, hypoxia or an acute confusional state may all lead to relative disinhibition. As a junior doctor, you are likely to be on the receiving end of anger from patients, relatives (and even colleagues). Expressed anger appears to be very status conscious: as a junior doctor, you are less likely to be shouted at than the ward clerk but much more likely to be shouted at than your consultant. It is worth thinking in advance about the strategies you will need to deal with anger. These can be divided up into two categories: strategies for defusing anger in the other person (Figure 37.1) and personal coping strategies.

How to defuse anger

- Apologise: It is very difficult to be angry with someone who is saying sorry. If you know that a patient is likely to be angry (e.g. because your clinic is running an hour late), make the apology the first thing you say to the patient. Apologising when something has gone wrong is not synonymous with accepting blame: many complaints and court cases arise because 'Nobody ever said sorry.'
- Use body language constructively: Avoid squaring up to any angry person – try to adopt an assertive but open stance. If you can encourage the angry person to sit down, they are more likely to calm down.
- Listen: Many people regain their composure once they have had a chance to vent their frustration. If you show a genuine interest in the patient's or relative's problem and make an effort to understand, they are unlikely to be angry for long.
- Clarify any points you don't understand.
- Empathise (if possible): 'I'd be upset too if this happened to my relative.'
- Avoid transferring blame: Either to the patient – implying that it is in some way their fault is likely to make them more angry – or to a colleague. Sometimes patients will invite you to agree that the treatment they received was unacceptable. In this situation it is helpful to be empathetic ('It sounds like you had a really difficult time.') while remembering that you only have one side of the story.
- Take time out: It may sometimes be appropriate to leave a situation to give either the patient or yourself an opportunity to calm down.
- Call for help: If the patient or relative is still angry despite your best efforts, it is entirely appropriate to enlist the help of someone more senior on the team. Offering to contact your registrar or consultant may be helpful in that it shows that you are taking the angry person seriously. Indeed, if complaints are made and your seniors did not have a chance to deal with them at the time, they may be justifiably annoyed. If things have gone wrong, patients have a right to complain and it may be helpful to explain to them how this can be done (or pass them on to someone who knows).

Looking after yourself
Physical safety

Your physical safety is paramount and it is important that you recognise when you could be at risk. Hospitals employ security staff whose job is to help you stay safe and you should not hesitate to ask for their help: it is much better to err on the side of caution and have back-up which is not needed than to get hurt. It will be a matter of judgement whether the security person needs to be in the consultation room with you or outside the door. Explain who they are and why they are there to the patient.

If you are interviewing someone whom you suspect may be violent, as well as enlisting the help of security, think about the set-up of the room. You should be nearest the door, remove any potential weapons or missiles (sharps, coffee cups) and make sure you know where the panic buttons are situated.

Your feelings

Most people find it very unpleasant to be shouted at. How bad it feels depends a bit on how responsible you feel for the situation and also how threatening the episode is. Some people respond to anger by getting angry back. While this is sometimes understandable, particularly if the patient is being very unreasonable, shouting back is unprofessional and unlikely to help. If you can avoid tears until you are away from the patient (even if that involves making a very quick exit), this will help you to preserve your professional front.

Our ability to cope with other people's anger, and how likely we are to express anger or tears ourselves, depends also on the stresses we are under: when you are tired, hungry, feeling overburdened by a huge list of jobs to do and scared that something may go wrong, it is much harder to remain calm.

It is important to debrief with colleagues after an unpleasant interaction with a patient, to acknowledge you own feelings and get their support.

Colleagues

With the exception of instructions in an emergency, there is no place for shouting in the workplace. Although staff may sometimes feel angry with each other, particularly when things are going badly, angry shouting is always unprofessional and usually counterproductive. Being able to express the fact that you are angry in a calm manner, maintaining your self-control, is an important skill. It can be particularly distressing for patients to witness discord in the team looking after them.

38 Talking about sex

Figure 38.1 Talking about sex

Medical Ethics, Law and Communication at a Glance, First Edition. Edited by Patrick Davey, Anna Rathmell, Michael Dunn, Charles Foster and Helen Salisbury.
© 2017 John Wiley & Sons, Ltd. Published 2017 by John Wiley & Sons, Ltd.

For many people, sex is a very important part of their lives and of how they see themselves, and it is often affected by their mental or physical health. We cannot predict for whom it will be important: contrary to the stereotypes, some people are not sexually active in their twenties and many people remain sexually active into old age.

Most people find it uncomfortable and embarrassing to discuss worries they have about sex or problems they are experiencing but, as doctors, we are often in a position to help with advice, treatment or referral. It is therefore part of our job to make it as easy as possible for the patient by being open, straightforward and unembarrassed ourselves (Figure 38.1).

When sex is clearly the subject of the consultation

In some situations, sex is clearly going to be discussed in the consultation, for example in a genito-urinary medicine (GUM) clinic. We can make it easiest for patients by being matter-of-fact in the questions we ask and making it clear that these are routine questions for us (however unusual a situation it may be for them). In these consultations, in judging risk of acquiring or passing on infection, it is often important to know exactly who has done what with whom. Clear and explicit language rather than euphemisms are required and patients will usually find it easier if the doctor uses words that they might find embarrassing first. Offering patients options such as 'Was that vaginal, anal or oral intercourse?' may help them to be clear about what happened. It is important not to make any assumptions about a person's sexuality and it is helpful to ask routinely whether a partner was a man or woman.

Language must be unambiguous and non-judgmental if we want to gain an accurate history and help the patient. Sexual contact may be a more useful phrase than intercourse as there are sexual activities that might not be termed intercourse but which are still relevant to transmission of infection. If you are surprised by the number of partners or the activities described, do not let this show on your face.

Talking about sex in other settings

Most doctors will not spend much of their careers in GUM, but we all need to be comfortable talking about sex (see key points). Although there are some specialties where the subject may be more routinely discussed, for example urology or gynaecology, there are very few areas of medicine that involve talking to patients where it will not arise. Questions about the genito-urinary system in a routine systemic enquiry should include 'Are you sexually active?' as well as questions about bladder function. Any routine review of a male patient with diabetes should include questions about erectile function as its loss may be an indicator of small vessel disease, and patients with depression should be asked about libido.

When patients are worried about sexual function, it can be difficult for them to raise the topic during a consultation. They may be too embarrassed, or may not be sure that this doctor is the appropriate person to talk to.

Normalisation

This is a very useful technique, particularly if a worry is quite common. So, for example, when a patient has had a heart attack it should be part of your routine to ask about worries and provide information: 'Many people who have had heart attacks worry that having sex again may make things worse for their heart. Has that been a worry for you at all?' (Obviously it is sensible to find out first whether the patient was sexually active before their admission.) Make sure that you do know the medical facts so you are in a position to answer the questions that are likely to follow.

Normalisation serves several purposes: it helps the patient to feel that they are not alone, that this is something other patients have been through; it explains to patients why you are raising the subject (which may otherwise risk seeming prurient); and it opens up the topic for discussion – you may not have identified exactly the patient's worry but they may now feel able to express it.

Drug side effects

Many medications have adverse effects on erectile function (e.g. beta blockers) or on libido (e.g. selective serotonin reuptake inhibitors [SSRIs]). It is important to check whether people taking these and similar medications have experienced these side effects, because the patient may not have realised the connection and thus not raise the topic. It may come as a huge relief to them to discover that the problem can be explained.

Lists

If it is not clear whether sex is an issue for a person, it can be included in a list of possible worries or topics for discussion. For example, returning to our example of the patient post-myocardial infarction, you could say: 'Some patients worry about getting back to their usual exercise routine, going back to work or having sex again. Have any of these been concerning you?' The patient is then completely free to ignore the topic if it is not relevant or to pick it up if it is.

Disability and sex

Many physical disabilities have an impact on how easy it is to have sex. Sometimes this is a direct physical issue: for example, how severe hip arthritis limits sexual positions or where a suprapubic catheter should be sited to be least inconvenient during sex. Society as a whole, and many doctors too, finds it difficult to think of disability and sexuality together but we do a disservice to our patients by not considering the possibility that this may be an important part of their lives.

Effects of surgery

Many patients who have required significant surgery worry about the effects on their appearance and their relationships. Women who undergo mastectomies or patients who need stomas may have difficulties recovering a sense of themselves as sexually attractive. Sometimes referral for psychological input or couple therapy may be needed, but the ability to listen empathetically in order to identify the problem initially will be greatly appreciated by patients.

39 Communicating across cultures

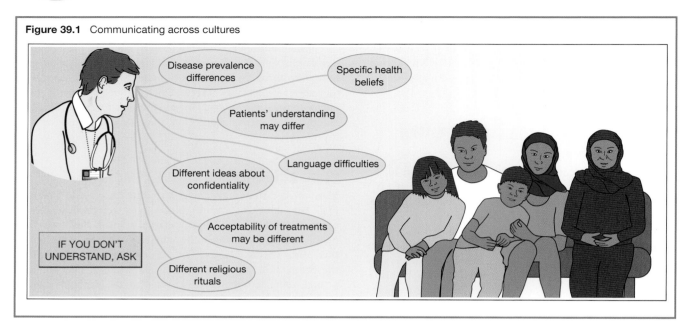

Figure 39.1 Communicating across cultures

- Disease prevalence differences
- Specific health beliefs
- Patients' understanding may differ
- Language difficulties
- Different ideas about confidentiality
- Acceptability of treatments may be different
- Different religious rituals

IF YOU DON'T UNDERSTAND, ASK

Cultural competence

The GMC document *Good medical practice* (2013) states: 'You must not unfairly discriminate against patients by allowing your personal views to affect your professional relationships or the treatment you provide or arrange', and that and to fulfil your role in the doctor–patient partnership you must:

- be polite, considerate, honest;
- treat patients with dignity; and
- treat each patient as an individual.

Looking specifically at cultural issues, 'tomorrow's doctors' require the following competences in that graduates must be able to:

• communicate effectively with patients regardless of their social, cultural and ethnic backgrounds; and
• communicate with individuals who cannot speak English including the use of interpreters.

What is culture?

Culture is surprisingly difficult to define. It is not possible to know every single variation in culture and language. Even within a culture of which you feel you may have some understanding, individual expression and interpretation varies widely. A helpful way to think about it is to see each person as having their own unique identity, which is shaped by the many different influences to which they are exposed. Culture has often been described as a lens through which we view and understand the world. It may also be seen as the way in which a social group collectively makes sense of the world (Figure 39.1).

What factors influence culture?

Language and ethnicity are the more obvious areas of cultural difference but there are many more ways groups of people get together and share a culture. Other factors include age, religion, sexual orientation, socioeconomic class and education. Culture can be thought of on a large scale, for example twenty-first century European culture, or on a small scale, such as the culture in an individual workplace or family.

An individual's culture is defined by their heritage as well as by individual circumstances and personal choice.

What cultures do you belong to?

It is important to understand our own cultural influences because these will affect our approach to patients. We are not 'blank slates' or neutral parties in the doctor–patient relationship. We bring our own biases as well as our own assumptions. Being aware of these factors can mean that we mitigate any possible adverse influence these factors may have on our relationship with the patient.

Medical Ethics, Law and Communication at a Glance, First Edition. Edited by Patrick Davey, Anna Rathmell, Michael Dunn, Charles Foster and Helen Salisbury.
© 2017 John Wiley & Sons, Ltd. Published 2017 by John Wiley & Sons, Ltd.

Why is it important to consider cultural issues?

There are many who would argue that our overriding core professional principles of treating patients with dignity and respect should include our attitudes and approaches to all patients. We should always treat patients as individuals.

However, cultural beliefs and influences can impact on behaviour such as communication styles, health beliefs, family roles, lifestyles, rituals and decision-making processes. Perception of health and ill health, as well as access to healthcare, can all be influenced by culture.

For example, rituals around death can vary enormously between cultures. Some cultures require burying their relatives within 24 hours of a death, which means that a timely completion of a death certificate is important. Some cultures do not eat gelatine: many capsules contain gelatine and this may affect patients' compliance.

Morbidity and mortality rates vary markedly between different cultures and it is important to have some broad understanding of how culture can influence access to and compliance with medical care.

Consulting across cultures

A good clinical history should always answer the following:
- Who is this person?
- What constitutes their life?
- What is important to this patient?
- What are their values and fears?
- How might their culture affect understanding, access to and compliance with good healthcare?

It is not possible to know everything about every culture. If in doubt ask. It's good for you and good for the patient.

How can we improve communication with patients who don't speak our language?

Non-verbal

It is still possible to show interest and concern for your patient. Many of the skills to show active listening are just as important in this setting. Maintaining eye contact, showing patience, nodding and open body language. Miming can also be a useful tool.

Written

Use diagrams and written material in the patient's own language. There is a wide range of literature available in different languages. For example the Royal College of Psychiatrists produces information on mental health problems in several different languages.

Verbal – use of interpreters

Many patients who do not feel confident enough of their English to consult a doctor nevertheless do speak a little and understand more. Check before you start what the situation is because this will affect your interaction.

Interpreters can be family or friends or a professional interpreter.

Use of a professional interpreter

Professional interpreters are trained to interpret exactly what the patient says and to relay the health professional's question exactly as asked. The replies should be given in the first person and the interpreter is acting only as a conduit for translated language.

Tips for using interpreters

- Allow time
- Emphasise confidentiality within the consultation.
- Always address your question to the patient and maintain eye contact. The interpreter will be happy to be ignored during the consultations. You can place the interpreter anywhere in the room to be least intrusive.
- Check the interpreter and patient speak the same language.
- Check the interpreter is acceptable to the patient. Many interpreters come from the same small communities within an area and patients may worry about sensitive information getting out (despite reassurances of confidentiality).
- Respect the role of the interpreter.
- Use simple language and be careful only to ask one question at a time.
- Check the patient's understanding and encourage asking questions.
- Do not forget to ask about the patient's perspective, what they think might be causing the problem and what they are worried about. This is sometimes omitted in interpreted consultations because they already seem complicated and may be lengthy. These questions can be especially important if the patient may have unfamiliar health beliefs.

Use of a family member or friend

This situation can be more difficult and requires the doctor to be more directive to the interpreter as to how exactly they would like them to help.

You may need to explain that you want a word-for-word translation (or as near as possible) and also offer time to hear the family member's own viewpoint. It can sometimes be difficult to get the patient's own story because their relative who speaks English may try to speak for them. Be firm but polite about what you need: 'Thank you very much for coming to interpret for your ... It would help me a lot if you just repeat my question to your ... and then let me know exactly what they say in reply.'

Use of a telephone translation service

Many healthcare organisations have access to telephone interpreting services that can provide translators in most languages with no notice. These services are cheaper than having an interpreter physically present and may be seen as more confidential by patients.

40 Communicating with people with disabilities

Figure 40.1 Communicating with disabled patients

DO...
Treat them as a well-functioning person
Maintain eye contact
Touch them where appropriate (e.g. handshake)
Adjust your speech content as appropriate for their ability to understand
Be patient and kind

DON'T...
Be condescending
Talk over them in the third person
Assume that they do not have capacity
Talk too quickly or in overly complex language
Gloss over their disability
Make their disability the dominant theme in your conversation unless it is relevant

Medical Ethics, Law and Communication at a Glance, First Edition. Edited by Patrick Davey, Anna Rathmell, Michael Dunn, Charles Foster and Helen Salisbury.
© 2017 John Wiley & Sons, Ltd. Published 2017 by John Wiley & Sons, Ltd.

'Disability' is an umbrella term that covers many aspects of impairment. The definition of disability under the Equality Act of 2010 is 'physical or mental impairment that has a "substantial" and "long-term" negative effect on your ability to do normal daily activities.' For the purposes of the Act:

• 'Substantial' means that the effect of the disability is neither minor nor trivial – it does not have to be a severe effect.
• 'Long-term' means that the effect of the impairment has lasted or is likely to last for at least 12 months (excluding terminal care).
• Normal day-to-day activities include everyday things like eating, washing, walking and going shopping.

It is unlawful to discriminate against people with disabilities without justification or to treat a disabled person less favourably than others because of their disability. The GMC expects doctors to have an 'anticipatory duty' and to make 'reasonable adjustments' (Figure 40.1).

Medical students often avoid asking about disability and its impact. This is especially an issue when verbal and non-verbal communication are difficult. Students also worry about using the wrong language or causing offence.

Positive language is important. Always speak to and about the patient as an individual. This is important when communicating with anyone, but needs a special emphasis when communicating with individuals with disability. Avoid phrases such as 'the blind' in favour of 'this individual/person/patient has a visual impairment'.

The GMC make very clear recommendations. For example, when gaining consent: 'You should check whether the patient needs any additional support to understand information, to communicate their wishes, or to make a decision …make sure, wherever practical, that arrangements are made to give the patient any necessary support … (Consent guidance, paragraph 21).

The following tips embrace all the gold standards of communicating with any patient.

General tips for communicating with individuals with a disability

• Introduce yourself and your role. You may need to also introduce yourself to a carer if appropriate.
• Don't be frightened to offer a handshake. People with limited hand use may still be able to shake hands. A left-handed handshake is acceptable.
• If a third party is present, check whether the patient is happy for this person to stay in the room throughout the consultation. They may be present purely as a help with mobility and it may not be appropriate for them to stay.
• Ask questions directly to the patient.
• Don't be frightened to ask questions. Respectful enquiry will never cause offence.
• If you offer help, always wait until the offer is accepted. Ask the patients for instructions on how you can help, for example with getting undressed or onto the examination couch.

Tips for communicating with individuals with mobility problems

• Ensure communication with a wheelchair user is at their eye level.
• Do not lean on the wheelchair.

• Do not assume the individual wants to be pushed – ask first.
• Be courteous – opening doors, removing barriers.

Tips for communicating with individuals who are blind or visually impaired

• Speak as you are approaching the patient.
• Introduce yourself and your role. Use a normal tone.
• Talk to explain what you are doing. For example, 'I am now getting up to get my stethoscope from my bag.'
• Be descriptive if you are examining the patient. Tell them what you are doing – and why.
• Ask if they wish to be lead. Allow the individual to hold your arm.

Tips for communicating with individuals who are deaf or hard of hearing

• You may need to gain the individual's attention. A gentle touch on the shoulder or arm is appropriate.
• Try and find out the best way of communication.
• If the patient is lip reading, look directly at them. Use simple short sentences.
• Diagrams and gestures can supplement speech.
• If the individual is using a sign language interpreter, then talk directly to the individual not the interpreter (see Chapter 14 for tips on how to use an interpreter).

Tips for communicating with individuals with speech impairment

• Don't rush, slow down, be patient.
• Say one thing at a time.
• Ask short questions that only need short replies.
• Ask what helps.
• If you do not understand what the patient is saying, do not pretend you do. Ask them to repeat it. Most people with speech impairment are used to this.
• Do not try to finish the patient's sentences.
• If you are having difficulty understanding, consider alternative means of communication – for example, using a pen and paper to draw diagrams and write down key words.
• Check understanding.

Tips on communicating with individuals with a learning disability

• Allow time. Be patient.
• Don't forget to introduce yourself and your role.
• Make eye contact and try to build a rapport and establish trust.
• Ask questions and talk directly to the patient.
• Bring the carer into the conversation if needed for clarification. Ask for permission first: for example, 'Is it ok if I ask your carer a few questions?'
• Explain what is happening in the consultation.
• Do not avoid an examination because of concerns about capacity to consent. Work hard to establish trust and consent should follow.

41 Communicating with colleagues

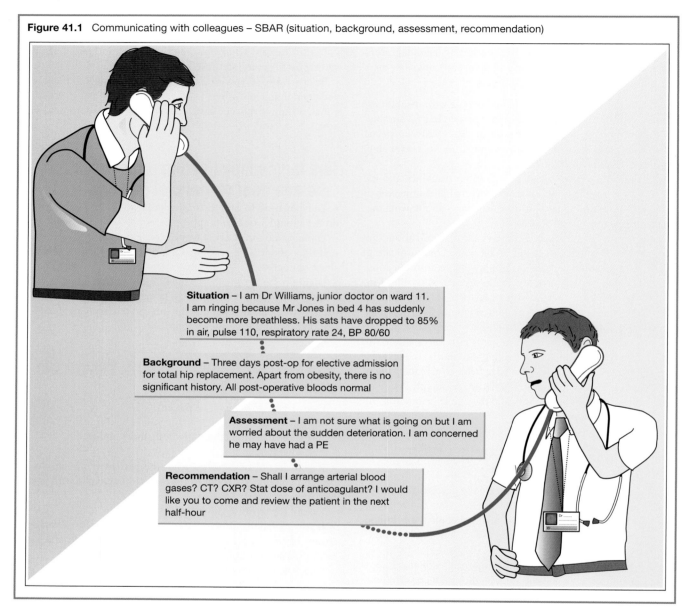

Figure 41.1 Communicating with colleagues – SBAR (situation, background, assessment, recommendation)

Situation – I am Dr Williams, junior doctor on ward 11. I am ringing because Mr Jones in bed 4 has suddenly become more breathless. His sats have dropped to 85% in air, pulse 110, respiratory rate 24, BP 80/60

Background – Three days post-op for elective admission for total hip replacement. Apart from obesity, there is no significant history. All post-operative bloods normal

Assessment – I am not sure what is going on but I am worried about the sudden deterioration. I am concerned he may have had a PE

Recommendation – Shall I arrange arterial blood gases? CT? CXR? Stat dose of anticoagulant? I would like you to come and review the patient in the next half-hour

Communicating effectively with colleagues is vital for the smooth and safe running of the health service. Ineffective communication is recognised as the most common cause of serious error.

Working patterns have changed. Junior doctors are working shifts and now mostly work as part of multidisciplinary teams. These teams are made up of many different disciplines and levels of staff. There exist different models of communication, different assumptions and different hierarchies, all of which complicate the work of such teams. Accurate, concise transfer of information is vital to the effective safe running of these teams to ensure the best possible patient care.

Working in a team

Everyone in the team has a responsibility for patient safety. This does not change your personal accountability or the care you as an individual provide. The GMC lays out clear guidelines on how to work within a team.

- Respect the skills and contributions of your colleagues.
- Make sure your role and responsibility within the team is understood.
- Participate in regular reviews.
- Support your colleagues.
- Communicate effectively with colleagues. Use clear, accurate language.

Medical Ethics, Law and Communication at a Glance, First Edition. Edited by Patrick Davey, Anna Rathmell, Michael Dunn, Charles Foster and Helen Salisbury.
© 2017 John Wiley & Sons, Ltd. Published 2017 by John Wiley & Sons, Ltd.

Human factors

Healthcare professionals are human beings and, like all humans, they can make mistakes. In a healthcare setting, the consequences of these mistakes can be catastrophic. There are still an unacceptable number of patients harmed as a result of their treatment or as a consequence of their admission to hospital. The aviation industry was the first to recognise the role of human factors in making mistakes.

Human factors are all the factors that exist that may influence human behaviour in a work context.

Common human factors that increase risk

• Stress: We bring our whole selves to work. Personal pressures as well as workload stresses can all have an effect on how we behave. Be self-aware because your concentration may be affected and you need to achieve total focus on high-risk tasks.
• Physical demands: Junior doctors frequently work intensive shifts that allow little time to eat properly. Tiredness and hunger can affect cognition and may have an impact on patients' safety. Getting adequate rest and eating properly is good for you and for patients.
• Memory: The human brain can only really keep seven or eight things to the forefront of the mind at any one time. Think about producing a written list.
• Physical environment: Are there noise distractions? Is the lighting good enough to complete a procedure?

A positive safety culture

We need to move away from the 'hint and hope' model of communication to the 'see it, say it, and fix it' model. In one study, 84% of healthcare workers saw colleagues making dangerous short cuts. Only 10% confronted their colleague. Silence kills. It is sometime difficult to assert yourself as a junior member of the team. Remember that patients' safety is paramount. This is a helpful way of focusing on the correct thing to do.

A safe culture should be:

• Open: All team members should feel safe in raising safety issues with their colleagues.
• Just: Staff and patients should feel treated fairly when issues of safety are raised.
• Encouraging to staff reporting: No one should be blamed or punished when they report incidents.
• Promoting learning: Constructive feedback and safety lessons learned should be shared by the team involved.

The most dangerous mistakes are the ones that are ignored or covered up, because these cannot be rectified. Even if no harm has arisen as a result of a mistake, in a positive safety culture, 'near misses' are discussed in a no-blame atmosphere so that everyone can learn and future errors can be avoided.

A framework for accurate communication

In practically every area of medicine, multidisciplinary teams work together for the common goal of patient care. Communication is much more effective when there is a standard system of communication. Good healthcare staff can often fail in their work because of bad systems. One such tool that has been developed is the SBAR system: the acronym stands for 'Situation, Background, Assessment, Recommendation'. SBAR helps to structure team communication (Figure 41.1).

How does SBAR work?

Situation

• Identify yourself and where you are calling from.
• Identify the patient and the reason for your call.
• Describe your concern – for example, 'I am Dr Williams, junior doctor on ward 11. I am ringing because Mr Jones in bed 4 has become suddenly more breathless. His sats have dropped to 85% in air, pulse 110, respiratory rate 24, BP 80/60.'

Background

• Patient's reason for admission.
• Relevant past medical history.
• Relevant test results – for example, '3 days post-op for elective admission for total hip replacement. Apart from obesity, there is no significant history. All post-operative bloods normal.'

Assessment

• Clinical impression and concerns – for example, 'I am not sure what is going on but I am worried about the sudden deterioration. I am concerned he may have had a pulmonary embolism.'

Recommendation

• Explain what you need. Be specific and clear about the time frame.
• Make suggestions if you can.
• Make sure you repeat back any instructions given to you over the phone so it is clear you have fully understood.
• Don't be afraid to restate your concern and look more actively for the response you would like if you don't think you are being heard – for example, 'Shall I arrange arterial blood gases? CT? CXR? Stat dose of anticoagulant? I would like you to come and review the patient in the next half hour.'

When is SBAR useful?

This tool can be used at any stage of the patient journey, both in urgent and non-urgent communication. It is a good format to adopt in your verbal and written communication, in all emergency situations, in more routine handovers and in your less formal emails.

Why is it useful?

• It reduces communication errors and therefore improves patients' safety.
• It saves time at handovers.
• It is effective in breaking down the traditional hierarchy between doctors and other healthcare professionals.
• It is a good way of prompting your own memory.
• It is an excellent method when you need to pass on information to a colleague who has been sleeping.

42 Professionalism

Figure 42.1 Professionalism

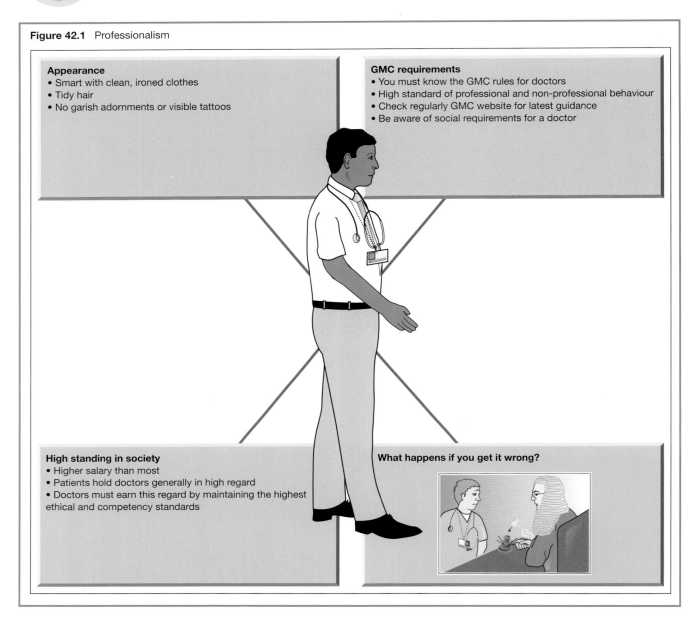

Appearance
- Smart with clean, ironed clothes
- Tidy hair
- No garish adornments or visible tattoos

GMC requirements
- You must know the GMC rules for doctors
- High standard of professional and non-professional behaviour
- Check regularly GMC website for latest guidance
- Be aware of social requirements for a doctor

High standing in society
- Higher salary than most
- Patients hold doctors generally in high regard
- Doctors must earn this regard by maintaining the highest ethical and competency standards

What happens if you get it wrong?

Medical Ethics, Law and Communication at a Glance, First Edition. Edited by Patrick Davey, Anna Rathmell, Michael Dunn, Charles Foster and Helen Salisbury.
© 2017 John Wiley & Sons, Ltd. Published 2017 by John Wiley & Sons, Ltd.

What is professionalism

Professionalism is a set of values and behaviours that shape and define how we form our working relationships with patients and colleagues. The GMC receives more complaints about doctors' behaviour than they do about their clinical abilities.

The word 'profess' means to 'proclaim something publicly'. Many medical students at graduation recite the Hippocratic Oath. The Oath requires doctors to practise ethically and honestly, and signals a passage from student to doctor.

When you qualify as a doctor, you enter into a privileged position of trust with which come responsibilities to behave and act in a certain way.

It is important to use the many opportunities spent observing doctors as a student to reflect and think about the values and behaviours you see and whether they meet professional standards (Figure 42.1).

Professional virtues

- **Compassion/empathy:** This is a deeper awareness of suffering, relating not only to patients' symptoms but also to their circumstances.
- **Trustworthiness:** It is important to be honest, reliable and dependable.
- **Intellectual honesty:** Admit when you don't know.
- **Conscientiousness:** Achieving and maintaining good clinical practice is clearly important. It is also important to do what you say you'll do, even if this is a simple administrative task.
- **Courage:** To stand up for what you think is right for your patient. If you think your colleague's actions are putting patients at risk, it is important to act promptly
- **Equity/non-discrimination:** It is important not to allow personal views to affect the way you treat patients or colleagues.

Professionalism towards patients

Patients must be able to trust their doctors quite literally with their lives. Patients and their families invest a lot of trust in their doctors and it is this trust that is the cornerstone of the doctor–patient relationship. The moment we ask 'how can I help you?' we enter into a trusting relationship where certain behaviours and attitudes are expected by the profession and by patients.

We have to justify that trust and the GMC as the regulatory body for doctors has written clear guidelines in its document 'Tomorrow's doctors':

- Make the care of your patient your first concern. Patients' welfare and well-being are paramount.
- Protect and promote the health of patients and the public.
- Provide a good standard of practice and care:
  - Keep your knowledge and skills up to date.
  - Work within your limits of competence.
  - Work with colleagues in ways that best serve the patient's interests.
- Treat patients as individuals and respect their dignity:
  - Respect confidentiality.
  - Treat patients politely and considerately.
- Work in partnership with patients: listening, giving appropriate information, supporting and respecting their right to make decisions about their own care.
- Be honest and open and act with integrity.
- Remember you are personally accountable for your own professional actions and must be prepared to account for them.

The GMC also requires doctors to dress in an 'appropriate and professional way'. This is clearly open to interpretation. Patients and their relatives often feel frightened and vulnerable and need to trust the doctor caring for them. This may be harder for them if you look scruffy or unkempt. The key principle of 'Make the patient your first concern' is important and acts as a guiding principle in all we do, including how we dress.

Putting your patients first also means valuing their time and not keeping them waiting unnecessarily. There are often unavoidable delays in hospital because of the unpredictable nature of our work but, whenever possible, you should arrive in good time to start your clinic or ward round without keeping patients or colleagues waiting.

Principles of trust

It is right to consider the principles that underlie the trust patients invest in us. After qualifying, there will be many stresses and demands both personally and professionally, and it is easy to see how these principles may be eroded. Keeping the principles clear in your mind will serve as a rock in challenging times, as well as giving clear direction on how to behave and act.

Professionalism teaches us to maintain patient confidentiality. Clearly we have to communicate important information to colleagues that affects clinical care, but caution is needed when we discuss patients outside this context. It may be appropriate to discuss specific cases – for example, when you are teaching others and technically speaking there is no breach of confidentiality if you do not use names or other identifiers. However, when you are discussing a case with a colleague, friend or relative, stop to think about what the patient would feel if they overheard you. Have you honoured that trust?

The majority of complaints about doctors are because of miscommunication. Think carefully about the language you use with patients and how your attitude towards them will make them feel. Treat patients in the way in which you would like yourself and your loved ones to be treated.

Professionalism towards colleagues

We must work with colleagues in ways that best serve the patients' interests. Patients' interests are often served best when we are working in a multidisciplinary team. To work effectively in a team, it is important to understand and respect the expertise of other health and social care professionals. Behaviour that might once have been seen as merely arrogant or bad-tempered (failing to listen to colleagues, shouting on ward rounds) is now clearly identifiable as unprofessional.

Handing over care in a careful, concise and effective way is considered in another chapter.

Behaviour outside the workplace

The requirement to avoid behaviour that might bring the profession into disrepute extends outside the hospital grounds. The GMC takes an interest in instances of financial irregularity or issues of academic integrity even if they are not related to your employment. You are also required to obey the laws of the country in which you are practising.

(43) Feedback

Figure 43.1 Feedback

(a) Take control of your learning

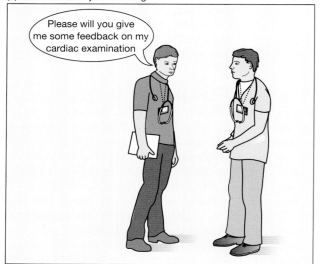

(b) Try not to be defensive

(c) Reflect on the feedback you receive

(d) Decide what you will do as a result of feedback

Medical Ethics, Law and Communication at a Glance, First Edition. Edited by Patrick Davey, Anna Rathmell, Michael Dunn, Charles Foster and Helen Salisbury.
© 2017 John Wiley & Sons, Ltd. Published 2017 by John Wiley & Sons, Ltd.

What is feedback?

Feedback is any information provided about any aspect of a student's learning and performance with the purpose of improving them. How we give and receive feedback is important (Figure 43.1). Feedback is often provided by senior and more experienced colleagues although increasingly peers are asked to provide feedback both in a teaching setting and also in work settings.

It's also really important to develop the critical skill of reflecting and feeding back to yourself about your own learning and performance. This is crucial for long-term professional development and learning, which relies on learning from our experiences – what went well and what didn't go so well.

Feedback has been described as a 'critical condition for excellence'.

Good feedback will help you improve your performance.

Students also need to become independent of their teachers and learn from their own experiences. This is particularly important in clinical medicine, not only for professional development but also for patients' safety.

The word 'doctor' derives from the Latin 'doceo', which means 'I teach'. Not only will you become lifelong learners but also lifelong teachers.

Effectiveness – the evidence

There have been several studies on the subject of feedback and its importance in students' learning. The evidence on the role of feedback in promoting learning is convincing. Students want feedback and recognise how valuable it can be in improving their performance.

The studies also show that the positive effect of feedback is more obvious when related to a clinical task. Feedback relating to 'self' is much more difficult to hear and act on. Feedback on a clinical examination of the chest is much easier to act on than feedback about how empathetic or respectful you were when performing the examination.

It's important, therefore, to give some thought to how we give and receive feedback.

So how do we do it?

Initial steps

1 Take control of your learning. Ask for feedback and be specific about what it is you would like feedback on. Learning is not just about transmission of knowledge from teacher to pupil: it is about actively engaging with opportunities to learn and making the most of them. Be honest. Think about what is going well and what was difficult. Seek out opportunities to practise and really think about your own performance.

2 Be clear about what makes a good performance. Use as many opportunities as possible to observe doctors at work. Use these opportunities to really think about what makes a good doctor. Reflect and think: what works well, what doesn't work well and why.

3 Practice makes perfect – use as many opportunities as possible to practise your skills. This may be a clinical skill-based task or simply taking a history. The more you repeat the cycle of doing, reflecting and learning, the better you will become. Ask to be observed by a peer as well as a teacher.

How to give good feedback

Feedback relies on describing a performance. The language we use is important.

Good feedback should be:

1 Non-judgemental: Describing a specific behaviour rather than the result of the behaviour works better. For example, instead of saying, 'You ignored the patient when she tried to tell you …', try 'I noticed that you lost eye contact with the patient when she was trying to tell you …' Offer some suggestions for how the task or performance could have been done better.

2 Directed towards behaviour rather than personality: We can change our behaviour more easily than our personalities.

3 About something that has been observed.

4 Timely – as soon as the task is completed is most effective.

5 Sensitive to the recipient. Allow them to select specific areas for feedback. Make sure they want feedback. Provide information as to what was good as well as what could be improved. It is important to be supportive and well intentioned.

6 Prioritised – there may be 10 things that you could discuss but the student will probably only remember three or four. Work out which are most important learning points.

How to frame good feedback

As well as the language we use, it is important to think about how we structure the feedback we give so that it is helpful and able to be received and acted on. Inevitably feedback on clinical performance can feel personal, which can have a negative impact on learning. You can be left feeling demotivated and demoralised. A lot of feedback is given on an ad hoc basis and so there may not be time to structure feedback in a formal way.

However, if you are asked by a peer to feed back on their performance, ask them before you start what particular problems they are hoping to address and what they want to achieve. After the task has been performed, ask, 'How do you think it went?' This then allows the student to identify themselves what was difficult. It also helps you to frame the feedback appropriately. If a student knows that they made a mistake, you can move straight on to discussing how to improve. If they are completely oblivious, you will be starting from a different point. With careful use of language, this then becomes a conversation about performance. The 'feedback sandwich' – what you observed that was good, followed by what didn't work so well, finishing with more positive messages – is a popular method of giving feedback.

How to receive feedback

It's harder than you think. It is very easy to feel criticised by feedback and become defensive. Approaching feedback in a positive way is very important.

1 Believe in the importance of feedback for learning and development.

2 Ask for feedback. Be specific about what you want feedback on.

3 Listen to feedback – don't react immediately. Often things are harder to hear if we feel there is some truth in them.

4 Decide on what you will do as a result of the feedback.

44 Looking after yourself

Figure 44.1 Looking after yourself

(a) Discuss emotions

(b) Eat well, drink modestly

(c) Exercise regularly

(d) Take holidays and time off

Medical Ethics, Law and Communication at a Glance, First Edition. Edited by Patrick Davey, Anna Rathmell, Michael Dunn, Charles Foster and Helen Salisbury.
© 2017 John Wiley & Sons, Ltd. Published 2017 by John Wiley & Sons, Ltd.

Culturally, as medics, we are not always encouraged to consider our own well-being as a priority or even as having any importance. It is well known that medical students have increased rates of anxiety and depression compared with the general population. Baseline depression measurements on entering medical school seem to be consistent with the general population. There is something about the process of being a medical student that increases the risks of anxiety and depression. Personality may play a role. Medical students are often self-critical and perfectionists, which is sometimes unhelpful in the imperfect world of medical science.

Students and doctors are exposed to a lot of challenges and difficult situations. Unless these experiences are processed properly, they can lead to negative coping strategies.

How we process our own feelings can have an impact on the way we care about and care for others (Figure 44.1).

Here are some examples of unhelpful coping strategies:

Suppression
- Fighting to suppress any difficult thoughts or feelings.
- Arguing with yourself.
- Using up a lot of energy having conflicting conversations with yourself: 'I am useless', 'No, I am not', 'Yes I am.'
- Taking charge.
- Telling yourself to 'snap out of it' or forcing yourself to feel happy when you are not.

Self-bullying
- Telling yourself you are a loser or idiot, and criticising or blaming yourself.
- Hiding or escaping.
- Avoiding people or situations that raise difficult feelings.
- Distraction or zoning out.

A high proportion of medical students regularly exceed the recommended weekly limits for alcohol intake. There is also concern about the high rate of cannabis use among medical students. While these strategies can initially numb difficult feelings, they can set up long-term issues and problems including legal ones.

Emotional well-being
If you worked on a building site, you would have to wear a hard hat. We work in emotional, dangerous and challenging situations so it is important to consider how we develop protection for ourselves. We have to allow time and space to process and reflect on difficult emotions. Other disciplines working in emotionally challenged areas have long recognised the need to 'debrief' and have regular 'supervision'.

Why?
With proper reflection and through our experience – and mistakes – we can learn about ourselves and our role as doctors. We are then better balanced and more equipped to cope with the demands of our role.

It deepens our understanding of emotion and its importance for our patients. This ultimately will give us a better insight into our patients' difficulties.

How?
There are many healthy ways to process the difficulties and challenges of work. As individuals, we have to find what works best for us.

Examples might be listening to music, going for a walk, and talking to friends and colleagues. Other methods include debriefing and mindfulness-based stress reduction.

Debriefing
This is a semi-structured conversation usually set up following a stressful situation. You may need to be proactive in seeking a debriefing.

It involves discussing an event and reflecting on what went well, as well as what was difficult. If done properly, it can deepen our understanding of our colleagues as well as enhance our clinical learning. The process of reflection is a helpful way of learning from difficult encounters, which informs how we might approach similar situations in the future.

Mindfulness-based stress reduction
Mindfulness is a mental state achieved by paying attention to the present moment while calmly accepting your own thoughts and feelings. It acknowledges that many of our anxieties relate to fears about the future. It is widely used as a therapeutic technique to help respond to pressures in a calmer, more helpful way.

Physical well-being
'To keep the body in good health is a duty … Otherwise we shall not be able to keep our mind strong and clear.' (Buddha)

Physical activity
At a physiological level, the benefits of exercise to our physical health are well researched and understood. Physical activity can be loosely described as anything that requires using muscles to expend energy. Activity can be structured and competitive, such as sport, but equally can be just done for fun.

Physical activity has also been shown to have a strong and positive influence on mental well-being. The way in which exercise affects mental health is complex and multifaceted. It reduces stress, depression and anxiety as well as enhancing mood and quality of life.

Eating well
A healthy balanced diet is essential for our body's physical function. There is also an increasing awareness of the role of 'food and mood'. The demand and workload of the medical day does not always lend itself to three regular healthy meals a day. Missing meals, especially breakfast, can lead to low mood, irritability and fatigue. Sugary snacks can provide a quick fix but are associated with increased insulin production that ultimately lowers the sugar levels, leaving you tired and low. Having access to healthy snacks is a good strategy.

45 Kindness

Figure 45.1 Kindness

Kindness is easy to recognise but difficult to define. If you are in any doubt as to whether a phrase or action is kind, imagine someone you care about being on the receiving end and ask yourself if this is what you would choose for them. When people feel ill or scared, are in an unfamiliar environment or facing an uncertain future, kindness from those around them can make a huge difference to how difficult that situation is to bear. Unfortunately, when we are stressed or anxious ourselves and in a hurry, our will and ability to be kind, and to be the sort of doctor we aspire to be, is easily eroded. Behaviours that are spontaneous when we are rested, relaxed and confident may need to be more deliberate when this is not the case: kindness is too important to be dependent on our mood; rather, it must be a practised, dependable attribute of our professional behaviour. It may be useful, therefore, to examine it a little more closely.

Attentiveness

Part of kindness is attentiveness, making the patient our first concern. In practice, this means giving our whole attention to what the patient is saying, and demonstrating our interest in their story with verbal or non-verbal signals.

Empathy

Another element is empathy, which can be shown in facial expression or in words. This is easily lost because, in our eagerness to make a diagnosis, there is a risk that our only reaction to a story of excruciating pain is to find out all the details of where and when it occurred, and forget to say, 'That sounds horrible for you.'

Time

Skilled doctors often have a knack of appearing to have time for their patients, which in turn gives the message that the patient matters to them. On a ward, this impression is helped by, whenever possible, sitting down to talk to a patient, so that you are both on the same level. Avoiding outward displays of impatience (looking at your watch, drumming your fingers) when the patient is slow and you are late also helps.

Gentleness

This can be expressed in your tone of voice and the pace at which you speak as well as the words you use. When examining a patient, be careful not to cause pain, watch their face attentively for wincing and apologise if you do inadvertently hurt them.

Non-judgemental acceptance

Patients often feel bad about themselves, about their weight, their poor diabetic control, their alcohol, smoking or drug use. Whatever your own personal opinions, part of your job as a doctor is to hold your patient in unconditional positive regard. In practice, this means guarding against facial or verbal expressions that undermine this, and finding out from the patient what they want or intend to do, rather than jumping in with your advice. It also means avoiding the use of dismissive labels about patients to others in the medical team, because even in joking, these legitimise an 'us versus them' culture based on stereotypes and value judgements.

Medical Ethics, Law and Communication at a Glance, First Edition. Edited by Patrick Davey, Anna Rathmell, Michael Dunn, Charles Foster and Helen Salisbury.
© 2017 John Wiley & Sons, Ltd. Published 2017 by John Wiley & Sons, Ltd.

Index

ability to benefit 51
abortion 11, 12, 37–39
  actions to prevent 39
  ethical debate 39
  failed 39
  genetic testing and 55
  regulation 38–39
Abortion Act 1967 12, 38
Abortion Regulations 1991 38–39
absolute risk 85
abuse, child/vulnerable adults 46, 47
activities of daily living (ADLs) 58
advance care planning 60
advance decisions 62
aggression, dealing with 92–93
AIDS 67
Airedale NHS Trust v Bland (1993) 17, 63
anger
  dealing with 92–93
  reaction to bad news 90, 91
anorexia nervosa 43–44
apologies 93
appeals, tribunals 15
artificial nutrition and hydration (ANH) 60, 62
'Ask three questions' 83
assault 24–25
assisted reproduction technologies 10, 11, 35–36
assisted suicide 63, 64
attentiveness 108
attitude, of doctors 79
audit 67
autonomy 29
  children 33
  older adults 59
  reproductive 35
  respect for 6

bad news, breaking 88–89
  patient reactions to 90–91
battery and assault 24–25
behaviour(s)
  ethical healthcare management 67
  kindness and 108
  lifestyle change management 87
  outside the workplace 103
beneficence 6
  procreative 35
best guess 31
'best interests' 6, 19, 27, 44
  assisted suicide and 63, 64
  mental incapacity 30, 31
  older adults 59–60
best outcome 31
blame, transferring 92, 93
blindness 99
body language 77, 93
Bolam test 11, 17, 20, 21
Bolam v Friern Hospital Management Committee 11, 20
'Bolitho gloss' 21
Bolitho v City and Hackney Health Authority (1997) 20
boundaries, patient–doctor relationship 75
breach of duty 17, 21
breast cancer, familial 53, 54
British Medical Association (BMA) 19
bureaucrats 66, 67

cancer, bad news 89, 91
capacity *see* mental capacity
capacity view, embryo/foetus status 35
Care Act 2014 47
care order 47
care planning, older adults 60
carers, informal 59

case law 14
casuistry 8–9
'categorical imperative' 5
causation, breach of duty 21
change management, lifestyle 87
chaperones 25, 75
children
  abuse 46, 47
  consent and 33, 41
  genetic testing 55
  legal protection 47
  primary care 69
  reproductive decisions, impact 35
  research involvement 57
  safeguarding 46–47
  welfare 33
Children Act 1989 33
chunking, in explanations 79
civil law 11, 17, 47
Clinical Commissioning Groups (CCGs) 52
clinical efficacy 51
'clinical equipoise' 83
clinical ethics committee 19
clinical genetics 53–55
clinical governance 19
Clinical Leadership Competency Framework 65
clinical management 66–67
clinical negligence 11, 12, 20–23
  claims 21, 22, 23, 29
  consent, failure 29
  stages 21, 22, 23
  timing, parties, procedures 23
clinical trials 57
'coercive healthism' 49
colleagues
  anger with 93
  communicating with 100–101
  professionalism towards 103
collegial consensus 66–67
commissioning 52, 69
'common assault' 25
communication 72–108
  across cultures 96–97
  anger and aggression 92–93
  bad news *see* bad news, breaking
  with colleagues 73, 100–101
  in consultations *see* consultations
  diagram use in 79, 85
  errors 101
  ethical decisions and 19
  explanations (to patients) 78–79
  feedback 104, 105
  good, importance 19, 72–73
  on lifestyle changes 86–87
  listening and questioning 76–77
  non-verbal 77, 97
  older adults 59, 60
  people with disabilities 98–99
  resource allocation in NHS 52
  of risk 84–85
  shared decision making 82–83
compensation 10, 11, 12, 23
complaints against doctors 73, 103
computers 81, 85
computers on wheels (COWs) 81
confidence 67, 69
confidentiality 12, 17, 26–27, 103
  consent for information disclosure 27
  duty to maintain 26, 27
  genetic information 55
  older adults 59
  in primary care 69
conflicts
  emotion *vs* duty 66–67
  of family members, primary care 69
  value 3, 5, 6, 19

conscientious objection 38
consent 11, 25, 28–33
  assisted reproduction 35
  battery/assault avoidance 25
  breaches 27
  care/treatment types 31
  children and 33
  by courts 33
  definition 29
  disagreements, management 33
  disclosure of confidential information 27
  ethical foundations 29
  general principles 29–31
  informed 29, 80
  intimate examinations 25
  legal obligation to breach 27
  mental capacity 11, 30, 31–35, 44
  older adults 59–60
  organ donation 40–41, 42
  people with disabilities 99
  persons with parental responsibility 32, 33
  for procedures/investigations 80
  refusal 31, 33
  surgery 25
  therapeutic research 57
  treatment without 44, 45
  valid 29
  voluntary 29
consequentialism 5, 26
consistency, resource allocation 52
constitution, UK 14
consultand, genetic testing 54, 55
consultations 75
  across cultures 97
  bad news and 89, 91
  computer use 81
  doctor–patient relationship 75
  explanations, advice on 78–79
  explanations of procedures 80
  interpreted, and interpreters 97
  lifestyle changes and model for 87
  listening and questioning 76–77
  patient-centred 73, 74, 81
  sex, talking about 94–95
  structure 77
continuity of care 69
contraception 39, 83
Convention on the Rights of Persons with Disabilities, UN (CRPD) 31, 33
coping strategies 107
cost-effectiveness 51
costs, resource allocation 51
courts 13, 14–15
  consent by 33
  end of life care 63
criminal law 11, 15, 47
cues, in consultations 77, 80, 89
cultural competence 96
culture, definition 96
cultures, communication across 96–97

data protection 27, 69
deafness 99
deaths
  clinical negligence 23
  rituals and cultures 97
debriefing 107
decision aid 83
decision making
  older adults and informal carers 59, 60
  primary care 69
  reproductive 34, 35
  resource allocation 51
  safeguarding children/adults 46–47
  shared 82–83
  see also ethical decision making

Declaration of Helsinki 56
defendants 23
dementia 58, 59, 60
denial, reaction to bad news 90, 91
deontology, Kantian 5, 6
detention, under Mental Health Act 44, 47
diagnosis, making, communication 73
diagrams, use 79, 85
diet 107
direct-to-consumer genetic testing (DTC-GT) 54
disability 99
  communication in 98–99
  foetal, pregnancy termination 38
  sex and 95
disclosure of information 27, 57
discrimination 99, 103
doctors
  building relationship with patients 75
  explanations by 78–79
  looking after yourself 91, 93, 106–107
doctrine of binding precedent 14
'do not attempt cardiopulmonary resuscitation' (DNACPR) 60, 63
'do not resuscitate' (DNR) orders 62, 63
'double effect,' doctrine 63
dress code 75, 102
drug side effects 95
duty-based ethics 5
duty of care 21
duty to disclose information 57
duty to maintain confidentiality 26, 27

'eggshell skull principle' 23
electronic patient record 81
embryo, status 35
emotional well-being 107
emotions, patients', to bad news 90, 91
empathy 89, 91, 92, 93, 103, 108
empirical methods 3
empowerment 33
end of life 10, 11, 12
end of life care 61–64
  decision making flowchart 61, 62
  definition 62
English legal system 13–15
equality of opportunity 51
equality of outcome 51
errors 11, 101
ethical conflicts 3, 5, 6, 19
ethical decision making 5, 6, 8, 9, 19
  context 19
  in practice 18–19
  see also decision making
ethical issues 5, 19
  assisted reproduction 36
  clinical genetics 55
  identification 19
  transplantation 41–42
ethical reasoning 5, 7–9
ethical theories and principles 3, 4, 5, 19, 33
  application 6
ethical values 3, 5, 8, 19
ethics *see* medical ethics
ethnicity 96, 97
European Convention on Human Rights (ECHR) 1950 12, 14
European law 14
euthanasia 10, 10, 11, 11, 12, 63, 64
exceptions, in resource allocation 52
explanations 78–79
  good, criteria for 79
  of procedures 80
explicit framing 77

Medical Ethics, Law and Communication at a Glance, First Edition. Edited by Patrick Davey, Anna Rathmell, Michael Dunn, Charles Foster and Helen Salisbury.
© 2017 by John Wiley & Sons, Ltd. Published 2017 by John Wiley & Sons, Ltd.

familial adenomatous polyposis (FAP) 55
family
    interpretation of language 97
    primary care 69
    sharing information with 19, 55
fears
    reaction to bad news 90, 91
    relieving, doctor's role 73, 74
feedback 104–105
'feedback sandwich' 105
fiduciary 66, 67
financial loss, damages for 23
fitness to practice 15, 17
foetus
    abortion, ethical debate 39
    disability, pregnancy termination 38
    status 35, 39
foreign languages 97
formality 75
Fragile X syndrome 53, 55
framing, explicit 77

gametes 35
gatekeeping 69
gender reassignment surgery 52
General Medical Council (GMC) 8, 11,
    15, 17, 19
    breaches of confidentiality 27
    end of life care 62
    Good Medical Practice 25, 68, 83, 96
    informed consent 29
    Tomorrow's doctors 96, 103
general practice see primary care
general practitioners 68–69
    communicating with, bad news 91
genetic counselling 53, 54
genetic origins, right to know 35
genetics 53–55
genetic testing 54, 55
gentleness 108
Gillick-competent child 33
good communication 72–73
good practice 25
'gradualist' approach 35, 39
greeting, the patient 75
grief, reaction to bad news 90, 91
guidelines 25, 29

harm, dealing with 67
health-affecting behaviour 49
health management 65–67
    behaviours for 67
    clinicians' role 66
    framework 66–67
health promotion 87
hearing impairment 99
hedonistic utilitarianism 5
history taking 77
housekeeping (after giving bad news) 91
human factors 101
Human Fertilisation and Embryology
    Authority (HFEA) 35, 55
human research 56–57
human rights 12, 14, 27
Human Tissue Act 2004 40–41, 42
Human Tissue Act (Scotland) 2006 41
Human Transplantation (Wales) Act
    2013 41

ideal utilitarianism 5
information see medical information
informed consent 29, 80
inquisitorial behaviour 67
intellectual virtues 9
interpreters 97
intimate examinations 25, 75
investigations, explaining 80

jargon 79
jurisdictions 14–15
justice 6, 59
justification 3

Kant, Immanuel 5
kindness 108

language
    breaking bad news 89
    communication across cultures
        96, 97
    communication of risk 85
    for explanations 79, 80
    for feedback 105

positive, people with disability 99
talking about sex 95
law see medical law
learning, student's 105
learning disability 99
legal knowledge 8
legislation 14
life expectancy 58, 59
lifestyle changes 86–87
life-sustaining treatment 25, 62
    English law rulings 61
    refusal 25, 64
    withdrawal 32, 33, 63
listening 76–77, 93
litigation 12, 17, 23, 73
looking after yourself 91, 93, 106–107
loss or damage, negligence and 21, 23

MacIntyre, Alasdair 6
Magistrates' Courts 13, 15
medical ethics 2, 3
    content and methods 3
    law and professionalism relationship
        16–17
    principles 3, 4, 5
    scope, and boundaries 3
medical information
    breaking bad news and 89
    confidentiality see confidentiality
    disclosure 27, 57
    ethical decisions and 19
    incorrect, negligence 11
    older adults, informal carers and 59
    primary care 69
    sharing with family 19, 55
medical law 10–12
    ethics and professionalism
        relationship 16–17
Medical Practitioners Tribunal Service
    (MPTS) 15, 17
medical records 75, 81
medicinal products, human research
    57
mental capacity 11, 12, 31
    artificial nutrition and hydration 60
    assessment in mental disorder 44
    children and 33
    consent and 11, 30, 31–35
    consent to disclosure confidential
        information 27
    definition 31
    'functional' test 31
    life-sustaining treatment 62
    older adults 59–60
    persons lacking see mental
        incapacity
Mental Capacity Act 2005 11, 31, 33,
    41, 57, 63
    advance decisions 62
    Mental Health Act vs 44
    principles 45
    substitute decision making 31, 330
    vulnerable adults, protection 47
mental disability 11
mental disorders 11, 12, 43–45
    capacity assessment 44, 45
    treatment without consent 44
mental health 12, 43–45
Mental Health Act 1983 12, 44, 47
mental incapacity 11
    decision making 30, 31, 33
    human research and 57
    life-sustaining treatment 62–63
mindfulness-based stress reduction 107
minimally conscious state (MCS) 62, 63
misconduct 11, 17, 25
mobility problems, communication
    in 99
models, use in explanations 79
Montgomery v Lanarkshire Health Board
    (2015) 28, 29
moral dilemma 3, 4, 5, 7, 18–19
moral duties 5
moral reasoning 8–9
multidisciplinary team 19, 100, 103
murder 63

need, resource allocation 51
neglect, child 47
negligence see clinical negligence
NHS, reports into 65
NHS Constitution 51–52

NHS resources 12
    allocation 50, 51–52
    procedural requirements 52
non-judgemental acceptance 87, 107, 108
non-maleficence 6
non-therapeutic research 57
non-verbal skills 77, 97
normalisation 95
'notifiable disease' 31
numerical communication of risk 85

older adults 58–60
    advance care planning 60
    care planning 60
    confidentiality 59
    consent, capacity and best interests
        59–60
    ethical dilemmas, resolving 59
    justice, fairness and rationing 59
opportunity cost 51
organ donation 40–42
    deceased donors 41, 42
    incentives 42
    living donors 41
    opt-in vs opt-out systems 41, 42
    reciprocity-based system 42
Organ Donation Register (ODR) 42

pain 23
    warning patients 80
pain-relieving medication 63
palliative care 63–64
parentage 35–36
parental responsibility, consent 32, 33
paternalistic attitude 79
patient(s)
    bad news 89, 90–91
    explanations for 78–79
    interests 66, 67, 103
    known wishes 31
    professionalism towards 103
    safety 101
    shared decision making 82–83
patient-centred consultation 73, 74, 81
    see also consultations
patient-centred explanation 80
patient–doctor relationship 75
patient records 75, 81
persistent vegetative state (PVS) 62, 63
personal autonomy 6, 29
physical activity 107
physical safety 93
policy and policy making 8, 47
'preference-sensitive choices' 83
preference utilitarianism 5
pregnancy termination see abortion
pre-implantation genetic diagnosis
    (PGD) 55
prenatal testing 55
preventative medicine 85
primary care 68–69
    ethical frameworks 68–69
principlism 6, 66
privacy 27
proband, clinical genetics service 54
procedures, explaining, and consent 80
procreative beneficence 35
professionalism 16–17, 75, 102–103
professional standards hearings 15
professional virtues 103
'pro-life' approach 35
proxy decision making 31
public health 48–49
    'intervention ladder' 48

quality, investigating 67
questioning skills 76–77
questions 79, 87

rationing 59
    see also resource allocation
referrals 17, 21, 69
    genetic service 54
refusal of consent 31, 33
refusal of treatment see treatment
    refusal
regulation(s)
    abortion 38–39
    human research 56
relative risk reduction 85
reproduction 10, 11, 34–36
    genetic testing and decisions 55
reproductive autonomy 35

research 56–57
resource allocation 12, 50–52, 59
    clinical management and 66
    decisions 50, 51
    equality and fairness 51
    gender reassignment surgery 52
    legal and policy aspects 51–52
    NHS procedural requirements 52
    older adults 59
    primary care 69
respect for autonomy 6, 26
restorative behaviour 67
'right not to know' 55
'right to refuse' 31
risk
    changes with interventions 85
    communication of 84–85
    human factors increasing 101
Roe v Wade (1973) 38
Royal College of General Practitioners
    (RCGP) 68
rule of law 14

safeguarding children/adults 46–47
safety culture 101
'savour sibling' 12
SBAR (situation, background,
    assessment, recommendation)
    100, 101
Scanlon, Thomas M 5
'sectioned,' under Mental Health Act
    44, 47
security 93
self-bullying 107
self-control 91, 93
separation of powers 14
sex, talking about 94–95
sex selection 55
Sexual Offences Act 2003 69
shared decision making 82–83
shared management plan 74
shouting 93
smoking cessation 84, 87
sovereignty of parliament 14
speech impairment 99
statistical calculations 85
stoicism 86, 90, 91
stress (doctors') 93, 101, 107, 108
substitute decision making 30, 31
substituted judgment 31
suicide 12
    assisted 63, 64
summary, in consultations 77
supervision order 47
Supreme Court 13, 14, 15
surgery
    consent 25
    sex affected by 95
surrogacy 10, 12, 36
symptoms, patient-centred consultation
    73, 74

team working 100
telephone translation service 97
templates, electronic patient records 81
termination of pregnancy see abortion
therapeutic parsimony 69
therapeutic research 57
time, requirement 79, 83, 108
tort law 11
translation service 97
transplantation 40–42
transtheoretical model of change 87
treatment refusal 11, 25, 30
    communication 73
    mental ill-health and 43
treatment without consent 44, 45
tribunals 15, 17
trust 26, 29, 59, 67, 103
    principles of 103

utilitarianism 5, 6, 49

virtue-based ethics 5–6
visual communication of risk 85
visual impairment 99
vulnerable adults 47

ward rounds 81
welfare, child's 33, 35
well-being, of medics 106–107
'well-being,' as value 5
worry, relieving, doctor's role 73, 74